Food Culture in
Sub-Saharan Africa

Food Culture in
Sub-Saharan Africa

FRAN OSSEO-ASARE

Food Culture around the World

Ken Albala, Series Editor

GREENWOOD PRESS

Westport, Connecticut · London

Library of Congress Cataloging-in-Publication Data

Osseo-Asare, Fran.
   Food culture in Sub-Saharan Africa / Fran Osseo-Asare.
     p. cm. — (Food culture around the world, ISSN 1545–2638)
   Includes bibliographical references and index.
   ISBN 0–313–32488–3 (alk. paper)
   1. Cookery—Africa, Sub-Saharan. 2. Food habits—Africa, Sub-Saharan.
   I. Title. II. Series.
   TX725.A4O7 2005
   394.1′2′0967—dc22   2005005498

British Library Cataloguing in Publication Data is available.

Library of Congress Catalog Card Number: 2005005498
ISBN: 0–313–32488–3
ISSN: 1545–2638

First published in 2005

Greenwood Press, 88 Post Road West, Westport, CT 06881
An imprint of Greenwood Publishing Group, Inc.
www.greenwood.com

Printed in the United States of America

The paper used in this book complies with the
Permanent Paper Standard issued by the National
Information Standards Organization (Z39.48–1984).

10 9 8 7 6 5 4 3 2 1

Illustrations by J. Susan Cole Stone.

The publisher has done its best to make sure the instructions and/or recipes in this book
are correct. However, users should apply judgment and experience when preparing recipes, especially parents and teachers working with young people. The publisher accepts
no responsibility for the outcome of any recipe included in this volume.

This book is dedicated to Auntie Sika (Barbara Baëta), pioneering culinary professional of sub-Saharan Africa for over half a century—colleague, inspiration, and friend.

Contents

Series Foreword

The appearance of the Food Culture around the World series marks a definitive stage in the maturation of Food Studies as a discipline to reach a wider audience of students, general readers, and foodies alike. In comprehensive interdisciplinary reference volumes, each on the food culture of a country or region for which information is most in demand, a remarkable team of experts from around the world offers a deeper understanding and appreciation of the role of food in shaping human culture for a whole new generation. I am honored to have been associated with this project as series editor.

Each volume follows a series format, with a chronology of food-related dates and narrative sections entitled Introduction, Historical Overview, Major Foods and Ingredients, Cooking, Typical Meals, Eating Out, Special Occasions, and Diet and Health. Each also includes a glossary, bibliography, resource guide, and illustrations.

Finding or growing food has of course been the major preoccupation of our species throughout history, but how various peoples around the world learn to exploit their natural resources, come to esteem or shun specific foods and develop unique cuisines reveals much more about what it is to be human. There is perhaps no better way to understand a culture, its values, preoccupations and fears, than by examining its attitudes toward food. Food provides the daily sustenance around which families and communities bond. It provides the material basis for rituals through which people celebrate the passage of life stages and their connection to divinity.

Food preferences also serve to separate individuals and groups from each other, and as one of the most powerful factors in the construction of identity, we physically, emotionally and spiritually become what we eat.

By studying the foodways of people different from ourselves we also grow to understand and tolerate the rich diversity of practices around the world. What seems strange or frightening among other people becomes perfectly rational when set in context. It is my hope that readers will gain from these volumes not only an aesthetic appreciation for the glories of the many culinary traditions described, but also ultimately a more profound respect for the peoples who devised them. Whether it is eating New Year's dumplings in China, folding tamales with friends in Mexico or going out to a famous Michelin-starred restaurant in France, understanding these food traditions helps us to understand the people themselves.

As globalization proceeds apace in the twenty-first century it is also more important than ever to preserve unique local and regional traditions. In many cases these books describe ways of eating that have already begun to disappear or have been seriously transformed by modernity. To know how and why these losses occur today also enables us to decide what traditions, whether from our own heritage or that of others, we wish to keep alive. These books are thus not only about the food and culture of peoples around the world, but also about ourselves and who we hope to be.

Ken Albala
University of the Pacific

Acknowledgments

It has been both a thrill and a challenge to write this book, to my knowledge the first of its kind since Laurens van der Post's two classics: the 1970 *African Cooking* followed by *First Catch Your Eland in 1977*. Much has changed in sub-Saharan Africa in the past several decades. The thrill came from being able to contribute to a glaring void in the culinary literature, the challenge from the immensity of the task. Despite more than three decades of a love affair with sub-Saharan African food and culture, this book has required numerous trips to the edges of my comfort zone. Ideally, almost every sentence should be footnoted to acknowledge the huge debt to others for information in it. Since my editor, Wendi Schnaufer, tells me that is unfeasible, included is an extensive bibliography of sources consulted during the book's preparation.

However, I offer apologies in advance for any errors, omissions, or misrepresentations that may appear. This book is a foundation on which to build, and comments and corrections are welcomed to remedy any inadvertent errors or distortions (www.betumi.com).

I have received support and assistance from many individuals, particularly those who traveled to Africa and brought me additional books, especially cookbooks, which were unavailable outside the continent. Thank you to Virginia Ciminelli, Joan Thomson, George Ofosu-Amaah, and Abena, DK, Augustus, and K. Osseo-Asare. I also benefited from helpful interactions with Dialla Konate, Judith Mukaruziga, Angèle M. Kingue,

Pashington Obeng, and many other sub-Saharan Africans both on the continent and outside of it, as well as North American colleagues with experience living in Africa. Special thanks to Doug Himes for sharing his knowledge, as well as photographs from Gabon, and to Igor Cusack for his e-mails and reprints. I am particularly indebted to Dorah Sitole, writer and culinary professional in South Africa, and her publisher Anita Pyke at Tafelberg Publishers, for moral and concrete support, including permission to reprint and/or adapt photos from Sitole's *Cooking from Cape to Cairo*. Thank yous are due to Oyeeman Wereko Ampem II for permission to use a photograph taken in Ghana at the Amanokrom Odwira; to Julie Letourneau for assistance with French translations; to Bryna M. Freyer, curator at the Smithsonian Institution, for the information she provided on central African Woyo pot lids; and to series editor, Ken Albala, for his encouragement when I needed it most. I also benefited from conversations with and resources provided by my anthropologist sister Patricia Banach.

This book was enriched by the participation of my children: Abena, fellow Africanist; Masi, muse, who helped steady me during the hard work; DK, advisor and research assistant; Ernest and Sam, recipe tasters. As always, the last should be the first: I acknowledge the unwavering support of my critic, fellow scholar, and primary cheerleader—my husband, Kwadwo.

Introduction

Atannayita: y'atenda nnyina obufumbi (okufumba.)
The one who has not traveled widely thinks his/her mother is the only (best) cook.[1]

—Baganda Proverb (also Akamba, Kikuyu, Bemba, Haya, Igbo, Yoruba)

SOCIAL CHANGE AND FOOD CULTURE IN SUB-SAHARAN AFRICA

... the essential truths and probabilities yielded by research over the past few decades repeatedly insist on two great underlying themes, manifest or hidden, concerning all African development no matter what the region may be. These themes are unity and continuity of cultural growth among them all, and from an immense depth of time.[2]

Scholar Basil Davidson's quotation declares that two great recurrent themes of African history are continuity of growth and growth taking place within an "immense depth of time." While acknowledging this, this book has a slightly different emphasis. Two themes that flow throughout it are: first, the similarities and differences of sub-Saharan Africa's cultural and culinary landscape and, second, the tension between the conflicting needs for stability and holding on to traditions and for flexibility, experimentation, and adaptation in the culinary realm.

Food, like air, surrounds and sustains us and is not static. Food habits have always changed over time, although the pace of change has accelerated in recent years. Technology has particularly facilitated trends such as globalization, modernization, and migration. Improvements in transportation and telecommunications have shrunk the world and created a "global market basket." We all recognize a greatly increased reciprocal flow of information, goods, and people at all levels—local, regional, national, international, and intercontinental.

This book introduces a part of the world that is still, however, very different for many Westerners. The ability to see it clearly may be affected by many lenses we are unaware of using. One generally understands something new by comparing it with something already known. As a result, Africa has often been explained in negative terms. Rather than viewing Africans as active in creating their own history, a "Eurocentric" view of colonizers and the colonial experience has dominated writing about Africa the past 200 years, including culinary writing. Thus, writing about Africa has often provided a litany of stories of poverty, disease, malnutrition, famine, warfare, ethnic conflicts, and the need for outside help. While understanding poverty and its roots is critical to making sense of the realities facing sub-Saharan Africa today, material simplicity and the lack of accumulation of wealth have too often been taken as signs of intellectual inferiority. Similarly, oral traditions have been assumed to be inherently inferior to written traditions. Yet the equally distorted and romanticized tourist view of the Africa of "The Lion King," an exotic world of safaris, wild animals, and scenic beauty, is also an unhelpful foundation upon which to base a meaningful knowledge of African food and culture.

Paradoxically, not only are there ways in which Africa's food culture is foreign to Westerners, there are also many familiar points of contact whose origins lie in the unwilling arrival of sub-Saharan Africans in the New World during the slave trade. An estimated 425,000 to 650,000 Africans, primarily West Africans, were forcibly brought to the United States as slaves, while at least 9.5 million slaves and up to 12 million are thought to have been transported to the New World between the early 1500s and 1888, when slavery was abolished in Brazil. About 6 percent came to the United States and over 75 percent of the slaves were sent to Brazil and the Caribbean islands.

Familiar "American" cooking techniques such as deep-frying and slow cooking, or the use of ingredients such as peanuts, chili peppers, okra, or watermelon, or even the *cola* in Coca-Cola were in many cases introduced by sub-Saharan Africans. Similarly, new world foods such as corn, tomatoes, cassava, and chili peppers are part of the migration called the *Columbian Exchange* and are today integral to sub-Saharan African cuisine and culture.

The most striking common thread throughout the cooking of countries in sub-Saharan Africa is the basic format of a meal, which often consists of a thick, filling starch or porridge eaten with a sauce or stew, sometimes called a relish. The starch is generally a boiled or pounded form of roots, such as African yams, cassava, or cocoyam, or of plantains, maize, millet, sorghum, or rice. The stew or sauce components vary with the locality and availability but commonly include an oil, such as palm, peanut, or coconut oil, and some form of vegetable such as cooked green leaves, possibly hot peppers, tomatoes, or onions and possibly a small amount of a protein source such as fish, meat, poultry, seeds, legumes, or nuts.

A widespread African riddle asks: I have three children. If one of them is absent, the others are of no use to me. Who are they? The answer is: The three stones that support a cooking pot. It takes all three of them to balance the pot.[3] This riddle illustrates the most common traditional cooking technique throughout sub-Saharan Africa, that of stewing in a pot over a fire made within three stones put together.

Another thread running throughout hundreds or possibly thousands of years of sub-Saharan history is the multipurpose reliance upon the humble gourd, or calabash. Though they are gradually being replaced by plastic, enamel, aluminum, tin, and other containers, the calabash is still ubiquitous, whether known by its many local African names or by the English *calabash* or French *calabassa* (also *calebasse*).

While gourds have been found in numerous other societies, they have continued to play a special role in Africa. Some reasons for their long popularity include: they grow quickly and easily; are lightweight and portable, yet sturdy and waterproof so they can hold liquids as well as dry materials; and are inexpensive and accessible. They come in many shapes and sizes and are easy to cut, shape, and decorate. While they have long been used as instruments and in rituals and religious ceremonies, they have been perhaps most cherished in the domestic realm, where they have been indispensable to domestic life as plates, bowls and lids, cups, bottles, ladles, and storage containers for dry grains, seeds, nuts, fruit, and beans, and for liquids such as water, wine, beer, milk, oil, animal fat, or blood.

In addition, they have been basins or sinks for bathing; containers for laundry, cosmetics, medicine, tobacco, or snuff; scales and measures in markets; tree sap containers; floating buoys for fishing nets; and used to hold and sow seeds for farmers.

They have also provided a vehicle for showcasing creativity and imagination. Nomadic Wodaabe women carefully decorate the outsides of calabashes with geometric shapes, half moons, suns, and various other designs, and treasure them as family heirlooms, keeping them carefully nested in groups of 10 as they travel. In Cameroon, the calabashes might be covered with beads or raphia, wood, and string; in Kenya or Ethiopia, with leather and/or cowrie shells; and in Angola, colored and engraved with a hunting scene. One scholar has gone so far as to state, "The calabash is, unquestionably, the only natural medium which has transcended geographical, cultural, and social barriers in Africa."[4]

These observations involve oversimplifications but do point to similarities that cross from west to east and from north to south.

THE AFRICAN CONTINENT

Film producers often begin movies with a panoramic view of the setting, gradually moving the camera in tighter and closer to the subject. To understand the food culture of sub-Saharan Africa it is equally helpful to view the big picture, both geographically and historically.

Africa is the second largest continent in the world. At about one-fifth the world's total land area, or 11,668,000 square miles, it could hold Argentina (1.1 million square miles), all of the United States (3.7 million square miles), China (3.7 million square miles), India (1.2 million square miles), Europe (about 1.9 million square miles), and New Zealand (more than 100,000 square miles).

The equator runs horizontally through the center of Africa with the northernmost and southernmost tips equidistant from it. The temperate climates of the continent are found in these extreme northern and southern locations. Africa teems with diversity and striking extremes. In much of equatorial Africa there are great rain forests of valuable hardwoods such as mahogany and ebony. These rainforests have sometimes served as barriers to the movement of peoples. Almost 75 percent of the continent is tropical or subtropical. There are grasslands, savannas, mountains, plains, highlands and lowlands, and numerous islands. One of the islands, Madagascar, is the fourth-largest island in the world. Sub-Saharan Africa also has many mineral reserves, including diamonds, gold, oil, bauxite, and copper.

The climate patterns vary dramatically, with weather patterns north of the equator reversed south of the equator. The desert areas receive little rainfall and are dominated by constantly blowing hot, dry, dust-laden winds. As one moves from the Sahara desert into the tropical areas humidity increases, then semiarid steppe and tropical savanna give way to tropical rain forests that stretch across what is known as "equatorial Africa" from the Atlantic Ocean to the Rift Valley of eastern Africa. This pattern reverses as one crosses the equator and moves south, into the desert regions of South Africa and Namibia, and culminates in the relatively mild, temperate climate of the southwestern tip of the continent and eastern South Africa.

About one-third of the continent is made up of deserts, and the Sahara Desert in the north is the largest desert in the world. It alone covers more than one-fourth of the continent. The word *Sahara* comes from an Arabic word for desert, and the Sahara Desert is often viewed figuratively as a "sea of sand." The Arabic word *sahel* means shore or border, and the word *Sahelian* refers to the areas bordering the Sahara. As a result of drought, climate changes, overgrazing, and excessive farming leading to deforestation, the Sahara is creeping southward every year.

However, this was not always the case. Important to understanding the "unity and continuity" that Davidson alludes to is recognition that the Sahara Desert was not always a barrier. Although it was largely impenetrable through much of the Middle Stone Age, some time after 10,000 B.C.E., the environment changed. For about 3,000 years, between 5500 and 2500 B.C.E., the Sahara was a green and fertile land: as the climate cooled, rivers and pastures emerged, and peoples, ideas, and technologies intermingled. The land could support relatively large populations, and their lifestyles were recorded by artists who engraved and painted compelling pictures on stone of the people, gods, cattle, grains, and wild game. This wet phase is known as the *Makalian* time, and the Saharans who lived here experimented with farming, making this area the cradle of the farming cultures of the Neolithic (or "New Stone") Age.

Sometime before 2500 B.C.E. the pattern reversed, and the Sahara began reverting to desert as rainfall again decreased, rivers dried up, and pastures withered, forcing people to migrate east to Egypt and the Nile, south toward the Ethiopian plateau, and westward.

The Sahara Desert, a formidable entity, is commonly considered to separate northern Africa and sub-Saharan Africa. The more Arabic North African countries of Morocco, Tunisia, Algeria, Libya, and Egypt are strongly linked to the Mediterranean and Middle East, with histories, climates, and cultures that differ in many ways from those of the countries south of the Sahara. However, there are important links among all parts of Africa, such as languages and ethnic groups.

PEOPLES AND LANGUAGES

Africa is estimated to have a population of around 700 million. Roughly half of those people, almost 350 million, live in sub-Saharan Africa. The region has 47 countries, most of which have regained their independence from European countries since the late 1950s. The national borders of these countries were generally carved out in the nineteenth century by colonial powers during the infamous "Scramble for Africa" and make little sense geographically or culturally, a reality that has imposed serious burdens on newly independent nations. There are thousands of different ethnic groups, and estimates run from 1,000 to 1,700 separate languages. People speaking different languages and with different cultural histories and allegiances have often found themselves cut off from relatives who were arbitrarily assigned to other countries; conversely, people found themselves sharing a nation with their former enemies.

These ethnic groups and languages probably evolved from much smaller pools. In the Early Stone Age, perhaps 50,000 years ago, there were likely only a handful of types of people in Africa: the so-called little people, including the San (formerly labeled bushmen) of the southwestern deserts, and the ancestors of the Khoi (formerly labeled Hottentots) of southern Africa, and the predecessors of the pygmies of the equatorial forests; secondly, the ancestors of the dark-skinned Negroid peoples of western and central Africa; and finally, descendents from the mingling of indigenous peoples with neighboring Asians in the north and northeast, possibly as early as the Middle Stone Age.

There have been efforts to combine DNA-mapping and linguistic studies to untangle the early roots of people on the continent. Four main original language groups have been identified: the Niger-Kordofanian (sometimes broken into the Niger-Congo and Kordofanian), the Nilo-Saharan, the Khoisan, and the Afro-Asiatic (sometimes called the Hamito-Semitic). The Niger-Kordofanian is by far the most prevalent language family, and the vast majority of sub-Saharans speak languages that have evolved from this, covering a wide geographic area from western Africa through eastern and southern Africa. A sub-branch, the Bantu languages, includes Zulu, Xhosa, and Swahili, some of the better-known African languages. Khoisan, also known as the *click* language, is the smallest language family. The once-numerous San and Khoikhoi people of the dry regions of southwestern Africa and the Hadza and Sandawe of northern Tanzania are today facing extinction. The Nilo-Saharan family divides into six branches and is so widely dispersed that it has been difficult to study. The sub-branches are Songhai, Saharan, Maban, Furian, Koman, and the main sub-branch, Chari-Nile. Chari-Nile languages are spoken in Sudan, Congo, Uganda, Cameroon, Chad, The Democratic Republic of the Congo (DRC), Kenya, Tanzania, and Ethiopia. Afro-Asiatic comprises languages such as Arabic, Berber, Cushite, Hausa, ancient Egyptian, and Amharic.

In addition, there are parts of sub-Saharan Africa where today two other language families are represented: Indo-European and Malayo-Polynesian. Given its interaction with other nations over the past several hundred years, several Indo-European languages, including Afrikaans, English, French, Portuguese, Spanish, and pidgin English or a form of creole Portuguese, are used. In addition, Malagasy, from the Malayo-Polynesian family, is spoken on Madagascar. The famous language of trade in much of eastern and southern Africa, Swahili (or Kiswahili), is a kind of *creolized* language: although primarily a Bantu language, it contains many Arabic and English words and was first written in Arabic and later Roman script.

Today there are probably 50 or so languages on the entire continent with more than 500,000 speakers each, but many more that are spoken by relatively few people. A country such as Nigeria, the most densely populated country in sub-Saharan Africa with about 125 million people, has roughly 250 different ethnic groups, but only a few of them dominate: Hausa, Fulani, Yoruba, and Igbo (or Ibo). This branching out of languages and ethnic groups corresponds to the migration of peoples on the continent.

A discussion of language families is a reminder of the continuity as well as diversity throughout the continent. This book cannot possibly explore every country and culture in sub-Saharan Africa. Therefore, it is important to remember the interconnectedness of the land and its peoples even as one sets out to distinguish among them.

The following chapters will consider the "who, what, why, where, when, and how" of food within a variety of cultures in sub-Saharan Africa. Material is organized around the major geographical regions of sub-Saharan Africa: western, southern, eastern, and central. This device has the advantage of neatness and precedent but forces together some strange bedfellows. As was noted, the accidents of colonial history sometimes bear little relationship to cultural and geographical continuity. Another strategy would have been to consider the countries of what is called the "Horn of Africa" separately. These include Eritrea, Djibouti, Ethiopia, and Somalia, and are in many ways culturally separated from their East Africa neighbors. Or the islands such as Madagascar, with its Malaysian influences and language, could have been treated apart from southern Africa. Former Portuguese colonies such as Angola, DRC, Mozambique, and São Tomé and Principe could have been discussed together. In the end, simplicity and convention won out, but the reader should remember that national boundaries are not the only, nor always the most helpful, way to make sense of sub-Saharan Africa.

NOTES

1. http://www.afriprov.org/resources/explain.htm#aug1998.

2. Basil Davidson, *Africa, History of a Continent* (New York: Macmillan, 1966), pp. 10, 29.

3. Rebecca Dyasi (comp.) and Louise Crane (ed.), *Good Tastes in Africa* (Urbana-Champaign, Ill.: Center for African Studies, African Outreach Series, No. 3, 1983), p. ix.

4. Esther A. Dagan, *The African Calabash: When Art Shares Nature's Gift* (Montreal: Galerie Amrad African Arts, 1988), p. 15.

Timeline

Note: Many of these dates are approximations derived from the best estimates by historians and anthropologists.

About 4 million years ago (Paleolithic, or Old Stone Age)	Birthplace of first humans (East Africa).
By around 7000 B.C.E. (Neolithic, or Late Stone Age)	Hunters, gatherers, fishermen live in savannahs and forest areas. Use of stone tools and equipment such as grinding stones emerge.
5500–c. 2500 B.C.E. (Wet or Makalian Phase)	Sahara is green, fertile, and inhabited, including by Saharans who hunted and began experimenting with agriculture.
5000–3000 B.C.E.	Nubian and South African rock paintings and pottery document culture.
3000–1000 B.C.E.	Western Africa: Indigenous yam cultivation already well established. Before 60,000 B.C.E. probably wild yams were eaten and by 11,000 B.C.E. beginnings of cultivation; palm oil part of diet and culture before 3000 B.C.E. Sorghum, most important indigenous cereal grain cultivated in sub-Saharan Africa, cultivated in Sudanic and Guinean zone by 3000 B.C.E. Pearl millet (2nd most important indigenous cereal grain), cultivated by 1000 B.C.E. Finger millet (in southern and eastern Africa), also teff (East) and fonio (western).

3000–2000 B.C.E.	Cattle believed introduced from North Africa into Ethiopia by Cushites, who also became the first camel herders in Africa.
1500 B.C.E.	African rice (*oryza glaberrima*) domesticated in Niger and Senegal River Valleys (Sine-Saloum and Casamance rivers); origins thought to be more than 130 million years ago in Gondwanaland.
1000–350 B.C.E.	Nubian Kingdom of Cush (Kush) (commercial and cultural center linking Mediterranean and Middle Eastern civilizations with black African civilizations). Known for stone pyramids and iron-working center at Merowe. Metal technology greatly increases productivity in agriculture. As early as 1000 B.C.E. Arabs begin replacing donkey caravans with camel caravans.
500–100 B.C.E.	Nok culture in Nigeria (iron-working and terra cotta sculptures at height in 200 B.C.E.).
400 B.C.E.	Western Bantu migrations reachs the Democratic Republic of the Congo (DRC) in central Africa. Bantu speakers are associated with the spread of ironworking and agriculture and a distinctive pottery style.
200 B.C.E.	Increased use of iron in sub-Saharan Africa allowed development of tools such as iron hoes and knives to improve agriculture and hunting. Jenne (Djenne), the oldest known Iron Age city in sub-Saharan Africa, is supported by rice and trans-Saharan trade but established before that trade. The inhabitants domesticated sorghum and millet and kept cattle.
100 B.C.E.	Bantu-speaking peoples introduce iron-working into area south of Sudan.
1 C.E.	Beginnings of East African city-states and influence from Arabia in East Africa, eventually including Muslim dietary influences and Asian spices, foods, and cooking techniques. More Bantu migration.
	Probable existence of baobab trees, with their myriad social and culinary uses (about 1000–3000– year lifespan).

	Camels have revolutionized desert transportation and by 200–300 trans-Saharan trade flourishes in West Africa. Saharan and Malian salt deposits provide the precious mineral to West Africans in exchange for gold, ivory, slaves, cola nuts, and melegueta pepper. Horses, glassware, and Mediterranean goods also flow south from the north.
1–800	Semitic Kingdom of Aksum (Axum) (Ethiopia) (East Africa)..
200–900	Continued expansion of Bantu speakers.
250	Aksum controls Red Sea trade.
300–1076	Kingdom of Ghana (West Africa).
350–500	Bantu-speaking people have arrived in southern Africa. A pastoral people, they introduce cattle herding and the kraal.
400	Jenne-Jeno in Nigeria and Timbuktu are trans-Saharan trade centers. Aksum converts to Christianity, setting the stage for the Amharic state of Ethiopia and the Coptic church, with a diet dominated by numerous fast days and dietary restrictions.
500–900	Malaysian bananas and coconuts established in East African diet, probably spreading from Madagascar and East Africa to rest of the continent. Along with Malayo-Polynesian colonizers of Madagascar and the Comoros, Arabian and Persian traders also probably introduced mangoes, limes, black pepper, and ginger.
600–700	Muslims conquer northern Africa (Syria, Persia, Egypt) and continue to extend Muslim influence into sub-Saharan Africa, including dietary influences.
c. 600–1500 (or, 700 to 1911)	Arab–Indian Ocean slave trade: Extensive slave trade from sub-Saharan Africa (from East Africa to Mesopotamia, southwest Asia, Indonesia, and China) and the Mediterranean. Dhows were used by Arab and Persian (Iranian) Muslim traders to sail to the coasts to engage in trade, exchanging glass beads, glassware, ironware, textiles, wheat, and wine for gold, ivory, tortoise shell, rhino horn, and, primarily, slaves.

	An estimated 14 million Africans, many women and young boys, are enslaved, and urban cosmopolitan port cities along the coast from Somalia to Mozambique are established. Intermarriage with the traders become common, further increasing the cultural mix of foods, spices, religious taboos, and cooking techniques.
600	Coffee estimated to have been discovered growing wild in Kaffa in Ethiopia's southwest highlands or plateaus of central Ethiopia. It is reported commercially cultivated there during the 1400s. The early trade is closely monopolized by Arabs and by the middle of the sixteenth century has been widely accepted by Arabian Muslims who value its stimulating effects and are forbidden to drink wine (thus, its name "the wine of Araby").
900–1450	Great Zimbabwe: the most powerful southern African society in the eleventh century trades with Arab-Swahili partners—its agriculture and cattle feed at least 18,000 living near its granite walls.
1000–1505	Swahili coast city-states: blending of Bantu, Arab, and Indian cultures.
1100	Islamic invasion of Sudan.
1170–1900	Kingdom of Benin (by 1600 in decline) (West Africa).
1200–1360	Kingdom of Mali at its peak (West Africa).
1200–1800	Kingdom of Oyo (West Africa).
1250–1967	Lake Kingdoms (Lake Victoria/Lake Tanganyika); By 1750–1800 Buganda (East Africa) is the leading Lake Kingdom.
1250–1836	Kanem-Bornu.
1304–1368	Life of Ibn Batutta, scholar and culinary writer who describes foods of West and East Africa. In 1325 begins his travels in North and East Africa; in 1352–1354 crosses the Sahara to West Africa.
1324	Muslim Malian king Mansa Musa's pilgrimage to Mecca, where he gives the Egyptian sultan so many gifts of gold that its value plummets for a decade.
1400–1700	Kongo Kingdom (Central Africa).
1464–1591	Songhai (Songhay) Empire (West Africa).

1470s–1700s	Portuguese in Africa. Henry the Navigator encourages Portuguese expedition of raiders on Senegal River to capture black slaves from Senegal and take them to Lisbon.
1482	First Portuguese outpost, Elmina Castle (São Jorge da Mina), on coast of Ghana.
1480s	Portuguese successfully introduce cassava to central Africa via Kingdom of Kongo (present-day Angola); less successfully to West Africa, along with peanuts.
	Portuguese explorers and settlers likely introduce chili peppers from Americas into western Africa, where people and birds spread the seeds and plants throughout the continent.
1497	Explorer Vasco da Gama sails to East Africa.
1505	Kilwa destroyed.
1528	Mombasa captured.
1500s	Portuguese thought to have introduced sweet potatoes to West Africa from Brazil. Maize probably introduced to East Africa in 1500s by Portuguese traders. Maize probably travels from the West Indies to Gold Coast (Ghana) and by 1700s used to feed slaves. By the end of 1700s it spreads throughout West and central Africa. Portuguese may have introduced pineapple to coast of Kenya and Tanzania.
1520s–1860s	Trans-Atlantic slave trade (roughly 9.5 to 12 million African men, women, and children carried to slavery in Western Hemisphere). Often fed local African foods during trip, such as yams, palm oil, rice, and malegueta pepper. Also, they were fed peanuts, corn, and plantains. This transfer of foods between continents became part of what is called the "Columbian Exchange."
1600–1894	Kingdom of Dahomey (West Africa).
1680–1901	Ashanti (Asante) Kingdom (West Africa).
1652	Dutch settlers, ancestors of Afrikaners, arrive in Cape Town. These settlers bring slaves from Mozambique, Madagascar, and the East to work for them, introducing a Malaysian strand into southern African cooking.
1780	First "Kaffir War" between Bantus and Boers in South Africa.

1815–1828	Shaka becomes clan leader and reorganizes Zulu military to expand Zululand but spreads much terror and disruption throughout southern Africa.
1808	Britain and United States abolish slave trade.
1821	Liberia formed by returning ex-slaves (in 1824 first settlement named Monrovia after U.S. president James Monroe, and their colony, Liberia).
1834	Slavery abolished in British Empire.
1835	Boers begin "Great Trek" out of Cape Colony.
1870s–1902	"Scramble for Africa" (European colonial expansion of 90 percent of Africa).
1879	Cocoa introduced into Ghana from Fernando Po by Tetteh Quashie. Although cocoa originated in Central America, it reached Africa through the Spanish and Dutch via São Tomé and Fernando Po islands in the early 1800s. After commercial production began under Tetteh Quashie, West Africa quickly became a leading commercial producer of high quality cocoa beans in the late nineteenth and throughout much of the twentieth century.
1884–1885	Berlin Congress partitions Africa among European powers.
late 1800s	British lay the foundations of Kenya and Tanzania's coffee industries by introducing Brazilian coffee plants on plantations.
1900s	Former slaves returning to West Africa from Brazil spread cassava cultivation, teaching the making of farinha de mandioca (*gari* or *garri*).
1919	Treaty of Versailles: Germany loses its African colonies after World War I; subsequently the League of Nations gives them to Britain, France, and Belgium, adding to the cultural mix of European influences in the diet of the colonies.
1948–1949	Apartheid begins in South Africa with election of Afrikaner-led National Party.
1987	Beginnings of Nando's Chickenland restaurant chain in Johannesburg.

1957–the present   African colonies under European rule win indepen-
                     dence, beginning with Ghana in 1957 up to Namibia
                     in 1990. In 1993 Eritrea gains independence from
                     Ethiopia, and in 1994 Nelson Mandela is elected
                     president when South Africa holds free elections. Ris-
                     ing pride in indigenous cuisines occurs simultaneously
                     with urban interest in other culinary influences, es-
                     pecially Western fast food such as fried chicken and
                     chips or french fries, pizza, sweets such as ice cream
                     and frozen yoghurt, and "exotic" Western fruits.

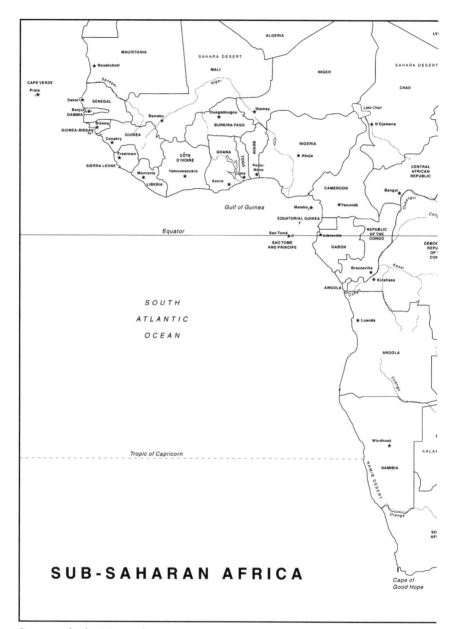

SUB-SAHARAN AFRICA

Cartography by Mapcraft.com

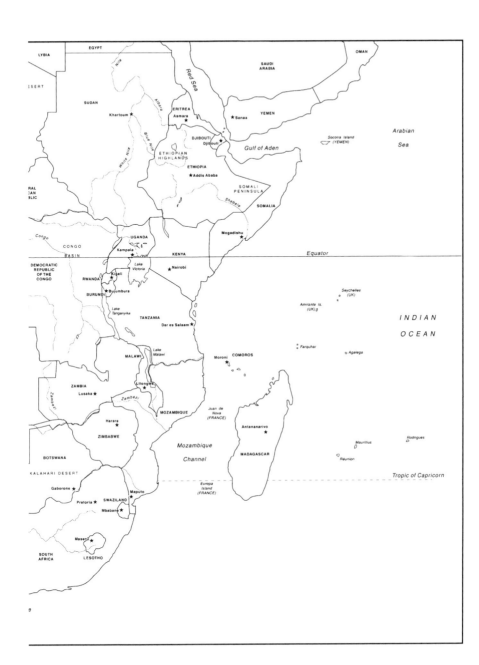

1

Western Africa

Wɔde ayaaseduru na ɛhyɛn abɛn.
It takes a heavy (full) stomach to blow the trumpet.[1]

—Twi Proverb (Ghana)

INTRODUCTION

What Is West Africa?

"Western Africa" or "West Africa" means different things to different people. It is intimately associated with the word *guinea,* derived from the Berber words *aguinaw* or *gnawa* for black man. Guinea is applied to everything from country names to a native African bird, from the coastal countries together to a type of GRAIN, even to a seventeenth-century English coin made from West African gold.

To some, West Africa refers only to 11 countries along the Guinea Coast from Senegal to Nigeria that have coastlines bordering the Atlantic Ocean and are part of the continent: Senegal, The Gambia, Guinea-Bissau, Guinea, Sierra Leone, Liberia, Côte D'Ivoire (Ivory Coast), Ghana, Togo, Benin, and Nigeria. Others include Cape Verde, the cluster of volcanic islands to the west of Senegal, or the nations bordering each of these countries. Still others include the countries north of the Guinea coastal nations, which border the Sahara Desert, the Sea of Sand. These are sometimes called the Sahelian countries and, along with Mauritania, are usually considered to include the semiarid countries of Mali, Niger, Chad, Burkina Faso, and the Sudan. Sometimes the western Sahara, adjoining Morocco, is included, too. This chapter will consider western Africa in a broad sense.

Simply assigning names to the countries of this region does not take one very far. Western Africa is a like a patchwork quilt. It is a world bursting with color, energy, and a lavish variety of smells, sounds, and images: these include arid and semiarid lands; palm-lined coasts with fishermen on painted boats tossing nets into the waters; dense tropical forests with squawking parrots, monkeys, and cocoa or oil palm plantations; grassy savanna with antelope and elephants and other wild game; and great curving rivers, mountains, and plateaus. Its music moves beyond the rain beating on the earth or the waves beating on the shore to include talking drums, flutes, stringed instruments, thumb pianos, bamboo xylophones, and the voices of griots telling epic stories, or groups of people engaged in call and response songs. There are Ashanti kings and queens being carried on palanquins under huge brightly colored umbrellas and Fulani men herding their cattle over wide arid spaces in search of food and water.

The earth itself comes in myriad colors and textures, from red lateritic soil to white sand, from gray to chocolate edible clays, holding within it sometimes gold, sometimes bauxite, sometimes oil, sometimes diamonds. It is home to giant anthills and massive baobab trees.

Western Africa is sometimes pounded by rains, with flooded riverbanks and rice fields, but other times subject to killing drought. The harmattan season, when dry, dusty winds blow west from the Sahara Desert, brings ubiquitous red dust. Small family farm plots are scattered throughout the countryside, where women and children fetch water from rivers, wells, or faucets; or gather wood for cooking fires or to make charcoal; or pound yams, plantains, cassava, and millet with mortars and pestles; or grind vegetables. Other enterprising women, with covered outdoor booths or small shops in the cities, are successful and powerful market women, selling their cloth, fresh or smoked fish, canned food, or a myriad of other items from beauty products to vegetables.

There are spotless rural homesteads with hard dirt floors and thatched roofs, modern roads with streetlights, as well as narrow country paths with lurking snakes. It is a place of generosity and celebration, with the smell of roasting goat or ripe plantain slices, of thick creamy peanut soup, of spicy meat kabobs or steaming plates of *jollof* rice, of vibrant music at outdoor patios, of people drinking beer, sipping palmwine under trees, or spooning soft meat from green coconuts.

There are also places of poverty to be seen and smelled: open sewers, rotting trash, rusting tin roofs, people weakened by malaria or AIDS, and children orphaned and left homeless by wars. Western Africa is a land of contrasts—from Western fast food chicken or pizza restaurants, BMWs, and air-conditioned hotels to dilapidated schools, broken fans, and roads choked with the exhaust from diesel buses and vans. There are tall trees, clustered earthen huts, and cement story buildings. While the rich have impregnable walled homes with watchmen and padlocked gates, ordinary folks may live in simple clusters of mud-walled buildings and earthen floors, with kitchens housing clay or plastic water pots, woven baskets, and aluminum cooking pots.

One sees food vendors in the cities or along travel routes selling bread, oranges, bananas, pineapple, coconuts, kola nuts, boiled yams, or steamed cornmeal balls with hot pepper sauce, fried fish, plantain cubes or chips, tiger nuts, bean fritters, deep-fried cookies and doughnuts, meat turnovers, eggs, and chewing gum. Women and children call out "ice water" as they hawk little plastic bags stored in plastic ice chests, or sell drinks of water from a plastic bucket. Others sell Fan icemilk from bicycles, or prawns strung on skewers. Babies sleep on their mothers' or sisters' backs, people balance huge headloads of stools, or foodstuffs, or a sewing machine, or cloth, or yams, or nuts, so gracefully the loads seem to weigh nothing. Colorful outdoor markets display piles of canned corned beef and sardines, cola nuts, bouillon cubes, peppers, cowpeas, tomatoes, onions, peanuts, dried fish and corn, bunches of plantains, yams, cocoyam, cassava, *gari*, okra, garden eggs, millet, sorghum, and various greens, spices, and herbs.

In the bursting cities, beggars call out or raise their hands alongside underemployed young men stationed along the roads with newspapers, maps, tapes, tourist art, CDs, dog leashes, watches, or chewing gum. One hears taxis blow their horns and sees overcrowded buses and minivans. People busily go about their daily lives, often cheerfully greeting people, shaking hands, snapping fingers, and touching.

The clothing is breathtaking: rainbow-colored traditional clothes from batik and tie-dyed indigo to coarsely woven cloth, brightly colored or in muted earth tones. Women dress in outfits that range from simple pieces of cloth to elaborate fashions with dazzling embroidery, crowned by the latest headties or elaborate hairdos that take hours and an entire crew to plait and style, and bodies adorned with stunning gold earrings or beaded necklaces. There is a mix of clothing styles: Muslim men from the north wear little round woven hats or pointed leather ones with wide brims, coarsely woven cotton cloth, and leather garments, leather sandals, and bags; people everywhere are incongruously dressed in recycled Western jeans and tee-shirts with eclectic sayings or polyester blouses and dresses alongside traditional handmade clothes. Cheap plastic jewelry, purses, thongs, and beads increasingly replace indigenous materials.

The region is pervaded by a deep spirituality. Visible and invisible worlds are closely united. Among the Muslim areas, concentrated in the northern parts of the region, the faithful stop to pray five times a day, and one hears Mullahs calling from the mosques, affirming the oneness of God and Mohammed as his prophet. This vital spirituality is seen among the Christian areas, too, especially in the spiritual churches where dancing and drumming go on day and night. Often there is a mix of beliefs intermingled, and traditional practices, gods, and healers coexist with or thrive within adopted faiths. Undergirding all of these approaches is a profound sense of God's (or gods') presence and efficacy in the world, of the reality of witches, wizards, and good and evil spirits in an environment that is often uncertain and hostile to survival. Always there is respect for, and frequently fear of, the ancestors who link the past, present, and future.

Diversity is incarnated among the myriad ethnic groups mingling together in each country, as well as among the variety of Westerners and non-Westerners speaking languages such as Arabic, German, French, English, Portuguese, Hindi, Lebanese, and Japanese.

The preceding images provide a collage of West Africa, a part of sub-Saharan Africa with many links to the Western world, particularly to the United States, the Caribbean, and Brazil.

HISTORICAL OVERVIEW

Early History and Geography

Western Africa has a distinguished history. It begins long before the slave trade and includes interwoven tales of salt and the *melegueta* pepper as well as gold and ivory, of trade routes and ancient powerful empires. More recent history incorporates tales of adopted foods such as corn, cassava, peppers, tomatoes, rice, peanuts, or cocoa into slavery and colonialism, all of which are also linked to the contemporary food culture.

The geography of this part of sub-Saharan Africa includes gradually merging horizontal bands: in the north the Sahara Desert blends into the Sahel, the semidry country bordering the desert; then into the savanna or tropical grassland, the largest vegetation zone in Africa; and finally into the tropical forest regions along the Guinea coast. Basically all of western Africa is below 5,000 feet (1,500 meters), with most of it made up of plains lying below 1,500 feet. There are some mountainous plateaus in Nigeria, Togo, Guinea, Liberia, Côte D'Ivoire, and Sierra Leone, but many smaller hills and ridges. Aside from the desert areas, the land is criss-crossed with great rivers—primarily the Niger that travels about 300 miles from the Atlantic coast in Guinea, northeastward toward the desert, then southeast and south through Niger and Nigeria. Other great river systems include Senegal, Volta, and Benue, and there are many short rivers as well. Western Africa has low muddy coasts with mangrove swamps and creeks as well as coastal areas with long, smooth, sandy beaches. Rainfall varies greatly. Usually there are one or two rainy seasons and a long dusty dry season.

A common thread stitching together the western Africa quilt is the centrality of water, whether from rainfall or rivers, to life and the cultures that develop around it. Around 10,000 years ago, people hunted, fished for food, or gathered wild plants. They tended to live in small, mobile groups, moving as necessary to obtain food. Those who lived in the sa-vanna areas hunted wild game and gathered plants such as nuts, berries, roots, and tubers. Those near rivers caught fish, and people living along the coast caught and ate shellfish. Most people probably did a mixture. Around 4,000 years ago when the Sahara Desert began to grow arid again, people who had become livestock herders and who were members of the Nilo-Saharan language group probably moved south as the climate wors-ened and population pressures increased. There they likely mixed with other groups that included both Nilo-Saharan speakers and members of the Mande and Atlantic branches of the Niger-Congo language group.

Water was the critical factor. The places most likely to support stable agriculture included rivers and the surrounding areas (i.e., the Niger River valley and its tributaries, the valley of the Senegal River, and Lake Chad, much larger then than it is today). It is not surprising that several countries in West Africa share names with the life-sustaining rivers or lakes that are within their borders: Niger, Nigeria, Senegal, The Gambia, Chad.

When people began making stone tools and equipment, such as grind-ing stones, and even more so when they could make metal tools such as hoes, agricultural communities developed and wild grains were domesti-cated. No one knows exactly how the agricultural development spread, but some of the Nilo-Saharan speakers were probably the earliest cultiva-tors of pearl millet. In the upper Niger River and Senegal River valleys agricultural production systems seem to have developed around African rice (the Senegambia), *fonio*, and guinea millet, while the Lake Chad area was likely where sorghums were first grown. Archaeologists believe that rice cultivation supported the ancient civilization of Senegambia and some of the early towns of the western Sudan such as Jenne.

Cattle, sheep, and goats came from outside of Africa in several waves from southwest and central Asian sources and likely spread across the area gradually from the Senegal River valley. Cattle may also have been introduced from the east, but it is also possible that indigenous varieties of a humpless type of cattle, *Bos primigenius,* were domesticated from within the Sahara and evolved into *Bos taurus.* Cattle herding was often the specialty of Fulbe or Fulani groups, who remain pastoralists throughout western Africa. Other groups, such as the Serer and Wolof of Senegal and the Soninke of Mali, may have originated in areas of southern Mauritania that became desert.

People first gathered wild tubers and other wild plant foods along the edges of the tropical forest zones. It is uncertain when they began domesticating them. It probably originated among some Kwa-speaking peoples (a branch of the Niger-Kordofanian language family) about 3000 to 2000 B.C.E. in the forest/savanna interface, rather than in the forest proper. African yams are neither well suited to the wet rainforest nor the grassland, but to the in-between area, because they have a vine that needs support to climb and also need some dry season time. Apparently poisonous versions of yam were planted around the nonpoisonous types, to keep out monkeys and thieves. Yam cultivation and the more intricate, stable social organization that tended to go along with it likely helped facilitate the Bantu speakers' dispersion across central, eastern, and southern Africa.

The oil palm, too, considered the second most economically valuable plant after yams, needs the moisture of the tropical rainforest zone, but also more sunshine than is available in densely forested areas. Pigeon peas and sesame, too, are probably native to and were first domesticated in western Africa.

Early Kingdoms

The environment ancient West Africans faced required flexibility and innovation to maximize the available resources, but it also forced them to develop communities that looked to the past and precedent to ensure stability. People organized themselves in different ways: some communities, especially those that were less sedentary, tended to be democratic and nonhierarchical; others, often the more stable communities, developed elaborate systems of kings and religious rulers and classes.

One of the oldest known cities in West Africa, and the oldest known Iron Age city in sub-Saharan Africa, was established before the influential trans-Saharan trade. It is the city of Jenne (Djenne) in present-day Mali, which was established around 200 B.C.E. Jenne, once a wealthy commercial and educational center, was a good place to grow rice. People forced down from the Sahara Desert as it became drier probably settled there, and archaeologists have found hulls of domesticated rice, sorghum, millet, and wild swamp grasses. By 450 the city covered more than 60 acres, and eventually people began working iron and importing both iron ore and gold, copper, stone grinders, and beads. Craft castes probably emerged. Jenne was at its height from 450–1100 but declined to a ghost town between 1200 and 1400 as the climate grew increasingly dry and unable to sustain agriculture and support cattle.

Islam, introduced by North Africans such as the Berbers, or Arab traders, began to exert increasing influence on sub-Saharan Africa from around the 700s. Islam was a force in Africa in the ninth century and greatly expanded in influence in the eleventh and twelfth centuries. Jenne's king converted to Islam in 1180, and Islamic Jenne was an important city in the empire of Mali. The city is remembered for its impressive mosques built out of fermented rice husks, earth, and water. The mosque there today is four stories high and has three minarets each almost 60 feet high. Its spires are topped by ostrich eggs, a symbol of good fortune and fertility.

Nok culture flourished in the forest region of southeastern Nigeria as early as 500 B.C.E. The Nok were renowned as artists, but also for their iron-working technology, including making iron hoes and other tools that made it easier to clear vegetation and prepare the soil, as well as to build more efficient weapons.

The introduction of both stone and iron tools enabled people to grow a surplus of crops in and near the forested regions of West Africa. They especially helped improve oil palm cultivation and that of root crops such as African yams. The changes in technology probably also contributed to more specialization of labor and more complicated, usually patriarchal, systems of social organization.

There were other famous centralized states, or kingdoms, some of which coexisted over decades. These early empires are referred to as the Sudanic Kingdoms because they developed in the large grassland region of West Africa that is often called the Sudanic belt—that is, neither in the harsh desert nor the dense rainforest environments.

Scholars differ on the exact dates, but the Ghana Empire flourished from 700 to around 1076. This proud empire was located in present-day Mali and Mauritania, and the contemporary nation of Ghana is named after it.

The city of Jenne was part of the empire of Mali, the inspiration for present-day Mali's name. Mali's founding is told in the epic poem "Sundiata" (or Sundjata), which chronicles the life of Mansa (King) Sundiata Keita (ca. 1210–1260), the king's son who defeated the Ghanaian king (Sosso) Sumanguru and founded Mali's empire. Mali was most powerful from the 1200s to about 1360 when it began to decline. At its peak it spread over large parts of today's countries of Mali, southern and western Mauritania, and Senegal. Mande-speaking people (including the Bamana, Senufo, and Dogon peoples) lived in the area since that time, although some have migrated throughout West Africa. This movement typifies the characteristic mobility of many sub-Saharan African peoples in response to changing climactic conditions, wars, work, or trade opportunities.

Mali's legendary wealth is illustrated by the story of Islamic Malian emperor Mansa Musa's pilgrimage to Mecca in 1324. He is said to have traveled with thousands of soldiers, officials, and attendants, 100 camels each carrying 300 pounds of gold, plus 500 maids and slaves to serve Mansa Musa's senior wife. Mansa Musa was reported to have given the Egyptian sultan so many gifts of gold that the value in Egypt fell drastically for a decade.

In addition to the mosque at Jenne, others were built in the cities of Gao and Timbuktu (or Tombouctou), other important stops along the trading routes that developed. The main ruling powers were also located in these major cities/commercial centers.

These descriptions are just a slice of the rich history of the region. There were numerous other early West African kingdoms, such as the Songhai (or Songhay, Songhey) Kingdom, with its beginnings in the 800s from a fishing community but most powerful from 1464–1591, the Asante Kingdom emerging in the late 1600s, and kingdoms of Dahomey (1600–1894), Kanem-Bornu (1250–1836), and the Yoruba kingdoms of Ife and Benin that rose to power in the eleventh and twelfth centuries.

The great Islamic states were distinguished by the ability to centralize the political and military power while letting the local rulers keep their traditional identities alongside Islam.

However, it was not only within the great kingdoms of centralized authority, wealth, and kings that the story of West Africa (or, indeed, all of sub-Saharan Africa) lies. Along with these urban cultures, in other places, such as among the Tallensi of northern Ghana, communities developed that were decentralized and had no interest in forming states. They continued to grow and develop intricate and flexible arrangements for individual and collective social life. Although some peoples sought to acquire and accumulate, others consciously chose not to do so.

Trade Routes (Salt, Gold, Slaves, and Islam)

Initially, Arab merchants used donkey caravans to transport goods. Possibly beginning as early as 1000 B.C.E., camel caravans began to revolutionize travel. The camels were able to travel long distances without water and to carry heavy loads. Their use also facilitated the spread of Islam. By 200–300 important trade networks flourished across the great sea of sand, the Sahara. This trade was partly stimulated by the African desire to obtain the precious mineral salt, found in large deposits in the Sahara but scarce in the forest and savanna regions of West Africa. The salt was mined in large slabs that weighed up to 220 pounds and was carried by camels to the great cities such as Timbuktu. Those who controlled the salt in the north, generally Muslim traders, traded it for gold, slaves, ivory, cola nuts, *melegueta* pepper, and other goods and food from these regions. The trading centers became important commercial cities besides promoting the spread of Islam. Mediterranean goods, glass, and horses flowed from north to south. It is said that salt set the value of gold and they were traded in equal weights. The development of the trade centers was a part of the rise of the great kingdoms of Mali, Ghana, and Songhai. Other sources of salt came from deposits in present-day Mali and were transported by the Niger River to river ports throughout West Africa. Alternative local methods of obtaining salt were by using ashes such as from the oil palm or baobab trees. Some areas evaporated sea water to get salt, but apparently the salt slabs were preferred. However, the salt obtained by evaporating the saline waters of Lake Chad was reportedly more highly prized for millet porridge than the slab salt.

The trading goods often corresponded to names given by western powers to the countries along the Guinea coast during the years of Western expansion and slavery from the fifteenth century through most of the nineteenth century. The former Gold Coast is now Ghana, Côte D'Ivoire is still the Ivory Coast, the general area of Liberia was called the Grain Coast (after the *melegueta* pepper, or Grains of Paradise), and the whole area along the Guinea coast bordering the Bight of Benin (Ghana, Togo, Benin, and Nigeria) was known variously as the Windward Coast, the Rice Coast, and the Slave Coast. Slavery, while known and practiced in Africa long before the arrival of Europeans, was more like serfdom or the indentured servants in medieval Europe and was of a completely different character than the racist version that became known as the transatlantic slave trade.

Raising Crops, Harvesting, and Division of Labor

In western Africa many families traditionally grow or raise the food for their own families, and there is a division of labor. Among agricultural peoples, in some areas rice is completely a woman's crop; in other areas men and women each have specific tasks, from selecting seed to hoeing, sowing, weeding, transplanting, and harvesting. A determining factor may be how important rice is as a dietary staple, with men more involved as the crop becomes more central. Among pastoral peoples, men and boys may have the primary responsibility for caring for cattle. Fishing is primarily a male job, although women may process, preserve, and sell the fish, as well as cook them.

Women play a vital role in growing, harvesting, and preparing food in West Africa. Sub-Saharan Africa as a whole is often cited as the "female farming" region of the world. Provisioning food for their families has generally been an important part of a woman's identity. Women tend to have small vegetable and/or fruit gardens near their houses and may also have larger farms that belong to them exclusively, although they may also provide labor for their fathers' or husbands' farms.

In polygamous households, where a man may have several wives, the wives will take turns preparing his food and will also be responsible for providing food for their children and other members of the household.

How yams are grown, harvested, stored, and prepared varies widely. Some yams may be considered men's yams, and other may be considered women's. In some areas, such as among the Igbo (or Ibo) of Nigeria, or Kabre of Togo, yams are primarily a masculine crop and the responsibility of men, while women are responsible for cultivating other crops considered more feminine. The novels of the famous African writer Chinua Achebe (*Things Fall Apart, No Longer at Ease,* and *Arrow of God*) are often set in the rain forests of Nigeria, where yam farming is central to survival and yams are king. His Igbo characters are farmers, and for men the successful cultivation of the prestigious and labor-intensive yam crops is the route to power and status in society.

In other areas, such as among the Tiv, a complementary division of labor exists. Men tend to clear the fields, prepare the mounds for planting, and stake the tall plants, and women do most of the weeding or harvesting. In other areas women may plant and care for one type of yams, men another.

MAJOR FOODS AND INGREDIENTS

Indigenous Foods

A number of the plant species and animals indigenous to Africa that were important both agriculturally and culturally in the past remain important sources of food in West Africa today. Some have diffused throughout the continent and the globe while others, such as the *melegueta* pepper and *fonio*, have almost disappeared from use.

Baobab (Adansonia Digitata)

If any tree can be said to symbolize Africa, it is probably the ancient and massive baobab tree, which grows on plains throughout sub-Saharan Africa from Senegal in the west to Zimbabwe in the east to South Africa at the extreme southern tip of the continent. The tree bears scented white flowers and has a gourd-shaped, hairy fruit about 30 centimeters long. Some baobab trees are believed to be older than 2,000 years. The trunk of the tree is huge, with a diameter up to 39 feet (12 meters) and the tree grows to be roughly 60 feet (18 meters) tall. Legends tell why the tree was planted "upside down" with its roots reaching the heavens. English explorer David Livingstone is said to have been reminded of a huge carrot planted upside down.

The low, spreading baobab grows in dry savanna areas and, like the oil palm tree, is wonderfully multipurpose. Its leaves are used to make soups and relishes with a prized slippery consistency; ashes from its wood contain enough chlorides to make it useful as salt; and the astringent seeds, with a taste similar to almonds, can be brewed in water to make a beverage, placed under the tongue to allay thirst, dried and ground and added to soups, or simply roasted and eaten. In South Africa the tree is known as the "cream of tartar tree" because the seeds can be made into a type of baking powder. The white spongy fruit is edible. The baobab's trunk usually contains enough water to sustain hunters, and a hollow baobab can even be used as a hut. Many animals, especially birds, rely on the baobab tree for their survival.

Cereals: Sorghum, Millet, and Fonio

Cereal grains most Europeans and North Americans are accustomed to, such as wheat and barley, thrive in temperate climates but do not do well in the tropical climate and soils of sub-Saharan Africa. Africa, however, is said to be the continent that has produced the most indigenous cereal grains. Three of its grains with a long and important history are millets, sorghums, and *fonio*.

Sorghum is now widely cultivated in India, China, and the Americas and is the fourth most valuable cereal crop in the world after rice, wheat, and maize. Sorghum and millet provide energy, protein, vitamins, and minerals for millions of the poorest people in Africa and Asia. Sorghums grow well even in saline soils and during periods of drought and do not require heavy applications of fertilizers. Some varieties of sorghum developed in West Africa, whereas others developed in southern, central, and eastern Africa. Sorghum (as well as millet) is made into *tuwo dawa* in Nigeria and eaten as a porridge, fermented to make sorghum beer called *burkutu* or *pito*, or made into flour and mixed with bean flour then fried to make *dawaki*. The most important indigenous African cereal is *Sorghum bicolor*. There is some confusion between sorghums and millets, because some of the common names of sorghum include "great millet," "guinea corn," "kafir," "milo," and "milo-maize." These cereal crops have been grown for thousands of years in western Africa.

Millet is a small-seeded grain that originally grew in wild grasses. It is rather unfamiliar in the United States, but it is often sold in ethnic or health food stores, as well as in pet stores as bird food. There are several kinds of millets. The earliest known cultivated kind (and the second most important after sorghum) is called pearl millet (*Penisetum glaucum*) or bulrush millet. Another type is the finger millet that prefers wetter and cooler areas and probably originated in Ethiopia. Millets and sorghums are labor-intensive crops, especially to harvest and prepare.

A hardy cereal grain whose popularity has declined is *fonio* (*Digitaria exilis or Digitaria iburua*, usually called *acha* in Nigeria). It is nutritious and still an important food in about 15 West African countries, from the Cape Verde Lake to Chad, and along the Guinea Coast in Guinea, Côte D'Ivoire (Ivory Coast), Togo, and Nigeria, as well as parts of Mali and Burkina Faso. However, removing the brittle husks from each sand-sized grain is tedious. It is said to take an hour of hard work and 15 liters of water to prepare only two kilograms of *fonio* using traditional methods. There is currently interest in the "lost crops of Africa" and ongoing research into the development of low-cost, efficient dehulling machines that could possibly revitalize the use of *fonio*. *Fonio* has been described as one of the world's best-tasting cereals.

Cola (Kola Vera)

Cola (or kola) nuts are seed kernels from an evergreen tree from the cocoa *Sterculiaceae* family in West Africa. Strictly speaking, they are not food, but they contain large amounts of stimulants like caffeine and are important in African ceremonial life. The fresh kernels, or cotyledons, of the seed are one to two inches long, are almost white, and taste bitter when chewed. After the bitter taste, a sweet taste and a feeling of well-being permeates the body. As the nuts dry they turn reddish-brown and lose some of their astringency. Some people allege cola to have aphrodisiac properties. When chewed, they are believed to lessen thirst and hunger. African Muslims, who are forbidden to consume alcohol, are allowed to chew them and may favor them for their stimulating properties. In West Africa they may be offered to a visitor as a sign of peace and hospitality. Before synthetic versions were available, the cola nut found its way around the world as a flavoring in many popular carbonated drinks, such as Coca-Cola.

Egusi (Agushi, Agusi)

Egusi are the seeds of a kind of melon native to Africa. The Latin name for the seeds, and the plant itself, is *Citrullus colocynthis*. They are called *egushi* or *agushi* in Twi, *egusi* in Yoruba, *agusi* in Hausa, and *ogili* in Ibo. Another name for them is bitter apple. The seeds resemble pumpkin seeds, and the hull is often removed so the seed can be roasted and ground. Cooking oil, similar to sunflower seed oil, is also extracted from the seeds. Roasted seeds are eaten as a snack or ground to use as nutritious thickeners for soups or stews. In Nigeria the whole seed may be soaked in water, fermented, then dried and made into a pungent soup ingredient called *ogiri*.

Guinea Fowl

One of the few indigenous food animals from West Africa, guinea fowls are related to pheasants. The most common in western Africa are the helmeted pearl guinea fowl, *Numida meleagris*, from the *Numididae* family, with feathers covered with a grayish/purplish pearl or dot. Although the noisy birds look large, they only weigh about 3.5 pounds and are favored for their delicious meat and wild game flavor. They never became as important as chickens as a food source, but they are eaten and may be found both domesticated and wild.

Melegueta *Pepper, "Grains of Paradise"*

Another early name for a coastal section of West Africa was the Grain Coast, after the *melegueta*, or *malegueta*, pepper, the small, spicy seed of the wild tree from the ginger family, of the species *Aframomum* (or *Amomum*) *Melegueta*. Related to cardamom, it has been called "Grains of Para-

Guinea fowl. Courtesy of the author.

dise," African pepper, British pepper, Jamaican pepper, *melegueta* pepper, and guinea pepper. *Melegueta* pepper was used to prepare both food and beverages and was thought to prevent dysentery and stomach disorders, major problems for slaves during the sea voyages of the Middle Passage. In Europe during the fifteenth century it was a highly prized substitute for the more expensive black peppercorns from Asia and was used both as a seasoning and a medicine. Today the pepper has been largely forgotten by the rest of the world, although it can be found in some health foods stores in the West.

Oil Palm (Elaeis Guineesis)

The official seal of the Republic of Sierra Leone features oil palm trees as a symbol of "strength and health-giving goodness." The oil palm, indigenous to West Africa, has been called the most useful tree in West Africa. Palm oil may have been part of the West African diets at least as early as 3000 B.C.E. The small datelike, orange-red fruits are an important component of many everyday dishes, ritual dishes, and medicines. A soup made using the palmnuts is integral to numerous festivals, such as the Ga Hɔmɔwɔ festival, and may be fed to pregnant or nursing mothers. Many sauces and stews, such as palaver sauce, traditionally include palm oil. Historically, all parts of the tree have been used—fronds, roots, sap, stems, flowers, fruits, kernels, pulp, and oil. Parts of the roots are used in Nigeria for headaches, the palm cabbage for menorrhagia or with peppers and salt to cure bronchitis, and the young leaves to treat gonorrhea. In parts of West (and Central) Africa the juice from young petioles is used to heal cuts, and the thorny bracts are burned to make ashes to put on scratches. Carotene-rich palm oil is found in many local medicines, and the oil of the palm kernel itself is used in ointments, enemas, and as an emollient for the skin and hair. In Côte D'Ivoire the roots are burned to ashes and mixed with salt and palm oil, then drunk by new mothers to help expel the placenta during childbirth. Other forms and parts of the plant are used to treat sleeping sickness or made into a paste to apply to skin ailments. The sap is used as a cooking yeast and the ashes as salt and to make soap.

In addition, the tree is a good source of building materials: from leaves for roofing and sides of huts, to rachis for hut poles, rafters, beds, carrying poles, or ladders. It supplies torches, tinder, toothbrushes or hairbrushes, and brooms. Palm trees, often as old as 50 years, are tapped to make palm-wine from the sap. Although this process usually involves cutting down and thus killing the tree, the decaying tree trunk provides a medium for growing edible mushrooms and insects. The palmwine is drunk fresh or allowed to ferment. Another, less obtrusive but more complex way of tapping the tree involves tapping the sap of a live palm through a cut at the base of the stem of the male flower. The sap is collected in a calabash every morning and evening by climbing the tree.

As with olive trees, there are varieties of oil palms, and the quality of oil varies with the type of processing and the variety of fruit. The quality of virgin palm oil depends on how quickly the palm nuts are boiled after picking, how ripe they are, whether the oil is pressed directly from the boiled seeds or the seeds are left to ferment before processing, and how the oil is extracted. There is soft, unrefined oil, which is liquid at room temperature; semisoft oil; and hard oil, which is solid at room temperature.

Americans are generally familiar only with refined palm oil used in processed foods, a process that removes the oil's natural beta-carotene, an important precursor of the antioxidants vitamin A and vitamin E. The carotene gives palm oil and traditional West African foods a distinctive red color. Limited quantities of palm oil and canned palm fruits for home consumption are imported into the United States.

Okra (Hibiscus Esculentus)

Okra is another indigenous West African vegetable that has spread globally. The English word *okra* is derived from the Twi word *nkuruma* and is famous in the United States as the thickening agent in the gumbo stews of Louisiana. The French word for okra is *gombo*, which, like gumbo, derives from a Bantu word. Okra is related to the hibiscus family, and its pods look a little like a matte version of green jalapeno peppers, with

Two types of palm fruits ("palm nuts") for sale.
Courtesy of the author.

raised ridges running along the sides. It has yellowish-white seeds, and when cut, is famous and (in Africa) much valued for its mucilaginous or sticky properties. It is primarily used cut up in soups and stews.

Rice (Oryza Glaberrima)

An area called the "rice zone" begins above the yam zone in northern Senegal. It is bounded by the Bandama River in central Côte D'Ivoire, then extends inland to Lake Chad. The yam zone and the neighboring rice zone to its north and east represent two distinct culinary and crop areas in West Africa. Both have existed for hundreds of years and still do today, although there are secondary coastal rice cultivation centers.

An indigenous type of West African rice, *Oryza glaberrima*, was first domesticated in the middle Niger area probably about 1500 B.C.E., with a secondary birthplace between the Sine-Saloum and Casamance rivers. The rice-growing communities developed two types of farming systems. The earliest, probably practiced by Mande speakers, used freshwater wetlands and later spread to rain-fed, upland areas. The second, known as the "mangrove" system, was based on irrigation along salty marine estuaries and was probably developed by West Atlantic language speakers. The unpredictable rainfall in these areas varies from 10 to 30 inches in the north where drought is an ever-present threat, to more than 40 inches in the south. African rice was part of the diet at Jenne-Jeno (the original site of

Jenne) by the year 50, and scholars estimate that it was being cultivated along the middle Niger in Mali 2,000 years ago.

Growing rice requires more water than drought-resistant crops such as millet and sorghum and is often part of a diversification strategy in high-risk environments. The rise of rice cultivation in western Africa is linked to the emergence of the states described earlier, such as the Ghana, Mali, and Songhai empires. These empires thrived long before the Portuguese explorers arrived in the fifteenth century.

Later, it was the skills and knowledge of West African men and women in cultivating and processing rice that made them particular targets of slave traders, especially for the lucrative markets of South Carolina rice plantation owners and in the eastern Amazon in Brazil. The West African Coast, as mentioned earlier, was also sometimes called the "Rice Coast."

The Portuguese later introduced a more productive Asian form of rice called *Oryza sativa* that was valued, although the African varieties continued to better handle the often inhospitable African soil conditions, including soil acidity, salinity, iron toxicity, phosphorous deficiency, and flooding. They also tended to grow more quickly, which gave them an advantage over weeds.

Rice Balls *(Omo Tuo)* (West Africa)

2 cups long-grain white rice (not precooked)

7 cups water

1 tsp salt (or to taste)

Bring the rice, water, and salt to a boil in a large heavy pot. Cover. Turn down the heat to low, and allow the rice to cook for about 20 minutes. When the rice is cooked (but not dry), turn off the heat and let it sit for a few minutes until it is cool enough to handle. Using a potato masher or a strong wooden spoon, mash the rice until it is fairly smooth. Fill a cup with cold water and put it next to the pan. Wet hands or dip an ice cream scoop into the water, then scoop up enough of the rice to shape into a ball, like a snowball. If the rice will not stick together, put it back on the stove and allow it to dry slightly before making the balls. Serve the balls in bowls of soup, such as groundnut or palmnut soup.

Shea Butter (Butryospermum Parkii)

Native to West African grasslands, the shea tree, also called the shea butter tree or Bambuk butter tree, produces a small chestnut-sized fruit

Shea-nut processing plant. Courtesy of the author.

high in oil. Its fruits are used in cooking, as a cosmetic emollient, to make soap, and to seal walls to keep houses from being washed away during the rainy season. One of the earliest written references to shea butter comes from the writings of the fourteenth-century Islamic travel writer Ibn Battuta. In 1351, 20 years after a famous trip to East Africa, Battuta traveled south from Morocco and through the Sahara to the Niger. Besides documenting the uses of a variety of food sources such as the versatile baobab tree, he describes shea nuts, calling them by the Arabic word *ghartī*. *Ghartī* likely gave rise to the Fulani word *karchi*, which evolved into its French name *karité*. Shea butter is used in cooking and will keep unsalted without going rancid. Shea nuts are a staple in Dogon communities such as those in Mali. Major producing countries in western Africa include Mali, Burkina Faso, Benin, Senegal, Côte D'Ivoire, Ghana, Gambia, and Nigeria. The trees do not yield fruit for about 20 years and only mature fully after about 45 years. They are said to continue producing until they are about 200 years old. Shea nut trees do not lend themselves to plantation growing and are well established as a "woman's crop." Outside of Africa, shea butter is known primarily for its use as a cosmetic.

Yam Culture

Yams, also called guinea yams, are a root crop believed to be indigenous to West Africa. They first grew wild in an area called the "yam zone," the interface of the forest and savanna zones, and were domesticated from wild varieties at least 3,500 to 4,500 years ago, although some scholars suggest it was more than 10,000 years ago. About 60,000 years ago hunter-gatherers probably ate many species of wild yam. Gradually people realized they could replant the tubers.

There are hundreds of kinds of yams, all belonging to the genus *Dioscorea*. A common misunderstanding outside of Africa is to confuse the yams or sweet potatoes *(Ipomoea batatas)* in the United States with African yams, a tropical plant from the morning glory family. Although sub-Saharan Africans also eat sweet potatoes, yams are from a completely different family and cannot simply be substituted.

West Africans recognize numerous types of yams. In Nigeria the main species grown are white yam *(Dioscorea rotundata)* and yellow yam *(D. cayenensis)*, followed to a lesser extent by the yams *D. esculenta* and *D. dumetorum*. Four commonly grown yams in Ghana include *D. alata, D. rotundata, D. esculenta, and D. dumetorum*, where they are known by local names. *D. alata* and *D. esculenta* are two types of southeast Asian yams that were probably imported during the 1500s by the Portuguese and have gradually replaced many indigenous varieties since they tend to have higher yields. The traditional white varieties are still required for ritual purposes, however. *Dioscorea* yams are larger than sweet potatoes and may weigh from 1 to 100 pounds. They may be short or as tall as a person, and their flesh commonly ranges from white to cream-color to yellow, although other types are red or almost purple. Their skin may be thin and brown, or

African yams for sale in an outdoor market. Courtesy of the author.

thick like bark, hairy, and almost black. They can be started from cuttings (seedlings), or from undamaged roots and vines remaining after the tubers are harvested. Yams were especially important in the forest regions along the Guinea coast, regions too wet to support growing grains.

The Wolof word for yam is *nyami*, which also means "to eat," while in Mende, the word *yambi* refers to a wild yam. The English word *yam*, as well as Portuguese *inhame* and Spanish *[I]ñame*, are likely derived from West African words.

Yams were fed to slaves on their voyages during the Middle Passage across the Atlantic Ocean to the Americas. Throughout what is known as the African Diaspora, descendants of West African slaves continue to incorporate yams into Afro-Latin (such as the Bahia of northern Brazil) and Afro-Caribbean cultures. Among the Gullah-speaking peoples, yams are called *nyam*. *Dioscorea alata*, also known as "water yam," became a mainstay of Haitian slaves' diet and eventually spread throughout the tropical New World.

Other Ingredients

The National Academy of Sciences of the United States estimates that throughout sub-Saharan Africa there are more than 2,000 native grains, roots, fruits, and other food plants. The preceding descriptions omit many important and interesting foods (both those native to West Africa and embraced from outside) such as: beans and seeds such as the African locust beans (used to make the *dawadawa* of Ghana, Nigeria, and Cameroon), sesame or *benne* seeds, spicy cedar (the *atiokwo* of Côte D'Ivoire), *fukungen* (a West African black pepper used in The Gambia and Senegal), fruits such as tamarind and ackee, various leaves such as bitter leaf, *ukazi* (or *utazi*), tea bush, bambara groundnuts, *chufa* (or tiger nuts), fluted pumpkins, custard apples, amaranth, Hausa potatoes, lemongrass, *roselle* (used to make *bissap rouge*, the Senegalese drink), *agbono* (*Irringia gabonsis*, also called African mango or bush mango), and potash.

Global Food Migration: Traders, Introduced Foods, and the Colombian Exchange

Several African foods, such as indigenous rice and yams, gradually began to share the soil with other varieties, such as Asian rice and yams. In addition, a number of tropical foods were adopted from other parts of the world before the arrival of Europeans in the fifteenth century.

Cowpeas are a legume that includes black-eyed peas. They most likely migrated down from North Africa, although some authorities believe they originated in South Asia. Cowpeas are another food that reached the New World via the slave ships of the African Diaspora.

Green Plantain Chips (All of Sub-Saharan Africa)
2 or 3 large green plantain bananas
vegetable oil for deep frying
salt

Peel the plantain as follows. Slice each end off, then make a cut around the circumference of the center of the plantain peel, but not the plantain itself. Next make a cut through the length of the peel. Use the tip of the knife to pry the peeling loose to get started peeling the plantain. Remove any fibrous strings on the plantain. The peeled plantain may be cut into chips in several ways: slice it into thin rounds or ovals on a cutting board, grate it into rounds on a grater or mandolin (as one would for potato chips), or use a vegetable peeler to cut horizontally along the plantain to "peel" long thin slices. Heat the oil in an electric deep fryer to about 365°F, making sure the fryer is not more than half full. Gently drop the pieces into the fryer one by one (do not add all at once or they will clump) and stir with a long-handled spoon to make sure they cook evenly. After a few minutes, remove the chips when they are golden and drain them on a paper towel or cloth-lined colander or tray. Salt the chips to taste while they are still warm. Eat immediately or store in an airtight container.

Many tropical foods, especially bananas and plantains, possibly cocoyams (also known as taro, dasheen, *edda,* or *eddo*), mangoes, limes, black pepper, and ginger, arrived from Malayo-Polynesian colonizers who came to the islands of Madagascar and the Comoros in the middle of the first millennium, as well as Arabian and Persian traders involved in establishing the Swahili civilization on the east coast of Africa. People in eastern Africa were already eating bananas and coconuts by the tenth century, and these foods gradually spread from Madagascar and the eastern coast of Africa throughout the continent. Sugar cane, although it is thought to have originated in the South Pacific and grows wild in eastern and northern Africa, probably reached West Africa via the Portuguese, after they introduced it into Madeira in the 1420s.

Among pastoral peoples in West Africa where cattle produce milk, such as the Fulbe of Senegal, a variety of milk products may be consumed, including fresh milk, yogurt, and butter. *Nebam* is a name for traditional butter in Mali, Mauritania, and Senegal. It is churned in gourds, and ghee (clarified butter) processed from it is known as *sirme* or *nabam sirme* in Pulaar, or *diiw ñoor* in Wolof. A fermented milk drink known as *kadam* or *kossam kaddam* is a popular thirst quencher during the hot season.

The prevalence of the tsetse fly in much of the region historically prevented cattle from thriving in the humid regions, and thus, fresh milk and milk products are not a traditional part of the diet in many places.

The "Columbian Exchange" is the phrase that describes the migration of foods and agricultural technology and know-how from Africa into the New World, the Americas, and from the Americas into Africa and the African Diaspora. It took place mostly during the fifteenth through nineteenth centuries, beginning when the Portuguese arrived on the west coast of Africa, landing first at the Cape Verde islands off the coast of Senegal and moving to Senegal and south along the Guinea coast. Eventually, the ships' captains discovered that the Africans being transported across the ocean in what is known at the Middle Passage coped better when they were fed familiar foods. They thus gave them things such as yams, palm oil, and rice, along with peanuts, corn, plantains, and *melegueta* pepper. Some of these foods, such as yams and peanuts, entered the diets of peoples in the West Indies, Brazil, and the southern United States. The slaves introduced okra into the North American diet, and the Portuguese brought it to Jamaica. Bananas and coconuts had already arrived in West Africa in the late 1400s, and the Portuguese transported them to the Canary Islands, then to Haiti in the early 1500s, which was their introduction into the Western Hemisphere. Similarly, as mentioned, many of the slaves who entered South Carolina to work on the rice plantations came from rice-growing regions in West Africa and were prized for their knowledge and skill, and are today credited with having known far more than their masters about how to grow, process, and prepare rice. The Brazilian slaves from West and Central Africa introduced palm oil into Brazilian cooking, and it is known there as *dendê* oil or *azeite de dendê*.

Akara (Black-Eyed Pea Fritters) (*Akla, Kose, Kosai, Accara, Koose*) (Western Africa)

1 cup dried black-eyed peas

water

2 Tbsp onion, coarsely chopped

1/2–1 tsp ground ginger (or 2 to 4 tsp fresh peeled ginger) (optional)

1/2 tsp salt

1/4 tsp ground red pepper

vegetable oil for deep-frying

Pick over the black-eyed peas to remove any stones or spoiled beans. Rinse with cool water. Cover the beans with warm water in a large bowl, and let them sit for 10 minutes. Dehull the beans by rubbing them between your palms to remove the skins, which will float up to the top and can be removed. The longer the beans soak, the more water they absorb, so try to complete the dehulling within half an hour. Continue removing the skins—placing the bowl in a sink and slowly running water into it will allow the skins to flow over the top of the bowl as they come off, leaving the beans in the bottom of the bowl. It does not matter if the beans break apart. After dehulling the beans, place about half a cup of them into a food processor or electric blender and blend them until they are a smooth paste (it may be necessary to add a little water to a blender, but use as little as possible, and stop the blender periodically to push the mixture down the sides with a spoon to get it well mixed, or remove the ground beans before adding more if it jams). Add the ginger (if using) and onion to the blender and mix until it is ground up. Taste the seasonings, and add more ginger, onion, salt, or pepper if you wish. Put the bean paste in a bowl, and mix with an electric mixer or a wire whisk for 3 minutes to incorporate air into the paste to make the balls light. If the paste is extremely thick, add a scant tablespoon or two of water. Heat an electric deep fryer (or a large, heavy pot less than half-filled with a couple of inches of vegetable oil on the stove if you can regulate the temperature to about 365°). Carefully slide the batter by tablespoonfuls into the hot oil, avoiding splashing (it helps to use two spoons—one to scoop up the paste, another to push it off the first spoon). Do not crowd the pan, and cook the paste in several batches. If they do not turn over by themselves, the balls should be turned over once with a long-handled wooden spoon halfway through the cooking process. Cook until they are golden brown and crisp and the inside is not soggy, and remove with a slotted spoon. Drain the balls in a colander or on paper towels. Keep them warm in a 200° oven (or they may also be eaten at room temperature). This is just one of many variations of *akara*. These cowpea paste fritters have traveled from Africa to Brazil and other parts of the Caribbean. They make a nice vegetarian snack and are also eaten as a breakfast dish with corn porridge. Sometimes they are eaten with a spicy tomato sauce.

Many of the most common foods in the West African diet today, including corn, cassava (also known as manioc or tapioca), peanuts, sweet potatoes, tomatoes, pineapples, pumpkins, and chili peppers, entered into the West African diet from the opposite direction: they are foods indigenous to the Americas that were introduced by the Portuguese, quickly adopted by the West Africans, and incorporated into their diet. In Ghana, for example, tomatoes, peppers, and onions are commonly known simply as "the ingredients" and are integral to most sauces and stews.

Corn, or maize, was probably introduced to eastern Africa in the sixteenth century and circulated around the Mediterranean and North Africa by Arab traders. In the 1600s maize was carried from the West Indies to the Gold Coast, current-day Ghana, to be used as a cheap food to feed slaves while they were awaiting transport over the ocean, as well as to feed them during the Middle Passage. In West Africa, white corn is generally preferred over yellow corn, and the corn tends to be hard, like Indian corn, rather than the soft sweet variety with which North Americans are most familiar. It has become a staple food of many West Africans along the Guinea coast. Africans were probably attracted to it partly due to its higher yield and resistance to bird attacks when compared with millets and sorghums.

In much of North America, cassava is primarily consumed as tapioca, a granular form of cassava starch used as a thickener and in puddings. However, cassava, or manioc (*Manihot utilissima* or *M. esculenta*), also known as mandioca, *aipim*, and yucca, is another food that has become an increasingly critical staple food in West Africa. This tropical root crop is a perennial plant that can grow as tall or taller than a person. Its leaves are often cooked as greens, but today the roots are the primary food. They may be a foot or two long and several inches in diameter and with several roots to each plant. Cassava is easy to grow, even in poor soils. It can survive storms and animal and insect attacks, plus the roots can be stored in the ground and harvested as they are needed. It can be processed into a dried form that keeps well and can be quickly prepared. Even though it is nutritionally inferior to grains or other root crops such as yams, its popularity as a crop is steadily growing.

The two major kinds of cassava are sweet and bitter. The sweet ones can be harvested in six to nine months and simply peeled and eaten as a vegetable without further processing, but they cannot be stored in the ground. The more common bitter ones can take up to a year or a year and a half to mature but can be stored in the soil for months and require relatively little attention while growing. However, this variety may contain high levels of cyanogenic glycosides, which can cause prussic-acid poisoning if the roots are not processed properly. In 1986 the Nigerian writer Flora Nwapa published a book called *Cassava Song and Rice Song*. "Cassava Song" is a poem praising "Mother Cassava," the staple food that has always sustained Nigerians, even in times of war, while the poem "Rice Song" is a condemnation of rice, an expensive imported food seen to impoverish the country and provide little benefit to the majority of the people.

It is unclear exactly where in the Americas cassava was first domesticated, but it is commonly agreed that the Portuguese carried it to the West African coast from Brazil. Cassava was successfully introduced in southern and central Africa in the late 1400s and had become important by the 1660s in northern Angola and other places where people lived in tropical rain forests of the Congo Basin, rather than in the savanna where maize, millet, or sorghum could be grown. Its West African adoption took place more slowly. From Portuguese Guinea and São Tomé, it became an important food crop in islands of Principe and Fernando Po by 1700, but not on the mainland until the 1800s, even though by that time West Africans were already growing sweet potatoes, corn, beans, and groundnuts. It has been suggested that the complicated process necessary to reduce the toxicity was only clearly explained to the West Africans when former slaves returned from Brazil in the 1840s and taught them how to process manioc into *gari* or *garri*. Also, cassava became a famine food when European interference disrupted traditional food production systems and as migrant workers spread knowledge of how to process it.

Taro *(cocoyam)* is another root plant introduced into the West African diet. It is said to have been brought to Sierra Leone by former slaves in 1792 who fled after the American revolution, and also that missionaries to Ghana brought the American variety in 1843. As with cassava, its leaves may be cooked as well as its roots.

Peanuts (which are actually legumes, not nuts) were introduced into the West African diet by the Portuguese and later were used to feed the slaves on board ships during the Middle Passage. The peanut is known as *groundnut* in the countries that were former British colonies and *arachide* in French-speaking countries. Peanuts found their way into the North American diet via slaves and slave ships. Preparation of peanuts in West African cuisine includes boiling them or dry roasting them and either eating them unsalted or grinding or pounding them into a paste to use as a thickening agent for soups or stews, or extracting the oil to use in cooking. *Goober*, an American word for peanut, is derived from a Bantu word, *nguba*. One reason West Africans so willingly embraced the peanut may be its similarity to the indigenous bambara groundnut.

West African cuisine is noted for the liberal use of hot chili peppers, such as habañero, scotch bonnet, or *piri piri* varieties. The fiery capsicum peppers were likely brought to the western coast of Africa from the Americas by the Portuguese explorers who first arrived in Ghana in 1471 and by the settlers who followed them. It is asserted that the peppers were a subspontaneous crop, spread not only by humans, but also by African birds that were attracted to the bright colors of the fruits, ate the pods, then helped scatter the seeds as they flew from place to place.

Another hallmark of much cooking of the West African coast and region is the use of smoked, dried, and/or salted fish and seafood, especially dried smoked shrimps, which are often pounded and added liberally to enliven soups, stews, and sauces. They are an integral part of the Ghanaian hot dried pepper sambal-like condiment known as *shito* or *shitor*.

West African fresh and dried chili peppers.
Courtesy of the author.

COOKING

Culinary Images and Family Relationships

Cooking, family relationships, and sex are often linked by culinary images, words relating to sexual intercourse, marriage, family, or fertility. In Twi, the Ashanti word for "to eat," *di*, also means to have sexual intercourse. If a husband refuses to eat his wife's cooking, a domestic quarrel is likely to ensue. Also, just as a delicious meal is "sweet," so is a good sexual experience.

Among the Kabre of northern Togo, the most common way to describe the members of a family or household is not those who are joined by blood, but those who feed one another. It means that children's parents are not simply biological parents or blood relations, but those who provide them with food to eat. Similarly, one definition of the family unit in much of West Africa is those who regularly eat from the same cooking pot.

Division of Labor

A sharp division of labor generally still exists in meal preparation throughout western Africa. There may be strict guidelines as to who in the family provides what foods for the family meal. Invariably, in the traditional home it is females, including girls, who are the cooks. The following description of Nigerian Yoruba peoples could be generalized throughout much of the region:

Most people have a few favorite dishes which they eat meal after meal and day after day with little variation. They are discriminatingly critical of the way in which these are prepared. Not only with regard to the ingredients, the method of preparation and the amount of seasoning, but also as to the stiffness or consistency of gruel, porridges, mashed vegetables, and vegetable loaves. . . . It is the duty of the Yoruba wife to learn the favorite dishes of her husband and to prepare them exactly as he wishes. . . . Yoruba men do not cook for themselves for fear of gossip and ridicule; it would be assumed that they were either so bad that their wives and their close female relatives refused to cook for them, or that they were so miserly that they were trying to save a little that their wives might waste.[2]

The quintessential image of food preparation in West Africa is a woman holding a tall wooden pestle and standing beside a mortar placed on the ground. She may be pounding a grain such as millet or a root crop such as yam. Or, she may be pounding boiled palm nuts to macerate the pulp and separate it from the hard kernels as when processing palm oil or palm butter, or perhaps pounding dried fish, shrimp, or peppers.

Other common sights in households are grinding stones or grinding bowls, although in urban areas with reliable electricity electric blenders are gradually appearing alongside the traditional equipment.

Increasingly, mass-produced plastic jugs or bags are replacing the traditional leather bags or brightly colored or earth-toned woven baskets for carrying or storing vegetables or fruits. Similarly, traditional clay pots for storing water (or cooking in) are becoming less common.

Cooking is likely still done over wood or charcoal fires, often in a brazier placed on the ground. The most common traditional cooking arrangement involves three stones around a wood or charcoal fire on which a cooking pot or pots are balanced. Soups and stews are often made using slow-cooking techniques and simmering the food for a long time over a low heat, particularly when cooking meat or beans. For roasting a larger animal, such as a goat, a pit may be used. In some parts of West Africa clay ovens are used for baking, or cooking tins are covered directly with coals to bake.

Knives for peeling yams or plantains may be long machetes, and a special wooden spoon or smaller wooden pestle may be used for grinding or mashing peppers, garden eggs, nuts, beans, tomatoes, and so on.

The most common cooking techniques include steaming; boiling; slow stewing; deep frying or shallow frying in vegetable oil, such as coconut, palm nut, peanut, sesame, corn, or shea butter oil; roasting; and grilling, with some baking.

Given the warm and often humid climate, meat, fish, and seafood are frequently preserved using salt, or by smoking or drying. Grains that keep well, such as rice or dried corn, or root crops that can be stored in the ground, such as cassava, or processed into a form that will keep indefinitely, such as *gari*, are prized. Fermentation of foods, the oldest biotechnology, is integral to the food culture, whether applied to corn to make staples such as the *kenkey*, *koko*, or *akasa* of Ghana and the *ogi* of Nigeria; or the sorghum of Sudan to make *nasha* or *kisra*, or to brew alcoholic beverages, such as millet beer or palm wine.

TYPICAL MEALS

In West Africa the basic meal pattern includes a filling starchy carbohydrate such as rice, or a stiff porridge-like substance from corn or a grain such as millet or sorghum, or boiled and pounded root vegetables such as yam or cocoyam, accompanied by a thick soup, stew, or sauce. Throughout the forest region of western and central Africa versions of *fufu* (also *foo-foo*, *fou-fou*, or *foutou*) are common. They are prepared by boiling a variety of starches alone or in combination, such as yam, cassava, green plantain, and cocoyam (taro). People elsewhere use other ingredients, such as rice. Once the ingredients are cooked they are placed in a wooden mortar and pounded with a pestle until they form a stiff mass somewhat like a cross between a dumpling and a thick porridge. *Fufu* is eaten with

West African women often earn money by growing and selling fresh produce. Courtesy of the author.

Small-scale mills (grinding machines) are common
in markets in West Africa. Courtesy of the author.

a thick soup, such as palmnut or groundnut (peanut) soup. Palmnut soup, also known as cream of palm fruit soup, is prepared using the small red fruits of the palm tree and has a distinctive orange-red color.

In many parts of the forested region of West Africa cattle have not been able to survive due to the presence of the tsetse fly. Therefore, milk has traditionally been uncommon in these areas, apart from canned evaporated milk, or, more recently, powdered milk. Thus, instead of thickening soups with milk or cream, in West Africa soups are often thickened by adding pureed legumes such as peanuts or other ground beans or seeds such as *egusi* or sesame seeds, or the pulp from the oil palm tree or even a slice of yam or plantain, or by using vegetables such as okra or egg-shaped eggplants known as garden eggs.

In rice-growing areas, the rice may be boiled alone or with cowpeas, coconut milk, or herbs, and eaten with a stew or sauce. Rice may also be boiled and mashed, or cooked into a one-pot dish such as *jollof* rice. Millet and sorghum are often pounded or ground as well.

Stews typically contain generous amounts of oil (from oil palm trees, peanuts, coconuts, corn, shea nuts, sesame, or other vegetable oils) and tend to include pepper, onions, tomatoes, and a variety of other ingredients, such as leafy greens, garden eggs, seeds, nuts, beans, okra, peppers, and salt. Sugar is almost never added to a main dish. Sources of protein, in addition to those already mentioned, include small amounts of fish, poultry, or wild game. For special occasions, mutton or goat may be prepared.

Beef is more likely to be a part of the diet in cattle-raising areas, although it may also be true that cattle is regarded as wealth and not slaughtered unless absolutely necessary. The meat and fish or seafood—fresh, dried, smoked, or salted—are added in small amounts as a seasoning. Fish and meat may be added in the same dish, as is often true in palaver sauce.

While heavy meals of *fufu* or steamed corn dough are common, a popular West African convenience food is a processed version of dried grated cassava flour, similar to the couscous of northern Africa. The steamed version of dried cassava granules is known as *attieke* in Côte D'Ivoire, whereas the most common version of roasted fermented granules is known in West Africa as *gari* (for example, in Ghana, Benin, and Togo). A version in southwest Nigeria is known as *lafun*. *Gari* or *attieke* are popular for their low cost, storability, satiety factor (the ability to make one feel full), and quick and easy preparation.

People in West Africa often only consider they have eaten when they have had a filling, or "heavy" meal. As the Akan proverb at the beginning of this chapter proclaims: "It takes a heavy stomach to blow the trumpet." Such a meal might include a soup and stew and a starchy accompaniment, such as soup and *fufu,* rice and stew, or steamed corn dough and a spicy sauce with fried fish. Lighter meals or snacks, sometimes called "small chop," might include fresh fruit such as pineapple, mango, or orange, or sugar cane, coconut, banana, and roasted peanuts, roasted ripe plantain slices, fried cowpea fritters, or skewers of meat or prawns. A morning meal might traditionally have been made from the same foods but is more likely today to include a porridge made from millet, corn, or rice, and a hot beverage such as tea. Most of the countries in West Africa were formerly British or French colonies, and the colonial heritage has resulted in a legacy of preferred foods, especially in urban areas. In urban areas such as Dakar, the capital of Senegal, or Abidjan, the capital of Côte d'Ivoire, wealthier people might breakfast on coffee and croissants or baguettes, whereas bacon or sausage and eggs with baked beans and tea is commonly served at hotels and guest houses in the cities of formerly British colonies such as Accra in Ghana or Lagos in Nigeria. As mentioned previously, in many of the wet forest regions of West Africa fresh milk is rare. Although this is not the case in the drier northern savanna and Sahel, milk has not been a traditional part of the diet of much of the region. However, colonialism resulted in the introduction of imported evaporated or "tinned" milk. Evaporated, or dried powdered milk, is commonly sold throughout western Africa and may be added to beverages such as tea, coffee, Bournvita or Milo (a malt-type beverage), or to porridges, along with sugar or honey.

If food remains from the previous day, the morning meal might also consist of dining on leftovers.

Palaver Sauce (Western Africa)

1/2 lb stewing beef

1 medium onion, chopped

salt to taste

1/4–1/2 cup palm oil (if unavailable substitute peanut or other vegetable oil and a teaspoon or two of paprika for the red color, but not the flavor)

1/2 lb fresh or frozen fish fillets such as cod or haddock

3 lbs fresh greens, washed and shredded by slicing thinly (any combination, such as spinach, chard, collard or mustard greens) OR 2 10-oz packages frozen chopped greens (Note: if using frozen greens, defrost them first in a microwave and drain in a strainer or colander to remove excess water, or else increase the cooking time)

1 lb fresh tomatoes, seeded (if desired) and chopped OR 1 16-oz. can tomatoes

1/4–1/2 tsp ground red pepper, or to taste

1/2 cup ground *agushi* or ground hulled pumpkin seeds (or substitute 1 cup Mexican refried beans or mashed cooked kidney beans)

1/2 lb smoked fish, such as whiting or mackerel (or substitute smoked ham cubes)

2 Tbsp dried ground shrimp or crayfish, if available

Cut the meat into 1/2-inch to 1-inch cubes and put them into the pot with a half teaspoon of salt, 2 cups of water, and a tablespoon of the chopped onion. Simmer in a covered pot for a few minutes. Add the palm oil and remaining chopped onions. If using fresh greens, wash them and remove any thick stems or ribs from the middle, then roll a few leaves at a time lengthwise, and slice them finely. Add the fresh or frozen greens to the pot. Prepare the tomatoes. If using canned tomatoes, break them up with your fingers into pieces or smash them with a spoon against the pot as you add them. Add the red pepper and fresh or frozen fish. If using whole agushi or hulled pumpkin seeds, put them in a blender and grind, adding a little of the liquid from the soup pot if necessary. To the ground agushi, add about 1/2 cup of the liquid from the soup pot in a small bowl and mix together before stirring into the soup. If using canned kidney beans, mash them before adding them to the pot. For the agushi, let the sauce simmer for a few minutes to "set" before stirring the mixture. While the sauce cooks down and thickens, prepare the smoked fish by rinsing it and removing the skin and bones, then break it into pieces and add to the pot. Simmer the sauce, uncovered, until most of the liquid is gone and the meat is tender, stirring occasionally. Adjust salt and pepper to taste. Palaver sauce goes well with boiled rice, potatoes, or African yams.

Red palm oil and green leaves are important ingredients in *palaver* or *palava* sauce (or *pla'sas* in the Sierra Leonean creolized version of the name) a popular West (and central) African stew. Palaver sauce may be eaten with rice or boiled starchy vegetables such as yams or plantains, or the dried grated form of cassava known as *gari* (or *farine de manioc* in French-speaking countries), or a stiff cornmeal porridge. The dish also often includes onions, tomatoes, meat, fish (fresh and smoked), greens, hot pepper, and ground *egusi* or legumes such as peanuts. The Portuguese word for "word" is *palavra*, and there are many explanations suggested for the name *palaver* to describe the dish. A *palaver* often refers to some kind of trouble, one that may take a lot of talking to resolve. Some have therefore suggested calling it "trouble stew" in English. Various explanations put forth for its African names include: that the stew's spicy ingredients mingle in the pot together as raised voices mingle in palaver discussions; that ingredients one might expect to get into trouble with each other (such as beef and fish) simmer well together; or even that trouble brews while people stand around waiting for the stew to cook or while serving themselves.

A variety of different kinds of leaves may be added to the palaver sauce, each with its own flavor and texture, such as spinach, cocoyam leaf, cassava leaf, bitterleaf, or sweet potato leaf. Among the Sherbro cooks of the coastal areas of southern Sierra Leone, cassava leaves and sweet potato leaves are a favorite. Women selectively pick the tender fresh leaves from their kitchen gardens, making sure not to stunt the growth of the root underground. The leaves are washed and bruised with a pestle in a mortar, then neatly bundled together and finely shredded with a knife before cooking.

A global contribution from West Africa is the humble cowpea fritter known in Nigeria by its Yoruba name *akara*, and in Ghana variously as *akara*, *ackla*, *accra*, or *kose*. It is found throughout the Caribbean with names such as *akkra* in Jamaica and *acarajé* in Brazil.

Eating (Times, Places, and Etiquette)

Morning meals tend to be lighter than later meals. People will typically eat a heavier meal in the middle of the day and in the evening. When food is scarce, they might only have one main meal a day, supplemented by snacks. In the 1850s, one observer commented about the Yoruba: "No people are so much in the habit of eating in the streets, where women are always engaged in preparing all sorts of dishes for sale to passers by."[3] In Ghana snacks include fried or roasted foods, such as a meal of chunks of roasted yam or thick slices of bananas or roasted ripe plantains and peanuts. The shelled peanuts are roasted in sand to distribute the heat evenly, and commonly sold with the skins still on.

In some places, all the family members may eat together out of a common bowl, using their hands. The etiquette for mealtime requires carefully washing one's hands before and after the meal and using only the right hand. The left hand is traditionally reserved for personal hygiene, and it is an insult to use it to eat, or to hand anyone anything. Conversation during mealtimes may be limited, with attention given to the food, and conversation follow the meal. As one proverb attests, "When the food is good, the people are silent." In some places, women and children may eat separately from the men, sometimes adults separately from children, other times guests and visitors may be fed separately, and sometimes each person may be given his or her own place setting. Traditionally food would be served in bowls rather than plates, and spoons or forks would not be included. However, today plates, cutlery, and individual glasses for water or other beverages are common.

Most meals are not served in courses, although there may be snacks, such as grilled meat kabobs and drinks, such as beer or ginger beer, soft drinks, or a hibiscus drink called *bissap,* before meals. A traditional format for the meal would be a one-pot dish, such as *jollof* rice, commonly called the "national dish" of the Wolof people of Senegal, but eaten throughout West Africa, or soup and pounded yam or *fufu.* While at least one observer calls groundnut stew the national dish of Sierra Leone, and others call *Thiebou Dienne* the national dish of Senegal, these labels are misleading because versions of these dishes are served in various West African countries and often cannot truly be identified with a single place. Water is more likely drunk at the end of the meal than throughout it.

The trademark "heaviness" of West African cuisine means that people generally believe that rich desserts are an unnecessary and excessive end to a meal. Most commonly when a dessert is served it would be fresh fruit, such as papaya and lime, or a fruit salad, possibly sprinkled with grated coconut or chopped peanuts. The appearance of custards (the British "fools") seems to be another colonial heritage.

Mango or Papaya Fool (Custard) (Sub-Saharan Africa, especially English-Speaking Countries)

1/3 cup (5 Tbsp) custard powder, such as Bird's

3 Tbsp sugar

1 cup canned evaporated milk plus 1 1/4 cup water(or substitute 2 1/4 cup whole milk for the canned milk and water)

2 15-oz cans mango

First prepare the canned mango: Place a strainer over a bowl and pour both cans of mango into the strainer. Drain well. Discard the liquid, and place the mango in the strainer back over the bowl. Using your hands or a large metal spoon, force the mango pulp through the strainer into the bowl, using your fingers or a second spoon to scrape the mango pulp from the underside of the strainer into the bowl. Set aside while preparing the custard. Measure the 1/3 cup custard powder and 3 Tbsp sugar into a medium saucepan. Mix the powder and sugar with a wire whisk and a couple of tablespoons of evaporated milk (shake the can before pouring out the milk) until a smooth paste is formed. Add the 1 1/4 cup water and the rest of the evaporated milk to the paste in the saucepan, and cook on medium heat, stirring constantly with the whisk. As soon as the custard comes to a boil, remove it from the heat, and stir the strained mango into the custard. Return the custard to the stove on medium heat, and stir it again with the whisk until it returns to a full boil. Immediately pour the custard into 4 to 6 serving dishes. Chill for at least an hour. Garnish with mint, fruit slices, whipped cream, chopped peanuts, or fresh grated or toasted coconut. (Note: this dessert is normally less sweet than a custard in the United States.)

*Variations: 2 fresh mangos may be substituted for the canned mango. They must first be prepared by stewing them before straining. Peel the mangos and cut the fruit from the seed into a small saucepan. Squeeze the fruit through your fingers or cut it into small pieces. Add a few tablespoons of water and 2 teaspoons of sugar (optional) if the fruit is ripe, more to taste if it is not quite ripe. Simmer the mango on medium low heat for about 5 or 6 minutes. Stir it frequently to make sure it does not scorch. Add a little water or lower the heat if necessary. Strain the hot cooked pulp using a spoon, not fingers. Set aside and proceed from step 2 above.

Papaya Fool: Substitute fresh or canned papaya for the fresh mango. Fresh papaya contains more water and is often less sweet, so if using it, use only 1 cup of water and 1 cup of evaporated milk. Adjust the sugar as necessary to achieve the desired sweetness. This custard is best eaten the same day it is prepared.

Easy version: chop or puree fresh fruit and mix it gently into whipped cream.

Herbal teas, such as lemon grass, are also popular beverages, along with all kinds of locally and commercially produced alcoholic drinks.

Some foods, or cuts of meat, have customarily been considered more desirable, and given first of all, or only, to the men. Others were traditionally considered appropriate for women or children. It was frequently considered good manners to leave a little meat on the bones for the person in the kitchen who would be doing the cleaning up after the meal.

Meat and poultry tend to be free-range and tough and require vigorous chewing, plus people tend to chew bones and shells of fish, poultry, and meat, which are good sources of calcium. The head or the eyes of a fish may be viewed as especially appetizing.

In some societies, such as among the Akan, eggs are a symbol of fertility. Dishes using boiled eggs, mashed yam, and palm oil may be served to a new mother, and dishes with eggs to twins. However, among other groups twins may be associated with evil and abandoned, or in some places there are taboos against eating eggs. Other groups, such as the Mbum women of southwestern Chad, not only do not eat eggs, they also are said to avoid chicken and goat for fear of pain or death when giving birth, or of becoming sterile, or giving birth to abnormal or sick children.

Practicing Muslims in West Africa refrain from eating pork or drinking alcoholic beverages.

EATING OUT

Most West African societies do not have a tradition of elaborate eating out in restaurants, although among the emerging middle and professional classes Western-style restaurants with fare such as fried chicken and chips or Chinese food are appearing in urban areas. Informal eating establishments, known as "chop bars," are places where one can get an inexpensive meal, such as rice and stew, soup and *fufu*, or fried fish and steamed corn dough balls. They may have colorful, religious, or humorous names such as "Don't Mind Your Wife Chop Bar." The restaurant provides simple family-style dining in a roofed but generally open-walled area. Seating is usually on benches and tables or chairs, and attention to presentation is minimal. Meals are served in bowls or on plates; a basin, soap, and towel is provided for washing and rinsing hands; and spoons and forks may or may not be provided. Chop bars tend to be frequented by travelers or workers unable to eat at home.

Hospitality is an important value throughout the region. A good wife is assumed to cook enough food to provide for any unexpected guests, and visitors may time their arrival to coincide with likely mealtimes. Children may eat at whatever household they happen to be when food is served. Hospitality is also tied to prestige issues. In order to maintain a particular social status, certain foods must be served to guests, regardless of what may be eaten in private. An example would be a family who eats cassava, cocoyam, or corn among themselves, but serves yam on "public" or special occasions.

SPECIAL OCCASIONS (HOLIDAYS, CELEBRATIONS, AND RELIGIOUS RITUALS)

There are numerous festive occasions when West Africans get together and eat special meals, such as naming ceremonies after the birth of a child; birthday parties (both for children and to honor milestone ages of adults, such as turning 50, 60, etc.); durbars to honor a new king; harvest or hunting festivals, such as the beginning of the new year and the harvesting of yams, or the "hoot at hunger," hɔmɔwɔ festival of the coastal Ga of Ghana. In addition, Christians celebrate Christmas and Easter, and Muslims observe the fast of Ramadan and the feasting that follows its conclusion. Marriages and funerals are also extremely important events where food plays a large role. The food for these public occasions may be prepared by members of the extended household or the community, or they may be catered. Often women engage in entrepreneurial activities, such as catering food for large gatherings. Foods for these kinds of affairs may include both heavier food such as *jollof* rice, roasted goat, lamb, or pork; stews made from chicken, fish, beans, or greens; and lighter snack food (also known as "small chop") such as cakes, cookies, and fritters or kebabs rubbed with ground peanuts and other spices (called *suya* or *tsire agashai* in Nigeria, *chichinga* in Ghana, *chachanga* in Togo). Drinks may include soft drinks with brand names such as Fanta, Malta, or Coke (note: the cola drinks in West Africa, such as Africola, are said to include up

Procession during a harvest festival (odwira) in Akwapem, Ghana. Courtesy of the author. Used by permission of Oyeeman Wereko Ampem.

to twice the caffeine and half the sugar of colas available in the West); drinks made from fruits or spices such as ginger (ginger beer), hibiscus (*bissap*), tamarind, or pineapple, orange, lemon or lime, or corn; and locally made alcoholic beverages such as palm wine or pito yeast beer from sorghum. Locally bottled beer is a popular alcoholic beverage, with brand names such as Lucky, Star (Ghana), Mamba (Côte D'Ivoire), and Ngoma (Togo). Apart from southern Africa, where the moderate climate provides a good environment for growing grapes, grape-based wine has not historically been part of the diet.

Bissap Rouge (Hibiscus Drink) (Western Africa)

Senegal and other West African countries use the dried flowers from a type of hibiscus plant to make a pleasantly tart-sweet beverage that makes a delicious herbal iced tea. When steeped in boiling water, the flowers turn the water a deep red. Many herbal teas sold in the United States, such as Passion, Red Zinger, or Orange and Spice, include hibiscus flowers. The flowers, also known as *bissap, roselle*, or *red sorrel*, are sold in many ethnic or health food stores. The flowers and the beverage are also known as *Jus de Bissap, l'Oseille de Guinee, Guinea Sorrel, Karkade*, and *Karkaday*, and the flavorings vary.

5 cups boiling water

2 cups dried hibiscus flowers (*bissap* or *roselle*)

1/4 cup fresh lemon grass (optional)

1/2 tsp vanilla or rum flavoring (or to taste)

sugar to taste (probably 1 to 2 cups)

Put the hibiscus flowers (and lemon grass, if using) in a large stainless steel or glass bowl and pour 5 cups of boiling water over them. Cover the bowl, and let it steep for at least 4 hours. Place a strainer over a large bowl and empty the liquid from the hibiscus/lemongrass mixture into the bowl. Return the herbs to the bowl they were in originally, and pour another 5 cups of boiling water into it. Stir the mixture well, and then pour it through the strainer again to add to the previously strained liquid, pushing down on the strainer with a spoon to remove as much of the water as possible. Add the flavoring and sugar to taste, and chill. Store in a covered pitcher or jar in the refrigerator. Pour into a glass and add ice and/or water as desired.

Note: Dried hibiscus flowers purchased in outdoor markets may need to be rinsed before using. Also, when straining and pouring the bissap into serving containers, be sure to leave any sediment in the bottom of the bowl and discard.

Variations: Mix or match any two of the following with, or in place of, the lemon grass or vanilla or rum flavorings: a cup of pineapple or orange juices; one-half cup lemon juice; a mint sprig; or one-half to one teaspoon of fresh grated ginger. Or, prepare the beverage using half the water and dilute to taste with chilled seltzer water or ginger ale when serving.

In West Africa, as in other parts of Africa, there is great respect for, and a sense of connectedness to, one's ancestors. There is a strong spiritual connection to those who have gone before, and they are often shown respect at ceremonial occasions when a little alcohol is poured on the ground or food is offered to them.

Often, as part of ceremonies such as pouring libation to the elders, or the naming ceremony for a new child, strong liquor, called *nsa* in Ghana (the name for locally made gin is *akpeteshie*), is used. During naming ceremonies in Ghana among some Akan, a week-old child is introduced to the world by dipping a finger in water and touching it to his or her tongue and describing what is being tasted, then dipping it in gin or vodka or *akpeteshie* and telling the child to know the difference between the two, although both are colorless and look the same. Among the Yoruba of Nigeria, variations include the symbolic use of a number of foods such as salt, honey, or cola nuts: in the same way that salt is important and makes food palatable, so the child should help to "flavor" the community; as honey is sweet, so should the child bring sweetness and happiness to the community, and it should continue to embrace him or her as the child becomes an adult; cola nuts can be used in both good and evil medicines, and their presence represents the hope that the child will be protected from bad medicines, as well as refrain from using cola negatively against anyone.

Yams are central to life and considered sacred in many parts of West Africa, where fertility rites, New Years, and thanksgiving festivals are often connected with them. Five groups especially noted for their rites and festivals surrounding yams include the Akan of Ghana, the Ewe and Kabre of Togo and Ghana, and the Igbo (or Ibo) and Yoruba of Nigeria.

Yam festivals are common in many West African areas and are closely tied to beliefs about soil fertility and survival. Nigerian author Chinua Achebe has written several books set in Yoruba communities, and these books provide insight into traditional yam culture. For example, in *Arrow of God*, after Europeans arrive and build churches, the chief priest of the community asks his people what the church bell that rings every Sunday morning says. They explain it is calling people to come to church, and he replies: "It tells them to leave their yam and their cocoyam, does it? Then it is singing a song of extermination." Later in the same novel, the community of Umuaro faces a crisis when the chief priest threatens to refuse to call the Feast of the New Yam that ushers in the harvest. People risk annihilation because if the year's yam harvest is left in the ground and dies, it means the people will also likely die or be destroyed, because the economic and consumption system is nonaccumulating and depends on year-to-year cultivation.[4]

Although yams may be the most prestigious vegetables, they may be reserved for social occasions and be too expensive for poor people or even for ordinary meals. Instead families may depend on cassava, cocoyam, or corn.

From *Things Fall Apart*

The Feast of the New Yam was held every year before the harvest began, to honor the earth goddess and the ancestral spirits of the clan. New yams could not be eaten until some had first been offered to these powers. Men and women, young and old, looked forward to the New Yam Festival because it began the season of plenty—the new year. On the last night before the festival, yams of the old year were all disposed of by those who still had them. The new year must begin with tasty, fresh yams and not the shriveled and fibrous crop of the previous year. All cooking pots, calabashes and wooden bowls were thoroughly washed, especially the wooden mortar in which yam was pounded. Yam foo-foo and vegetable soup was the chief food in the celebration. So much of it was cooked that, no matter how heavily the family ate or how many friends and relatives they invited from the neighboring villages, there was always a large quantity of food left over at the end of the day.[5]

West African culture is marked by a sense of humor and the ability to celebrate, evident during the many festivals at which drumming, dancing, and food contribute to the pageantry. The essence of West African cuisine, in fact, is difficult to discover in a Western-style restaurant, so much is it tied to such communal and ritualized events as naming ceremonies, weddings, and funerals.

As mentioned previously, although eating eggs is taboo in many West African societies, in Ghana they are highly valued. Ɔtɔ, a sacred dish made from hard-boiled eggs, mashed yam, and palm oil, is an Akan as well as a Ga tradition. Ɔtɔ is commonly served at the naming ceremony for a new baby (an "outdooring") or the purification of the mother after birth; at puberty ceremonies for girls; at festivals associated with twins, whom the Akan and Ga people consider sacred; at special occasions after the birth of the third, seventh, or tenth child of the same sex (sacred numbers in the Akan and Ga cultures); at harvest celebrations; after the first and third weeks of deaths in a family, when not only family members eat ɔtɔ, but the house is sprinkled with ɔtɔ to satisfy the dead; and on special days in the Akan calendar known as "Bad Days" or *Dabone*. *Dabone* is based on the belief that on particular days the spirits inhabiting forest or farmland will be offended if anyone invades their territory, so people stay home and away from their farms to avoid meeting or offending the spirits. Thus, ɔtɔ is served to both the living and the dead. In addition, ɔtɔ is served on other occasions such as escaping from accidents, on recovering from illness, or on birthdays. Ɔtɔ is the customary dish to thank the spirits by sharing a meal with them, and since it is believed that the spirits do not like spicy food, it is made without any salt or pepper. When used in fetish rites, onions and tomatoes, foreign foods, are also excluded.

Ɔtɔ is always accompanied by hard-boiled eggs. Eggs, a key symbol in Ghanaian culture, are often used for sacrifices, at purification rites, as pacification fees, as gifts, for thanksgiving after illness, and at numerous other occasions. Oval eggs are used to symbolize the ideal of feminine beauty, along with the idea of cleansing power, easy labor, and fertility.

Eggs may be carved on the staff of a linguist (the king's spokesperson) to announce that the king desires peace with everyone (just as the egg is soft and has no bones) as well as that he is a careful, patient, and prudent person. The carved hand holding an egg symbolizes the fragility of power, and that it is unsafe to hold it in one hand.[6] Another explanation of the symbolism is: "Power is like an egg: if you hold it too tightly it breaks, and if you hold it too loosely, it drops and breaks."[7]

Another example of celebration in the region is an exuberant harvest festival of the Ga. Legend tells of the hard time of drought in the southern Accra Plains, home of the Ga people. Famine spread throughout the land, and when the harvest finally arrived and there was food again, the people were so happy that they celebrated with a festival that ridiculed hunger. The festival is called Hɔmɔwɔ, which means to "hoot" or "jeer" at hunger. Hɔmɔwɔ begins with the planting of crops around the beginning of the rainy season in May and culminates in August. The final festivities begin on the Thursday before the main celebration, when Ga people return to their hometowns. A month before the festival there is a ban on noise, including drumming, to ensure a quiet environment for the gods to entice them to stay and bless the people. On the Thursday before Hɔmɔwɔ, which falls on the Saturday preceding the Ga new year, musicians parade through the streets, and people spend time visiting and courting. That Friday a memorial service honors anyone who died during the past year, plus celebrating the birth of twins and other multiple births and includes the preparation and consumption of ɔtɔ. On Saturday, the sub-kings in each city sprinkle kpokpoi (also known as kpekpele) mixed with palmnut soup at various places as offerings to God and to the lesser gods and the ancestors. Guns are fired into the empty sky, accompanied by prayers, music, dancing, laughter, and conversation. During *Hɔmɔwɔ*, *kpokpoi* is eaten with palm soup. The actual preparation of the *kpokpoi* involves first soaking and grinding corn. Some recipes call for fermented corn dough, some unfermented. Either way, the corn meal is sieved and steamed before mashed boiled okra, salt, and palm oil are added. *Kpokpoi* is eaten with palmnut soup; for *Hɔmɔwɔ*, the soup is made only with fish, both fresh and smoked.

Suya (Sooya, Tsinga, Chichinga, Kyinkyinga, Tsire Agashi, Chachanga) Spicy Grilled Kebabs (Western Africa)

This popular snack and party food is found throughout western Africa. Although commonly made from beef or liver, lamb, chicken, shrimp, or vegetables can also be used. The distinctive flavor comes from the powder used to coat the meat, called *tankora* in Ghana. Tankora, or "chichinga powder," includes a mixture of dried ground seasonings, commonly including cayenne, a special peanut powder called *yagi* in Hausa, ginger, and roasted cornmeal. The beef should be cut into slices and the chicken into cubes, and traditionally the kebabs are cooked alone threaded on wooden skewers or broom sticks. Today thin slices of onion or green bell peppers may be added to the skewers.

1 lb. round steak cut into strips about 1 1/2 inches wide by 2 inches long and 3/8 inch thick (about 28 strips) OR 1 lb. of boneless chicken cut into 1 1/2 inch cubes

1/4 tsp fresh finely grated peeled ginger root

1/4–1/2 tsp fresh garlic (about 2 cloves put through garlic press)

2 Tbsp plus 2 tsp finely grated onion

1 Tbsp tomato paste

1 beef, chicken, or shrimp Maggi (or other bouillon cube), crumbled (optional)

1 Tbsp peanut or other vegetable oil

1/4–1/2 tsp salt

3/4 tsp white pepper

1/2 tsp ground cayenne pepper (or to taste)

1/2–3/4 cup tankora powder*

8 short skewers

*To make a simplified version of tankora powder, pour 1/2 cup of dry, roasted unsalted peanuts onto a piece of waxed paper, cover with another sheet of waxed paper, and crush with a rolling pin or pound with a meat tenderizer until a fine

powder. Then mix together in a bowl with 1/4 tsp ground red pepper, 1/2 tsp dried ginger, 1/2 tsp salt, and 1/2 tsp white pepper.

To prevent bamboo skewers from catching fire while grilling the meat, put them in a shallow pan of water to soak for at least an hour before using them. Slice the meat into strips. Prepare and mix together the fresh ginger root, garlic, onion, tomato paste, and crumbled bouillon then add it to the meat or chicken, mixing well. Add the oil and salt, and mix again. Allow to marinate 10 or 15 minutes. Thread a few slices of meat or chicken onto each skewer. When all 8 skewers are ready, pour the tankora powder onto a plate and roll each skewer in the powder, evenly coating all sides, patting it with your hands if necessary, and shaking off any excess powder. Using a pastry brush, drizzle about a teaspoon of oil over each skewer from a pastry brush held over it as you shake the brush and turn it to coat all sides of each skewer. Place them over a hot fire, and grill for 5 minutes on each side. At this point the meat can be placed in a medium oven (350°F) to finish cooking, or it can be basted again with additional oil using the pastry brush to keep it from drying out. Alternatively, the meat can also be broiled in the oven a few inches from the boiler coil.

To serve: the kebabs can be served alone as an appetizer (especially nice with cold ginger beer or other beer, or with *Bissap Rouge*. Or they make a nice lunch when served with a simple tomato gravy (sliced onion and tomatoes or tomato sauce or paste fried in oil, a little water added and seasoned with cayenne pepper and salt) and a starch such as rice, roasted ripe plantain, or yam.

DIET AND HEALTH

Recent history has not been kind to West Africa. Traditional farming practices have often broken down, from factors as far-ranging as policies of former colonial powers (such as cash cropping, forced labor, and migrations) to environmental degradation or population pressures on the land, and people's diets have suffered. For example, traditional farming practices have often been abandoned, such as the practice of leaving a field to lie fallow for several years after the soil has been depleted to allow it to replenish itself. Migrations of workers, especially men, to the cities has left a scarcity of farmers and resulted in the substitution of easier crops to grow and store. For example, yams quickly deplete the soils, and farms need to be periodically left to lie fallow, but they are currently being replaced by nutritionally inferior, but easier to grow and store, food crops such as cassava.

Competition from farmers and larger populations has reduced the amount of pastureland for cattle and wild game, and chopping trees down for firewood has literally fueled the loss of topsoil and the increasing desertification of many parts of the land. The overall result is that countries that once were self-sufficient in food production now need to import staples, such as wheat, to feed themselves, and their diets are often deficient in adequate amounts of protein.

Fresh cassava root is primarily a source of carbohydrates. The leaf has protein and vitamin A, and the fresh roots may contain calcium, vitamin C, thiamine, riboflavin, and niacin. However, when the root is processed (soaked, dried, grated, etc.), it may leach out vitamins. Cassava needs to be supplemented with other foods to meet basic nutritional requirements. Currently, research is being done to develop newer strains of cassava with a higher protein content.

Most people in West Africa are slim. However, in many West African cultures the image of success and prosperity, fertility and nurturing, generosity, ripeness and health, is the literally "big man" or "big woman." If a man's wife is called "fat" it is a compliment: it reflects well on her husband's ability to care for her—she has everything she needs and more, and she need not fear tomorrow. While images in North America revere thinness as evidence of goodness: self-restraint, good health, energy, success—many West Africans, like rural Jamaicans, might view it negatively, or at least with suspicion.[8] Powerful matriarchs and patriarchs are expected to look after their extended families, and politicians their wider ethnic groups' interests. Wealth, generosity, and sometimes conspicuous consumption may go hand in hand.

However, after independence, when too frequently the colonialist administrators were replaced by greedy and corrupt self-serving African officials, literature and films began to caricature these same big men and women. There now exists alongside the positive image another, secondary negative image of those with expanding bellies who advise their poorer countrymen and women to tighten their belts. Examples may be found among the films of Senegalese Ousman Sembene, the "Father of African Cinema."

Diets in West Africa vary according to religion, who the country's former colonial masters were, ethnic group affiliation, and whether someone is male or female, young or old, rural or urban.

However, generally in the semiarid desert areas settled agriculture is less common, a more nomadic, pastoral way of life tends to predominate, and there are vast areas of uninhabited land. The tsetse fly does not attack cattle the same way it does in the wetter areas, and so cattle can survive. Drought-resistant grains such as millet and sorghum are staples, and people follow water. These groups of people tend to be more mobile, less hierarchical, and their social relations more democratic. They tend to rely more on leadership of the elders than on kings and city states. Because they need to be able to move around freely, they tend to produce items that are easy to transport and have short life spans. Cattle tend to represent wealth, especially for males, and women often show their wealth in adornment, especially in beads and jewels. Basically, all members of a community eat the same foods and share what they have. The closer one is to North Africa, the heavier the Arabic and Islamic influences, including prohibitions on alcohol consumption, limiting the amount of coffee and tea consumed, not eating pork, and moderation in all things, including portion control. Milk products, such as a kind of clarified butter, may be included in the diets.

In the wetter areas, such as the "yam region," cattle do not thrive, and milk is not integral to the diet. Lactose intolerance is common in West Africa. Traditionally, people have obtained calcium from sources such as cooked greens and the marrow of bones. Fish and seafood are important protein sources along coastal and river areas.

Health Concerns

Westerners, in particular those in Victorian England, in the eighteenth and nineteenth centuries labeled Africa the "Dark Continent," or the "White Man's Grave." Racist ideas and terminology were fueled by the continent's inhospitable and impenetrable appearance to Europeans. This reputation was buttressed by the few natural harbors along the West African coast where boats could dock and the inability to navigate its rivers from the sea, as was possible with the Nile.

Also, western Africa was home to the anopheles mosquito and tsetse fly. Anopheles mosquitoes carry parasites that infect red blood cells and cause malaria, an illness causing chills and fever. Europeans originally thought that literally bad (mal) air (aria) caused malaria and wanted to stay away from the (wet) places where such infected air occurred.

Africans had been living with the illness for centuries. There is even thought to be a connection between the spread of yam cultivation and development of sickle-cell anemia. Yams grow in wet areas under conditions that favor the growth of the anopheles mosquito. There was an adaptive response in the red blood cells of people that helps individuals survive when inherited from only a single parent, but that can be fatal when inherited from both parents. This adaptive response was a "sickling," an alteration of the shape of red blood cells to increase the chances that an individual will survive an attack by the malarial parasite carried by the anopheles mosquito.

The tsetse fly prohibited successful cattle raising in the wetter parts near the coastline that fostered the fly's spread, which resulted in the absence of milk from the basic diet in these regions. In addition to hindering cattle production, the bite of tsetse flies can transmit "sleeping sickness," a disease found in many parts of tropical Africa. Its symptoms include fever, lethargy, tremors, and weight loss, and it is caused by either of two trypanosomes. Europeans who tried to penetrate inland from the coastal areas often succumbed to one or the other of these diseases.

It has been explained that the contemporary diet of West Africans is heavy on carbohydrates and low in protein. In 1935 the term *kwashiorkor* was used to describe severe malnutrition in infants and children that is caused by a diet high in carbohydrate and low in protein. Kwashiorkor is a Ga term from the Kwa people of Ghana and literally refers to the "influence a child is said to be under when a second child comes."[9] This may refer to the common reality that with a second pregnancy and childbirth in a family, the first child, who has been used to primarily his mother's breast milk, will abruptly be weaned to a diet high in starch and not providing all the nutrients needed for good health.

Another diet-health connection is the prevalence of geophagy, or the practice of eating earthy substances such as clay. Often called pica, it has had negative connotations as an unhealthy and inappropriate form of eating. Recently, researchers claim there may be good reasons to eat clay that include meeting nutrient deficiencies such as iron-deficiency anemia and calcium deficiency, and of cleansing plant toxins from the body, especially during pregnancy. Some evidence suggests that while certain clays are unhelpful, other clays are easily digestible. Geophagy has occurred in many places and times but has often been associated with women and pregnancy, and in particular with rural communities, often in preindustrial countries where there is little consumption of meat and dairy products, the usual sources of many required minerals.

Geophagy has been linked closely to West African women and to African American women in the Southern United States. The clay that is usually consumed is not surface dirt which would be loaded with bacteria and parasites, but a fine clay preferably taken from roughly 10 to 30 inches below the surface and usually decontaminated by drying or baking it, such as the clay known as *eko* from Uzalla in Nigeria, tons of which are exported to Ghana, Togo, and Liberia each year. The finest of these clays are described as being like unsalted butter, not gritty, and it is argued that using them is no different from Westerners adding salt from a salt shaker to meet nutrient needs. At least one researcher has noted the striking similarity between eko and the pharmaceutical Kaopectate, used to counter gastrointestinal problems.

The widespread use of fermentation as a food-processing strategy not only helps preserve foods, such as corn and cassava, it likely improves the overall nutritional content by increasing the levels of proteins and amino acids, as well as possibly affecting levels of nutrients such as riboflavin, niacin, and tyrosine.

Mycotoxins, such as aflatoxins, are by-products of molds that may grow on staple food crops produced in hot, humid, tropical regions. In West Africa aflatoxins are ubiquitous and thrive in areas with poor food storage and harvesting conditions. They are known liver carcinogens and are especially harmful when the hepatitis B virus is present. The fungi on foods such as corn, sorghum, and peanuts have been shown to cause stunted growth in young West African children. Aflatoxins cannot be killed by exposure to heat during cooking, but there is research underway into the use of bacterial enzymes during the fermentation process of foods such as corn or sorghum to metabolize the aflatoxins and break them down into harmless substances.

Americans often assume that consuming tropical oils such as West African palm oil is unhealthy. However, it is important to distinguish between coconut or palm kernel oil and palm oil. Palm oil is rich in oleic acid and low in saturates relative to coconut and palm kernel oils and contains beta-carotene, an important precursor of the antioxidants vitamin A and vitamin E. In addition, research has shown that adding palm oil to the Western diet results in an improved low-density lipoprotein (LDL):high-density lipoprotein (HDL) ratio.

NOTES

1. This proverb means that it takes food to fortify and strengthen one to do work. From: C. A. Afrofi, *Twi Mmebusεm: Twi Proverbs* (London: Macmillan, 1958), p. 56.

2. William Bascom, "Some Yoruba Ways with Yams," in *The Anthropologists' Cookbook*, ed. Jessica Kuper (New York: Universe Books, 1977), p. 83.

3. T. J. Bowen, quoted in Bascom, *op. cit.*, p. 82.

4. Chinua Achebe, *Arrow of God* (London: Heinemann, 1974), pp. 42–43, cited in Emmanuel Obiechina, *Culture, Tradition and Society in the West African Novel* (Cambridge: Cambridge University Press, 1975), p. 249.

5. Chinua Achebe, *Things Fall Apart* (London: Heinemann, 1978), p. 26.

6. G. F. Kojo Arthur, *Cloth as Metaphor: (Re)-reading the Adinkra Cloth Symbols of the Akan of Ghana* (Legon, Ghana: Centre for Indigenous Knowledge Systems, 2001), p. 76.

7. F. Osseo-Asare, "We Eat First With Our Eyes: On Ghanaian Cuisine," *Gastronomica*, 2, no.1 (winter 2002), p. 56.

8. Somewhat parallel to Elisa J. Sobo's observations for Jamaicans in "The Sweetness of Fat: Health, Procreation, and Sociability in Rural Jamaica," in *Food and Culture: A Reader*, eds. Carole Counihan and Penny van Esterik (New York: Routledge, 1997).

9. Frederick C. Mish, ed. in chief, *Merriam Webster's Collegiate Dictionary*, 10th ed. (Springfield, Mass.: Merriam-Webster, Inc., 1996), p. 649.

2

Southern Africa

Ukapanda mano usamaswe phale.
If you have no teeth, do not break the clay cooking pot.[1]

—Nyanja Proverb (Mozambique, Zambia, Zimbabwe)

INTRODUCTION

As one moves south of the equator that cuts Africa in half, one observes essentially a mirror image of the top half of the continent: first the tropical rain forests near the western edge of the equator, followed by transitional semi-arid savanna, then savanna proper, then the Namib and Kalahari deserts, culminating with a narrow band of moderate, temperate Mediterranean-like climate along the southwestern tip of the continent. The climate also reverses—much of southern Africa's summer runs from about November to April, and the winter is from roughly May to August. The climate and seasons vary: sometimes hot and wet, or warm and dry, or hot and dry, or cool and wet, depending on where one is in the region.

More than 75 percent of the southern region of sub-Saharan Africa is made up of high plateau, also called "high veldt." This refers to mountains that have eroded over millions of years, and its surface rocks are among the oldest in the world. Several of its countries share a chain of mountains, such as the Drakensburg Mountains, that run from the southern African region west of the coastal plain in the east, through Malawi, Lesotho, and

Ancient and versatile, baobab trees are found throughout Sub-Saharan Africa. Courtesy of the author.

South Africa. There is a fertile coastal plain along the eastern coast and a narrow semiarid, western coastal plain.

Water is the lifeblood among peoples in this often harsh environment and is central to understanding the lives, histories, and cultures of the inhabitants. The three major river systems in southern Africa are the Zambezi, Limpopo, and Orange. Rivers and rainfall help determine countries' boundaries and people's occupations. For example, the Zambezi forms part of the boundary between Zambia and Namibia, runs briefly through Botswana, and then becomes the world famous Victoria Falls (so named by David Livingston) about a third of the way down its course. It continues into the Batoka Gorge to Lake Kariba, and beyond. Waterfalls such as Victoria Falls are common throughout many of the rivers in sub-Saharan Africa, and they are part of the reason that the rivers are often unnavigable by boats, another reason that colonizers often stayed near the coast. Other major rivers in southern Africa are the Kunene (Cunene), forming part of the border between Angola and Namibia, and the Okavango, beginning in Angola and flowing eastward into Botswana's Kalahari Desert, eventually forming the Okavango (Inland) Delta.

At the southern tip of the continent, in the country of South Africa, is a narrow area with a Mediterranean-like climate and soils, as well as great botanical diversity.

The contemporary national boundaries in the region reflect former European colonizers' or immigrants' power struggles and political maneuverings more than being the logical, practical delineations.

Countries that are commonly considered to make up the southern Africa region include not only the country of South Africa, but also Namibia, Botswana, Zambia, Zimbabwe, Lesotho, Malawi, Swaziland, and Mozambique. Madagascar, the large island to the east of the continent, is sometimes included.

Throughout this book, the term *southern Africa* will refer to the entire southern Africa region, and *South Africa* to the single country by that name.

HISTORICAL OVERVIEW

Early History: San and Khoikhoi

Most scientists believe that Africa is the birthplace of the earliest humans, *homo habilis* or *homo erectus*, who gradually became *homo sapiens*. Likely the cradle was somewhere in eastern/southern Africa millions of years ago. Evidence exists of early humans in South Africa more than 3 million years ago, and in Malawi there is a site dated to around 2.5 million years ago. These early peoples were nomadic hunters and gatherers. By 750,000 years ago they had developed simple stone tools such as axes, and by 150,000 years ago they had advanced technologically with better spears, knives, and so on. for hunting and gathering. The aboriginal (as in indigenous, or original) inhabitants of southern Africa are believed to be ancestors of the San or Sanqua people, formerly known as bushmen. Although *San* refers to their language, the word gradually came to be used to describe the people. Before that, the Dutch people who came to South Africa in the mid-1600s derogatorily labeled them *Bosjieman* from a Dutch word referring to bandits or outlaws. The San, who sometimes referred to themselves as "the harmless people," were treated badly. The Afrikaners attempted genocide against them; the missionaries viewed them as "dogs" whose very existence was a threat to civilization. They were also often crowded out by their African relatives, from the Khoi to Bantu-speaking peoples who settled in southern Africa.

By around 30,000 years ago, the San had evolved an organized society, mastered the use of fire, further improved their tools, and were using natural pigments to adorn themselves. Some 10,000 years later, or 20,000 years ago, the Microlithic Revolution (working of small stones) had taken place, and they had more time for leisure and artistic endeavors using wood, bone, and ostrich eggshell.

About 10,000 years ago the San people were producing pottery and rock paintings in shelters and caves throughout southern Africa. This artwork documents their way of life in pictographs that are now famous, especially in places such as the Tsodilo Hills in Botswana, as well as in Zimbabwe, Namibia, and South Africa. These paintings feature hunting and gathering scenes. The San people were of different stock from the so-called Negroid or black races. San were shorter and of a slighter build with skin color ranging from yellow to light brown. They also had slightly slanted eyes and clumps of thick, tightly curled hair.

However, unlike the people of other parts of Africa, the San never developed metal-working skills and thus remain relegated to the category of "stone age" rather than "iron age" peoples. They did not herd animals, nor did they rely on agriculture for food.

A second related early group of inhabitants in southern Africa is the KhoiKhoi (Koikoi) or Kwena, whom the Dutch disrespectfully labeled Hottentots, perhaps taken from the Dutch expression hotteren-totteren meaning to stammer or stutter. Another explanation suggests that it was a word in a dance refrain that foreigners appropriated to describe the dancers and then the entire people. The Khoikhoi were cattle herders and lived a more sedentary life than the San, with whom they often were in conflict. The Khoikhoi's cattle disturbed the environment that provided the nomadic San's livelihood, and the San were gradually forced deeper into inhospitable regions, such as the Kalahari Desert, to get away from them. Many of the South African people formerly labeled "colored" are likely partially Khoikhoi and/or San, although the tendency has been to deny a connection given the negative stereotypes about the people. The Khoikhoi were important trading partners for the early European explorers and traders who settled on the coast and intermarried with them. The Khoikhoi provisioned European ships with animals, especially sheep.

Most of the San gradually died out, and there are only roughly 55,000 of them still living, with about 60 percent of them in Botswana, about 35 percent in Namibia, and the rest scattered in the country of South Africa, Angola, Zimbabwe, and Zambia. Some of the San people work in the service sector, but like native peoples elsewhere, they have often been relegated to low-status, marginalized positions in their societies, and alcoholism has become a social problem. Ironically, the San people, despised and slaughtered from the mid-1800s onward, began to be celebrated by Westerners as romanticized noble savages and pure, primitive people, and in the late twentieth century became a resource for tourism.

The San people's traditional diet was varied and balanced, and they generally only needed to work a short time each day to meet their physical needs. The society tended to be democratic with communal ownership of land, animals, crops, property, and so on. and without the elaborate hierarchy of chiefs and kings of some other African societies. The San appear to have respected members' individualism and lived in harmony with the rhythms of nature. Men tended to do the hunting or help with food gathering, with women tending the children and gathering plants for food or water. Both the San and the Khoikhoi speak a distinctive "click" language called Khoisan. The South African motto on the coat of arms is written in Khoisan: "!KE E:/XARRA //KE" (diverse people unite), and the coat of arms also features two Khoisan figures derived from images of San healers taken from a rock painting.

Bantu Migrations

Although ancestors of the Khoi and San peoples were the original inhabitants of southern Africa, many other peoples have important roles in the region's culinary and cultural history. Most notable are the Bantu speakers. The word *Bantu* is used in a linguistic sense and does not describe an ethnic group. Literally, *ntu* means "a person," and *Bantu* refers to the language of the peoples probably coming from eastern Nigeria and adjoining Cameroon. Bantu is part of the Benue-Congo branch of the Niger-Congo family of languages (see introductory chapter on language families). Over a period of 2,000 years, and beginning roughly 4,000 years ago, Bantu-speaking peoples migrated throughout much of central, eastern, and southern Africa.

Bantu speakers are associated with the early Iron Age, with the spread of iron-working, agriculture, and a distinctive pottery style. Likely the earliest Bantu-speaking migrants were farmers who practiced a form of shifting cultivation of yams and oil palm, who fished in rivers, and who migrated in successive waves through the tropical rain forests and the savanna next to them near the equator. Later, after iron-working was discovered, they probably continued to migrate further east and south. It seems that although the migrating Bantu-speaking groups shared roots, they developed in isolated pockets and formed numerous broad ethnic groups with distinctive languages, traditions, and ways of cooking.

The Bantu migrations illustrate the theme of continuity and change. Eventually, the ability to work metal gave people a new technology that allowed more efficient tools and weapons to be developed, such as metal hoes and knives that could cut grain from the stalks. As in West Africa, this meant that a more sedentary form of society was possible in places with these improved tools and weapons. The Bantu-speakers were also a pastoral people, and cattle herding was a part of the tradition they often brought with them. Cattle, and the kraal, have played a central role in southern African society. It is well established that by at least 350 Bantu-speaking people had settled south of the Limpopo River.

Bantu Descendants: Nguni (Zulu, Swazi, Xhosa, and Ndebele), Sotho, Vendi, and Tsonga

Many of the black southern African ethnic groups have descended from the original Bantu speakers. It is thought that they followed at least three general routes into southern Africa: one group is believed to have spread from the Congo Basin east of the Tanzanian highlands and the Indian Ocean coast, then south down the coastal plain through Mozambique and into KwaZuluNatal, secondly coming along higher ground in the interior, then through western Tanzania into Zambia; others south from the DRC (formerly Zaire) directly into Zambia, Malawi, Zimbabwe and western Mozambique. The groups are subdivided into two main categories: the largest includes the Nguni and Sotho, and two smaller groupings include the Tsonga and Venda. These groups are further subdivided. The most well known ethnic groups within the Nguni are the Zulu, Swazi, Xhosa, and Ndebele. Bantu cultures tended to have strong kinship systems with important family and clan loyalties and dependencies, and they were usually ruled more or less loosely by a chief.

These groups were hunters, subsistence farmers, and herders of cattle, sheep, and goats. As is the case in many parts of sub-Saharan Africa, the agriculture and cultivation that ensured survival were primarily female responsibilities (with the help of children), although men might help clear land and organize reciprocal male work parties at which they generally served beer. Originally wooden, and later, iron, hoes were the primary tools for farming, giving rise to the name "hoe culture." The primary crop was first sorghum (also known as Kaffir corn), but later sorghum was replaced by maize. Pumpkins, gourds, and vegetables supplemented the grain/starch, which formed the center of the meal.

Cattle were, and in many places still are, very important in the society, with caring for them a male domain. Bantu languages have hundreds of words to distinguish the shape, size, and color of cattle, and the bull of the herd has often been especially praised. Cattle have been an important symbol of wealth and exchange and also a source of food, although primarily for their milk rather than meat. In addition, they have provided many valuable by-products, from dung used for fuel and for plastering walls and floors to skins for clothing and hides and horns for containers. Cattle are usually kept in a kraal, or enclosure, and the kraal has traditionally been the center of the community, both geographically and socially, and a meeting place and ritual center for men, although women might be barred from there.

In addition, communal hunting parties of men hunted and trapped wild game, such as leopards, for food and sport. Children might help in trapping guinea hens, termites, or soldier ants. In many societies, protein-rich termites or "winged ants" are considered a delicacy and are dried and roasted.

The family unit has been the main unit of personal survival, but as in many sub-Saharan African societies, the extended family includes a wider circle than Western society. For example, polygamy, in which one man has more than one wife, was common, and extended family members might also live in the household.

Despite variations, the housing patterns of many Bantu speakers show similarities. Early Nguni and Sotho huts were grass-thatched beehive constructions on a frame of bent saplings, while other groups had walled huts. Still, the image most common is of a cluster of walled circular huts with conical thatched roofs. A homestead usually has included a number of such huts for the household head, his wife or wives and children, and other close relatives, such as a parent or sibling. Sometimes homesteads are scattered, sometimes part of well-defined towns.

The societies tend to be patriarchal, with people tracing their lineage through male members of the family. There is commonly a close spiritual connection to one's ancestors, who provide a fluid link between the living and those in the spirit world, and who often can protect or harm one. Despite a general common belief in a creator, daily experiences are removed from this rather remote being, and people are seen as much more affected by evil spirits or witches. Animal sacrifice and pouring libations of beer have been usual ways of appeasing the ancestors.

In past decades Westerners considered the Bantu-speaking groups *tribal* people, and writing tended to view them as isolated, politically underdeveloped peoples with unsophisticated social identities. More recent writing recognizes that people's lives were shaped not just by their village life. They also had sophisticated multiple social identities joining language groups and regions, especially near roads and markets, simultaneously with their local concerns.

Early Kingdoms and Rulers

Great Zimbabwe

Southern African kingdoms emerged among the Bantu speakers in the interior. *Zimbabwe* is derived from a Shona word meaning "houses of stone" or "sacred (venerated) houses" and refers to the largest ancient stone construction in sub-Saharan Africa. This capital of the kingdom of Great Zimbabwe, from which present-day Zimbabwe takes its name, was built by Shona-speaking peoples who moved into the area around the 500s and began building major parts of the city's massive stone walls around the 1100s. The city was in today's Zimbabwe, located to the east of the Kalahari Desert and between the Zambezi and Limpopo rivers. The area is surrounded by plains that were able to support herding and some, but not all, of the agriculture needed to feed the estimated 18,000 to 40,000 people that lived nearby. Neither written records nor oral tradition tell its definitive story, but it is believed Great Zimbabwe's economy was based on gold mining and that by the eleventh century, it was the wealthiest and most powerful southern African society, trading with Arab-Swahili partners who had moved southward and westward from East Africa. The kingdom reached its height between the twelfth and fifteenth centuries. The granite walls of the buildings fascinate people for many reasons, from their obvious careful planning and uniform construction to the fact that the perfectly fitted stones use no mortar. The center, elliptical, building's outer wall is 32 feet high and up to 17 feet thick in places. It is more than 800 feet long, with a circumference with a maximum diameter of 293 feet. People in Great Zimbabwe likely cultivated millet, sorghum, and cotton, and kept domesticated cattle, sheep, goats, and dogs. The king, and perhaps religious leaders, probably lived within the stone walls, and a gold smelter was located there.

When European explorers discovered the ruins, they assumed that it could not possibly have been built by black Africans and was perhaps the "lost city" of the Queen of Sheba of the Old Testament.

The word *Zulu* means "heaven," and the Zulu people, or "the people of the sky," are today the largest ethnic group in South Africa. They trace their beginnings to the late seventeenth century. A Zulu officer named Shaka is credited with revolutionizing military warfare, transforming the local, loosely organized chieftains into a tightly organized and exceptionally ruthless military machine that allowed the Zulu to become the most powerful and feared people on the southern African subcontinent. Shaka was responsible for a wave of disruption and terror throughout southern Africa called the *difaqane* ("forced migration" in seSotho) or *mfecane* ("the crushing" in isiZulu) until two of his half-brothers killed him in 1828. Some historians view Shaka as a brilliant tactician, while others believe he was insane. For example, when his mother died he ordered thousands of his people killed for displaying too little grief.

Immigrant Groups and Colonial Powers in Southern Africa

In addition to the Bantu and Khoisan speakers who migrated into southern Africa and displaced the native San peoples, non-African immigrants and colonial powers have played crucial roles in the culinary heritage of the region. Besides the Arab traders linked to Great Zimbabwe, these include the Dutch, Malaysians, Indians, English, Portuguese, French, and Germans.

The Spanish and Portuguese rounded the southern cape in 1487 and 1498 respectively but were not interested in southern Africa—their attention was fixed on India and eastern Africa. In 1647 a Dutch East Indian ship was wrecked at Table Bay, and its crew built a fort and waited a year before being rescued. After this experience the Dutch East India Company realized the value of having a refueling base for their scurvy-plagued crews. In 1652 Dutch settlers, the people who became the *Afrikaners* (although Afrikaans ancestry also includes later French and German immigrants) arrived in Cape Town. These farmers were sent not to colonize, but simply to settle and grow food to provision ships as they reached the half-way point in their voyage between Holland and the Dutch holdings in the East Indies. Upon arriving, the Dutch met local Khoisan people who lived by hunting, herding sheep, gathering *veldkos* (wild plants such as mustard leaves, sorrel, and wild asparagus), and sometimes eating the sea's bounty. A related group, whom the immigrants named *Strandlopers*, kept no cattle and did not hunt but lived off the sea consuming things such as mussels, abalone, crayfish, seagulls, penguins, and seals.

Most of the Dutch settlers stayed on the coast for 200 years, until the mid-1800s. They quickly imported slaves to work in their fields and houses. Although the first slaves came mainly from west/central Africa, especially Angola and Guinea, soon slaves were brought from Mozambique and Madagascar. The most prized ones, though, are said to have been people from the East—Java, Bali, Timor in Indonesia, and the Malaysian peninsula, China, and India, especially Coromandel, Malabar, and Nagapatam. Most of the slaves spoke Malay, and, along with exiled Eastern dissidents who also settled in Cape Town, they exerted a strong far-Eastern influence in the cooking both by virtue of their Muslim faith and the Eastern spices and cooking techniques they carried with them. This distinctive cuisine came to be known as Old Cape Cookery or Cape Malay cuisine and blends a European heritage, especially in the vegetable cooking and baking, with lots of preserves reminiscent of the farmer traditions of the early Dutch pioneers (and also some Germans and possibly French), with Malaysian influences.

In 1688 about 150 French Huguenot Protestants, Calvinists fleeing religious persecution in Catholic France, brought vine cuttings with them to the temperate climate of the southwestern cape and established a fledgling wine industry. In addition, Asian indentured laborers (mostly Indian Hindus) were brought into Natal province on the eastern coast in the 1860s as agricultural workers, primarily on sugar plantations, and introduced their curries into the cuisine.

Some of the whites originally at Cape Town began moving away from the coast, and became the first of the *trekboers*, or "wandering farmers," later known as the Boers, who came into conflict with Sotho-Tswana peoples from around 1700, and who began the first of nine frontier wars in 1779.

At the close of the 1700s Dutch power faded, and the British invaded South Africa to keep it from the French. Upon arriving there they found a colony of 25,000 slaves, 20,000 white colonialists, 15,000 Khoisan, and 100 freed black slaves. By 1814 the British became an active presence, and immigrants began arriving in earnest. Eventually, as population pressures increased, and especially after gold and diamonds were discovered in parts of southern Africa, the racism, conflicts, and violence between the whites and whites, and whites and nonwhites, as well as indigenous peoples and Bantu immigrants, and various Bantu-speaking groups, escalated. This included notably conflicts between the British (Anglos) and the Boers and the Boers and the Zulu.

The history of coastal Mozambique, like that of other Portuguese-speaking sub-Saharan countries, reflects strong Portuguese influences. In Mozambique (as in Angola), Portugal fought a long, bloody war to retain control of its colony and only granted the country independence in 1975. The Portuguese role in bringing numerous foods into the sub-Saharan diet was introduced in the West African chapter, and much of the information holds true for southern Africa, such as their introduction of corn, cassava, peanuts, and hot peppers.

One of the better-known culinary influences from southern Africa is the use of chili peppers to flavor a marinade for a chicken or prawn dish that is known as *peri peri* chicken or *peri peri* prawns (*camarão*), respectively. *Peri peri* in Swahili and other African languages (aka *pili pili*, *piri piri*, *peli-peli*, or *uPeli-peli*) is a generic word for African chili peppers. In Africa it often refers to the fiery, piquin-shaped African bird's-eye chili (*Capsicum frutenscens*). African dried ground hot pepper is usually hotter than cayenne pepper sold in standard grocery stores in the United States. The Portuguese regard *peri peri* chicken as a Portuguese dish (which they call *Frango Piri-Piri* or *Frango à Cafreal*, using the Portuguese words *frango* for chicken and *cafreal* or *cafrial* for grilled). The dish spread from Angola and Mozambique to Portugal, as well as other places such as Goa, India. *Peri peri* using marinated and grilled seafood, fowl, or meat served with rice is sometimes called the national dish of Mozambique. *Peri peri* has also come to refer to a spicy African sauce used as a condiment, but made with other chili peppers.

MAJOR FOODS AND INGREDIENTS

The previous section of this chapter detailed some of the myriad influences on southern African cultures that have influenced the major foods and ingredients. This breadth of influences, and the bitter racial conflicts that have plagued the region historically, have resulted in a search for new ways to think about the regional cuisine. The country of South Africa is a good example. Apartheid activist Archbishop Desmond Tutu suggested the country be known as the Rainbow Nation, and in the interests of universality and unity in diversity, the culinary world has popularized the idea of Rainbow Cuisine as epitomizing the area's food culture. However, this name, despite its obvious attractions, such as inclusiveness and the promotion of harmony, can be misleading given the strong differences in the cuisines of the majority of black southern Africans and the white and so-called colored cultures in a place where economic apartheid is still a force. Much of the published writing on southern African cuisine has to date stressed the non-black influences in the cuisine, and there is a need to address that lack of balance.

Common foods among indigenous and black southern Africans include corn (maize) and curdled milk (*amasi*); millet and sorghum, made into a variety of thick or thin porridges or beer; beans, both dried and fresh; meat (*inyama* or *nyama*), traditionally including beef, goat, or sheep and wild game such as crocodile, hippo, elephant, impala (a kind of antelope), wildebeest (or gnu, another kind of antelope), springbok (a type of gazelle), ostrich, and kudu (another type of antelope); pumpkin; green leaves (*morogo*); *marula*, a kind of fruit; peanuts; an herb made into tea (*rooibos*); tamarind; and sometimes prawns, crayfish, fish, or *mopane* worms.

The San people's traditional diet was mostly vegetarian, gathered from a couple of dozen native plants such as wild fruits, nuts, berries, and tubers, with the remaining edible animal protein coming from about 17 of 55 animal species in their environment, including birds, eggs (especially ostrich eggs), lizards, locusts, and game.

Beans and Greens

As is true in other parts of sub-Saharan Africa, a variety of legumes, in-cluding beans, lentils, peanuts, and cowpeas, both fresh and dried, are integral to the diets of many in the region. Greens are frequently cooked as part of the relishes to accompany the main starch. In southern Africa, *morogo* is the generic name for a variety of greens cooked in stews. Many of them are wild, but leaves, from pumpkins to beetroot to sweet potatoes to bean plants, are also used. Examples of other names for the greens are *matapa* in Malawi, *cacani* in Mozambique, and *rape* in Zambia and Zimbabwe.

Corn

The history of corn's introduction into sub-Saharan Africa was dis-cussed Chapter 1. It has now overtaken sorghum and millet in the diet of much of southern Africa. For example, up to half of the arable land in South Africa is planted with maize, and it was already a well-established crop before the Dutch colonists arrived. The seed corn Cape Town's first governor, Jan van Riebeeck, imported apparently fared poorly in South Africa and the Afrikaans farmers and *voortrekkers* adopted the strains

Pounding maize into meal, Zamezi, Zimbabwe. © TRIP/J. and F. Teede.

available from black communities. Corn, or maize, comes in myriad forms. It is generally field or Indian, not sweet, corn, and may be yellow or white. When the corn is fresh it is called green and is commonly eaten boiled or roasted. The dried corn, when stamped or coarsely broken, but not ground, is known in English as samp, or it may be ground into a coarse flour called maize meal. In South Africa the ground flour is marketed as super maize meal, and a special, more highly refined version that is ground much finer is called Special Maize Meal #1. The maize is most commonly cooked into various versions of porridge. Maize is even formed into a rice-shaped maize-rice. Corn is fermented to make beer, such as the Zulu's *amarhewu*, a slightly fermented version served to women and children.

Samp and Beans (Southern Africa; Called Umgqusho by the Xhosa of South Africa)

1 1/2 cup dried white corn kernels (about 8 oz), such as Goya's White Hominy Corn (*Maiz Trillado Blanco*) found in Latin sections of grocery stores

1 1/2 cup dried small red beans or kidney beans

Rinse the corn and beans. Remove any stones or spoiled beans, and mix the corn and beans together. Cover with water and soak several hours or overnight. Drain off the water. Pour the beans and corn into a heavy pot, and cover the mixture with about 4–5 cups of fresh water and 1/2 tsp salt. Bring the water to a boil. Cover the pot, reduce the heat, and simmer about 2 hours or until tender. Add more water if the mixture becomes dry.

Note: This may also be prepared in a crockpot, without soaking the beans first. Cook about 4 hours on high, adding more water if necessary. Add the salt after the beans and corn have cooked.

Samp and Beans with Peanuts

1 cup dried white corn kernels (as above)

1 cup dried lima beans

1 cup unsalted peanuts (skins removed), raw if available

3 chicken bouillon cubes

salt and pepper to taste

water

1/2 cup skim milk powder

5 Tbsp butter or margarine

Kapenta drying in the sun, Kariba, Zimbabwe.
© TRIP/D. Davis.

Soak the corn and beans as in previous recipe, but when cooking, add the peanuts and bouillon cubes and omit the salt. Stir in the milk powder and margarine at the end and mash the mixture a little with a wooden spoon before serving. Serve with stew.

Fish

Although the diet in southern Africa is predominantly based on meat and maize, along the coasts of the country of South Africa, Angola, Mozambique, and the island of Madagascar, seafood and fish are more commonly included in the diet, including prawns, oysters, and crayfish. Some popular types of fish include an elongated fish found only off the coast of southern Africa, but which has been overfished, *kingklip;* as well as *snoek,* an oily fish that is eaten fresh, dried, or smoked; hake; and a type of mackerel called *maasbanker,* or horse mackerel. In landlocked countries, such as Zambia, bream are eaten, and in Zambia, Malawi, and Zimbabwe a tiny anchovy-like fish called *kapenta (Limnothrissa mioda)* is popular.

Meat and Poultry

The African savannah was once home to wild game such as various kinds of antelope (eland, impala, wildebeest, and kudu), gazelles (such as the graceful and swift sprinkbok or *Antidorcas marsupialis*), lions, elephants, rhinoceroses, hippos, smaller game such as jackals, hares, hedge-hogs, and mice, and wild birds such as ostriches and guinea fowl. The land was also home to crocodiles and insects such as locusts, flying ants, ter-mites, caterpillars, crickets, and beetles. Along with today's domesticated beef, game such as springbok and ostrich can be dried into a frontier-like food similar to jerky and called *biltong*. Wild game is no longer readily available, so beef or goat is often the meat of choice, both cooked into stews and grilled over an open fire. Among the Bathoso, if a healthy horse is killed accidentally, they will sometimes cook and eat it.

The ostrich, although it cannot fly, is the largest existing bird, with adults weighing about 300 pounds. Ostrich eggs are the largest eggs in the world and may weigh up to five pounds. They are low in cholesterol, and one egg equals about two dozen chicken eggs. The eggs are roughly a half foot in diameter and six or seven inches tall, and unlike thin chicken shells, their shells are around 1/8-inch thick.

At the beginning of the twentieth century the birds were easily hunted when their feathers were fashionable. While wild ostriches once roamed over vast areas from southern Africa to Syria in the Middle East, they are almost extinct outside of Africa. Ostrich farms have been established there to meet the demand for meat and eggs. Ostrich flesh is popularly made into *biltong*.

Chickens are commonly kept in individual households, and guinea fowls, indigenous to Africa, are also eaten.

Milk and Milk Products

As already described, milk and milk products have been an important component of the diet of many southern Africans, especially cattle herd-ers. The Hereros traditionally ate curds, and *amasi* (curdled milk) is popu-lar. Cape Malay and Afrikaans cooking also use milk extensively.

Mopane Worms

Mopane worms are a delicacy among the Venda, Tsonga, and Pedi peo-ples in northern South Africa, Botswana, and Zimbabwe. These worms drop from the *mopane* tree and are eaten sun-dried as snacks, fried or roasted, or cooked into stews. A classic preparation for them as a snack includes washing the worms under running water, putting them into a pot, covering them with salted water, and simmering them about 10 min-utes to plump them up. When all the water is absorbed, a little vegetable oil is added to the pan, and the worms cook for about five minutes, then are spread on a baking tray and roasted in an oven for 10–15 minutes until tender and slightly crisp. They are served this way at room temperature. As mentioned earlier, as in other parts of sub-Saharan Africa, other insect sources of protein include locusts and termites.

Peri Peri and Other Chili Peppers

There is much confusion and conflicting information surrounding chili (or *chilli*, as they are often known in Africa) peppers. There are estimated to be more than 2,000 cultivated varieties worldwide. Most experts agree that chilies likely originated in the Amazon Basin in South America and were called *achu* by the Incas and *chilli* by the Aztecs.

Chilies are members of the *Capsicum* genus, which is part of the *Solanaceae* family. The word *capsicum* is derived from the Latin word *capsa*, meaning case. The pepper, or fruit, encapsulates or encases, the seed. There are five species: *Capsicum annuum*, *Capsicum baccatum*, *Capsicum chinense*, *Capsicum frutescens*, and *Capsicum pubescens*.

Chili peppers arrived in Africa via several routes. The Portuguese and Spanish played a major role in first moving them out of South America to Europe and West Africa. It is said that Portuguese traders also traded the peppers for slaves. The spread of chilies from gardens throughout the region with the help of birds has also been mentioned. Chilies also traveled the intra-African trade routes. Chilies reached India via many spice routes, and the Dutch introduced them to their trading partners. As already mentioned, Indian workers entering the KwaZuluNatal regions carried chilies with them.

Chilies vary in size, shape, length, and color, but it is their heat that distinguishes them. The heat in chili peppers comes primarily from a colorless oil, called capsaicin oil. Capsaicin oil is located in the membranes and seeds of chilies rather than in the flesh of the fruit. Sweet, or bell or butter, peppers are also part of the *Capsicum* genus, but they have no discernible hotness to them.

Prawns Mozambique (or Shrimp *Peri Peri*) (Southern Africa)

Peri peri sauce

1–2 red chili peppers, enough to get about 2 tsp, plus 1 Tbsp paprika (can use red bird peppers, scotch bonnets, or habañeros, but note these are REALLY hot and should not be touched with bare fingers), finely chopped or crushed in a mortar. Use extreme caution when working with fresh hot peppers—see note below*) or

2 or 3 heaping tsp dried cayenne pepper flakes or ground red pepper. Note that red pepper from Africa, such as the Sands brand, is hotter than U.S. cayenne pepper (adjust the seasonings to taste, using more or less hot red pepper, or substituting more paprika if less heat is desired).

1/4 tsp salt

2–3 Tbsp lemon juice (wine vinegar or cider vinegar may partially replace part of the lemon juice)

1–2 cloves garlic, crushed

few sprigs of parsley (optional)

1/2 cup red onion, finely chopped (optional)

1/3 cup olive, peanut, or vegetable oil

1–1 1/2 lbs of (preferably) jumbo shrimp, defrosted if frozen

(*Note: to avoid working with hot fresh peppers, one may simply blend all the ingredients except the shrimp in a blender and pour the marinade into a glass or ceramic bowl.)

Wash, devein, and remove the shells of the jumbo shrimp (bigger is better for this dish), leaving the tails intact. Pat the shrimp dry with a paper towel or cloth. Place them into the *peri peri* sauce; stir. Cover the container, and allow them to marinate in the refrigerator for several hours or overnight, stirring occasionally. If using bamboo skewers, soak the skewers for at least 30 minutes before skewering the shrimp onto them, keeping the shrimp as straight as possible and grilling for just 2 to 3 minutes on either side a few inches from a preheated broiler coil (in a flat pan) or a few inches directly over hot coals, basting them with the marinade. Do not overcook.

Variations: if the above recipe is doubled, and half kept separate from the sauce used to marinate the shrimp, it may be heated, cooked for a few minutes, and used as a dipping sauce for the cooked shrimp.

Peri Peri Chicken: In place of the shrimp, 2–3 lbs. of chicken pieces may be used, in which case the lemon juice can be replaced with 1/2 cup coconut milk.

The most common way of categorizing the different capsicums is to use a scale known as SHU, or Scoville Heat Units, developed by the chemist William Scoville. SHU rate the amount of capsaicin oil in chilies and ranges from 0 to hundreds of thousands of units. The scale has been simplified to a 1 to 10 rating that is usually used to express differences among peppers. The Scoville scale is a very useful device, but it is not completely accurate. The intensity or pungency of the same variety of pepper can vary widely depending on the soil or climate, or sometimes even on its location on the same bush.

Peppers are used in red, green, orange, fresh, and dried forms. They require great care in handling, and western cooks are sometimes advised to wear rubber or latex gloves when handling the hot peppers to keep from getting the capsaicin oil or their hands.

Hot peppers are used in many parts of southern Africa. The most common peppers include bird's eye, habañero, scotch bonnet (all rated 9–10 out of 10 in hotness, or 100,000 to 300,000 SHU), and cayenne (30,000–50,000 SHU, or an 8). The African Bird's Eye pepper is usually designated as from the species *Capsicum frutescens*. This was traditionally the pepper referred to as the *peri peri* pepper. Habañero or scotch bonnets are from the *Capsicum chinense* family, and cayenne pepper is *Capsicum annuum*. As a means of comparison, jalapeno peppers common in Mexican cooking only rate a 5 on the heat scale, and paprikas rate a 1 or 2. The section on diet and health later in this chapter describes some of the benefits ascribed to eating chili peppers.

Rooibos

A global export indigenous to southern Africa is *rooibos* (literally, red bush), a slender stemmed shrub, *Asplanthus linaris*, first found growing wild in the Cedarberg region of the western Cape in South Africa and now cultivated. The young and tender green bushes are cut back in summer and the branches, with their fine, needle-like leaves, are chopped into small pieces and bruised with wooden hammers, before being allowed to ferment in piles and then dried. The dried leaves make a tea that is high in vitamin C and minerals, contains no caffeine, and is purported to relieve allergies, especially in babies. The leaves may be steeped in boiling water or milk to make a beverage served either hot or cold, added to punch, or used to flavor other drinks. Hot, it can be served with lemon, cinnamon, or honey; cold with a sparkling mixer, fruit juice, or lightly sweetened with a hint of lemon and ice. It can also be used in cooking pork or chicken stew, or flavoring breads or desserts.

Sorghum

Sorghum (see Chapter 1) is eaten in numerous forms, primarily as a thin or thick porridge accompanied with milk or relishes. Zulu men sip the highly intoxicating sorghum beer known as *umqomboth* or *ithlodlwa*; *mageu* is a milder version for the rest of the family. Malawi or Zimbabwe have *chibuku*, "the beer of good cheer," also made of sorghum.

COOKING

As is the norm in sub-Saharan Africa, females are traditionally the cooks within households. However, when cooking is done in the bush or outdoors at barbecues, men may be involved with cooking, generally grilling the meat. Some scholars have suggested that there is a private/public distinction where women are relegated to private domains in the home, such as the cooking pot, and men are able to participate in more public activities, such as barbeques. However, since women are often roadside vendors and preparers of snack foods (in other words, in public), it is helpful to consider in addition a formal or nonformal (informal) distinction, where women are more likely to cook in the informal sector, and men may be found employed as chefs or servers in restaurants in salaried positions in the formal economy.

Among the Malagasy of Madagascar there is said to be a distinction between cooking in a pot and cooking over a fire, and there is also a hierarchy of the cooking liquids, with water the least and milk the most prestigious liquid.

Southern African beer, commonly brewed from maize, is an important staple and source of nutrition. Traditionally women not only grow the grain, but also prepare the beer: they soak the maize until it sprouts, then dry, grind, boil, ferment, and strain it. Beer is a part of many rituals and drunk on all important occasions, as well as being an everyday beverage.

Women are often the potters and traditionally create a variety of pots, from a large vessel for brewing beer, which is generally undecorated, to one used specifically for drinking beer, water, and *mahewu* at home (called *chipfuko* in Zimbabwe) and frequently decorated with chevron patterns. The types of decorations vary. For example, chevron patterns and vertical strips of contrasting graphite blacks with haematite red-ochres, or incised patterns of bands, triangles, and vertical stripes, for example, are typical of Shona traditions.

In Zimbabwe, as in other countries in the region, before the advent of durable aluminum, cast iron, or iron-enamel cooking pots, food would be cooked in a clay *shambakodzi*, or *sadza* cooking pot, that was generally undecorated and was larger than other food cooking pots because the starch was always the main component of the meal. Its sides and bottom were made substantially thicker than other pots to enable it to withstand the heat during cooking and stirring the porridge. In addition, there are several traditional wooden spoons and ladles. In Zimbabwe, every home would probably have what is known in Shona as a *mugoti*, or stirring stick, made from a strong wood that will not fray or splinter. If a thin porridge is being made, a wooden whisk known among the Shona as a *musika* would be used first, then the

Venda woman stirring porridge. Used with permission
of Tafelberg Publishers.

mugoti, and the *sadza* would be ladled into a serving dish with a *mugwaku.* To
give the *sadza* an appealing smooth rounded finish, a *chibhako* or flat smoothing spoon is used. An empty corncob is sometimes used as well.

Potjiekos

Early European traders are credited with most likely introducing a distinctive three-legged pot made from cast iron and commonly known as
potjiekos, a term coined by food writer and restaurateur Peter Veldsman.
These pots, which are sometimes huge, cook evenly and slowly and con-
serve energy. They are especially popular for outdoor entertaining, for
large feasts, or for celebrations. In the early settler days the white immigrant farmers cooked food in pots with legs that were placed over coals in
the kitchen's open hearth. The trek farmers carried these pots with them
as they traveled, cooking meat, vegetables, and spices together in the pots
when they made camp.

TYPICAL MEALS

A stiff, maize porridge, somewhat like Italian polenta, eaten once or
twice a day with a sauce the way many Westerners once ate bread, or the
rice of Asian cultures, is a common meal pattern throughout sub-Saharan

Africa, including southern Africa. Similar to Kenya's *ugali*, the porridge has many regional variations and names. In Zimbabwe the porridge (or dumpling) is known as *sadza*, and is made from either maize flour from white field corn or *rapoko*, a flour made from red millet. *Sadza Ne Muriwo* describes *sadza* served with a sauce, not a soup, which may be made simply from a few vegetables, or a stew containing meat or beans. Zimbabweans have a proverb: *"Hunge rakatsigir wa nemuto"* that means "For sadza to enter it must be supported by the sauce—always!"[2] In South Africa, cornmeal (or any other staple grain) porridge is known by the Dutch word *pap*. A crumbly version is called *putu* or *phutu* (in Zulu), or *umphokoqo* (Xhosa). Maize is also called *mealie* (or *meilie*). In Zambia porridge is called *nhsima*, in Malawi *nsima*, in Botswana *bogobe* and in Mozambique corn and cassava versions are *xima* or *upshwa*.

There are numerous variations on the preparation of porridge: how thick or thin it is, whether or not to add salt, how to combine the flour and water, how long to cook it, when and how to stir it, and so on. If the porridge is eaten as a morning meal, it is likely thinner and may be mixed with a little fresh or curdled milk, possibly also sweetened with sugar or honey.

Traditionally men tend to eat separately from women and children, especially when visitors are present. There is a common platter or bowl for the *sadza* and another for the relish, and people use their hands (always the right hand) to eat, rather than forks or spoons.

Maize porridge takes many forms, including these stacked layers of *vhutetwe*, or *vhuswa*. Used with permission from Tafelberg Publishers.

Swazi *isijabana* (spinach porridge) and *namazambane* (tripe and potato stew). Used with permission from Tafelberg Publishers.

The sauce or relish may include a variety of vegetables. These could be pumpkin leaves *(bowara)* eaten fresh or dried. They may be cooked and mixed with the pulp from ingredients such as baby pumpkins; meat such as goat, beef, or chicken; okra *(derere)*; *kovo*, a cabbage-like leaf; *nyovhi*, a wild plant indigenous to Zimbabwe, with small, narrow, green leaves; or mushrooms. Wild game, including eland, kudu, or impala, more available in southern Africa in former days than now, once formed an important source of protein.

Meals and Social Change

The description of South Africa's cuisine as a "rainbow" is helpful in the sense that there are distinctive classic meals of various ethnic groups that have been embraced by the region and transcended their origins. These include things such as samp and beans by the Xhosa or the *vetkoek* (the fat cakes of Dutch/Afrikaans origin, known as *amafekuku* by the Ndebele). A sampling of the diversity in heritages includes the following.

Cape Malay and Dutch/Afrikaans Influences

The use of curry powder and onions and other Indian and Malaysian spices (including, for example, tamarind, ginger, cumin, turmeric, coriander, garlic, chili peppers, and allspice), pickling, as well as the combination of sweet and sour flavors in *sambals* and chutneys, typify Old Cape cookery. Some representative dishes include: *bobotie, sosaties, bredies* (stews), *boeber, chicken masala*, curry (or *kerrie*) served with yellow rice (*geel rys*), *roti, blatjang, biltong, boerewors*, and *atjars*. Grated or chopped fresh fruit or vegetable salads dressed with lemon juice or vinegar, sugar, chilies, and various other seasonings are also popular.

Tomato *Bredie* (Tomato Stew) (Southern Africa)

1/2 cup water

2 large onions, sliced (about 2 cups)

1 1/2–2 lbs stewing lamb (e.g., ribs or shoulder), cut into pieces

2 Tbsp vegetable oil

6–8 large ripe tomatoes (about 2 lbs)

1 tsp sugar (or to taste)

1 tsp salt (or to taste)

1 chili pepper, finely chopped (about 1 Tbsp), or 1/2 tsp cayenne pepper (or to taste)*

1 clove garlic, peeled and crushed

freshly ground black pepper, to taste

Peel and slice the onions, and cut the lamb into chunks. Remove excess fat from the lamb. Heat oil on medium heat in a heavy pot, pan, or skillet, and brown the onions and lamb until the onions are golden and the meat is seared on all sides. Cover and simmer the mixture on the lowest heat for 20–30 minutes, checking occasionally to make sure that it does not scorch. While the meat is simmering, peel the tomatoes by dropping them into a saucepan of boiling water for a minute, then into a bowl of cold water. The skins will split and slip off. Slice the tomatoes into rounds about 1/4 inch thick. Drain off all but about 2 Tbsp of the fat from the pan. Add the tomatoes, crushed garlic, chopped chili pepper (or cayenne pepper), salt, and sugar. Stir gently. Lower the heat to very low, cover the pan, and simmer for about an hour, stirring frequently to prevent the mixture from sticking and burning. Just before serving, remove the lid and spoon off any fat on the surface. Cook a few more minutes until the sauce is thick. Serve with rice or thick corn porridge, such as *Bidia* recipe.

Variations: This classic *bredie* is named after the main vegetable in it, but there are many other *bredies*, such as green bean *bredie* or pumpkin *bredie*. Also, the above version is simplified. More elaborate versions would include additional spices such as peppercorns, cinnamon, cardamom, cloves, fresh grated ginger, and whole black peppercorns, along with 5 or 6 potatoes (peeled, chopped, and added toward the end of the cooking time). Chicken can also replace the lamb, and the cooking time decreased.

*Note: Always use extreme caution when handling fresh chili peppers.

Bobotie is a traditional ground meat loaf, preferably made from ground lamb, flavored with curry powder, butter or oil, onions, garlic, and turmeric, and topped with a custard when baked. The topping is made from ingredients such as breadcrumbs, milk, lemon rind and juice, egg, salt, black pepper, apricots, apple, sultanas (a raisin made from a yellow seedless grape), and almonds. The shepherd's pie-like dish is said to be similar to one known in Europe in the Middle Ages after Crusaders carried turmeric from the East, and also by the influence in Holland of Italian cooks who had a favorite dish of hashed meat baked with a spicy curry sauce and blanched almonds. In South Africa, early cooks added tamarind water to the meat, whereas a modern adaptation uses lemon rind and juice.

The word *sosatie* is made from two Malay words, *sate* or spiced sauce, and *sesate* meaning skewered meat. It is a popular dish for a barbecue, or *braai* (rhymes with eye), and the marinade commonly mixes the flavors of onion, chili, garlic, curry, and tamarind. Sheep, or mutton, is a favorite type of meat, although ostrich or pork can be used. Recipes call for a kind of fat, such as bacon or fat slivers from around sheep's kidneys, to be threaded on the skewers with the meat, perhaps with plumped, dried apricots and onions from the marinade, before grilling them. In old Cape Town, taverns were called "Sosatie and Rice Houses" in honor of this grilled, skewered meat, and *sosaties* were popular *padkos* or road food.

Another classic Afrikaans dish that has spread in popularity throughout the region is *boerewors*, literally farmers' sausages (from the Afrikaans words *boere* meaning farmers and *wors* meaning sausage). Poet and food writer Louis Leipoldt claims the French Huguenots brought the recipe to the Cape, but others believe that it was German settlers, experts in sausage making, who introduced them. Or perhaps the pioneers, or *Boers*, created them about 200 years ago. They are known colloquially in South Africa as *Boeries*. These sausages are traditionally made from minced meat such as beef or lamb, *spek* (pork and/or beef fat), spices (such as coriander seeds, cloves, salt, black pepper, nutmeg, allspice, and brown sugar), vinegar or wine (as a preservative), and sausage casings. In the latter part of the twentieth century, experimentation with the classic *boerewors* took place, leading to cheap but lower quality products, made using inferior meat such as offal, bone meal, and *soya* and thicker sausage casings, but some of the innovations resulted in developing interesting new flavors such as garlic wors, chili wors, cheese wors, etc. *Boerewors* are often served with a tomato sauce made from oil, chopped onions, possibly garlic, peeled and chopped tomatoes, sugar, and perhaps fresh spices such as thyme, marjoram, or oregano.

Afrikaans influence is seen in the salty, spicy, dried meat called *biltong*, a kind of jerky that is a favored snack food throughout southern Africa and can also be used in stews. However, the Afrikaners have no monopoly on preparing dried strips of meat. The San undoubtedly dried strips of the wild game they hunted. The Shona call dried meat *chumukuyu* and the Zulus *umqweyiba*. In rural black southern African communities, although cattle were rarely slaughtered for food, animals that died accidentally or of some natural cause were cut up and dried. Before *biltong* in South Africa, Dutch immigrants rubbed strips of lean meat with salt and coriander, covered them in vinegar, then pan fried them to make *tassal* meat. Swazis call *biltong umcweba* or *umcwayiba*, and coriander seeds, originally brought from Asia, are an essential ingredient, along with salt and black pepper. Although beef is the most common source of lean meat for *biltong*, it is also prepared from ostrich or venison such as springbok, kudu, or impala.

Unlike in western or central (equatorial) Africa, sugar features prominently in southern African cooking. Desserts and sweets are popular and include dried and planked fruit (fruit leathers); *melk tert*, a sweet custard tart/pie; *koeksisters*, braided crullers deep-fried and dipped in cinnamon syrup, originally from Batavia centuries earlier; and spice cookies. Fruit and vegetable condiments are often served with curries. *Blatjans* are chutneys made from fruit or vegetables with spices, acids, and sugar. *Blatjang* is the Cape Malay version of the Javanese spicy *sambal blachang* and includes ingredients such as dried apricots, raisins, vinegar, onions, garlic, brown sugar, almonds, salt, ginger, coriander, mustard seeds, and chili powder. *Atjars* are hot, spicy, curry-flavored, pickled fruits.

Jams are popular, as are the preserves known as *konfyt*. *Konfyt* refers to a fruit soaked in lime water, then cooked in thick sugar syrup and spices. Such preserves can be eaten alone or to accompany tea. Favorites are ripe fig, watermelon rind, quince, and tomato *konfyts*. The popular green fig *konfyt* is seasoned with cinnamon and dried ginger. *Konfyt* origins are unclear, but some believe it was a contribution from the French component of the Afrikaner's ancestors and comes from the French word *confiture*.

Bredies, as in the recipe previously, refer to stews, such as a mutton stew, that may include onions, chilies, tomatoes, potatoes, or pumpkin.

Many foods eaten in southern Africa include versions of Indian foods, such as the savory deep-fried pastries known as *samosas*, as well as *roti*, a flat, round bread often eaten with curries. Small pieces of the bread are torn off and used to scoop up the meat and sauce. Chicken marsala is a dish in which chicken pieces are coated with a mixture of spices such as cumin, turmeric, coriander, garlic, ginger, chili pepper, salt, black pepper, oil, and the seasoning *masala*, and marinated, then roasted. Another popular dish is Tandoori *Murghi*, or Tandoori chicken.

Xhosa

The Xhosa in southeastern Africa include clans such as the Thembu, Bomvana, and Mpondo. Their language makes a distinctive clicking sound that the famous South African singer Miriam Makeba introduced to the West. Xhosa traditionally wore clothes made from animal skins. Later, they dyed blankets with a special kind of red clay and became known as the red blanket people. The women traditionally wore large turbans, beads, copper bracelets, and, for a mature married woman, a long pipe was a status symbol. Many Xhosa remain in rural homesteads, with women taking care of the home and land, and the men working, perhaps migrating to work in mines. However, in urban areas traditional clothing is rarely worn today, except for celebrations. In the area of cuisine, the Xhosa have contributed many corn recipes, most famously samp and beans (*umngqusho*). Other dishes include a popular soup called *isopho*, combining sugar beans and fresh corn with onion, curry powder, potato, and salt; and *ugadugadu*, which combines dried pumpkin and maize-meal. *Umqa* is fresh pumpkin mashed with corn. *Amarhewu* (a thin, drinkable, slightly fermented sour porridge made with yellow and white maize meal, and a favorite of the most famous Xhosa, former South African President Nelson Mandela), *imbila* (the version of sour porridge from maize-meal and sorghum), and *umvubo*, all have maize in them. Meat dishes include *inyama yegusha*, a casserole, with mutton, onions, carrots, tomatoes, flour, salt, and black pepper, that might be served with samp and beans; and *ulusu lwenkomo*, stewed ox tripe that pairs well with pap or dumplings. *Inyama yenkukhu* is a casserole with chicken, onions, tomatoes, salt, black pepper, and flour. *Intlanzi*, or *maasbanker*, is a firm white fish that may be fried and served whole on a bed of braised cabbage, accompanied by samp and beans, and topped with a tomato sauce/relish made from oil, onion, fresh tomatoes, and cayenne pepper.

Zulu

The largest ethnic group in South Africa, the Zulu nation originated in the late 1600s. As described, it was their warrior king, Shaka, who led them to unrivaled power. As do people in most of sub-Saharan Africa, the

Zulu place a high value on hospitality. One of their proverbs *"Isisu om-hambi asingakanai singang 'enso yenyonin' "* declares "A visitor's stomach is as small as the kidney of a bird."[3] In other words, there is never too little food to feed strangers. It is likewise considered impolite for those visitors to refuse to accept food that is offered to them. A popular Zulu food is *amandumbe*, similar to a sweet potato. Other typical foods include the ubiquitous maize-meal, sorghum, sweet potatoes, potatoes, melons, and pumpkin. As is true of much of the region, meat, in the form of chuck, steak, or brisket *(inyama eyosiwe)*, grilled over an open fire is especially popular among the men, served with pap or samp, and washed down with a sip of sorghum beer *(umqomboth)*. As mentioned previously, *amarhewu* is the milder version that women and children would drink. Typical meals include *phutu* (crumbled maize porridge) with *amasi* (Xhosa) or *maas* (Zulu), curdled milk, and a simple tomato relish. "Green" (fresh) maize is popular with almost all groups, boiled or roasted on the cob.

Part of the cultural heritage of KwaZulu-Natal homelands of the Zulu is the influence from the descendants of Indian settlers who were originally brought in to work on the sugar plantations or came later as merchants from Gujarat and other parts of India. Zulus have adopted curries as their own, although omitting the ginger. One classic South African cookbook from 1961 claims rice and curry as a national dish of the country. The Indian-influenced curries of the Zulus are hotter than those of Cape Malay cooking. The Zulus also cook in *potjiekos*, and purists believe that foods cooked over the open fire have a special flavor from the wood used in cooking. Porridges, such as *iphalishi lobhontshisi* (butter bean porridge), *iphalishi elimuncu* (sour milk porridge), or *isijeza* (pumpkin porridge), may be served with a relish/sauce over it, such as the common *umhluzi wetamatisine anyanisi* (tomato and onion relish). Vegetables such as sweet potatoes may also be peeled, thinly sliced, flavored with cumin and salt, and fried crisp, then served with stir-fried vegetables such as leeks, onion, cabbage, spinach, sunflower seeds, salt, and pepper. Maize-meal can also be cooked into a sweetened custard with a chocolate sauce made from chocolate, cream, and prunes.

Lesotho

The small land-locked country of Lesotho is dominated by the Maluti Mountains and populated mostly in its rural lowland areas. Moshoeshoe I created it in the 1800s by consolidating small chiefdoms torn apart by the Difaqane wars of the Zulu king Shaka. The Basotho people are known for their horses and patterned blankets, the distinctive conical hats the men wear, and the skill of their women weavers. Cooking tends to be nutritious, but simple and less spicy than along the coast, including dishes such as pap, steamed pumpkin with cinnamon, and spinach stewed in beef stock. Basotho are fond of well-stewed oxtail and often eat beetroot salad at meals, where beets are cooked, grated, and mixed with chopped onion, sugar, and vinegar. The beet leaves may be cooked either alone or combined with tomatoes and onions. Ginger beer, an unfermented drink made from water, sugar, yeast, ginger, and orange or pineapple in Lesotho, or perhaps raisins in place of the citrus fruit in Botswana, might be drunk as a beverage, or sour (fermented) porridge, called *ting*, made from maize-meal and maize-rice. Offal, chicken, pounded meat, and liver are different forms in which protein is eaten in stews. As do other ethnic groups, instead of porridge, maize-meal paste may also be made into a dumpling that is steamed separately, such as the fermented *leqebekoane*.

Zimbabwe, Mozambique, Zambia

As mentioned earlier, Zimbabweans commonly eat *sadza*. They also like meat or fish sauces made with things such as wild leaf (such as *rape*), okra, peanuts, *kapenta, mopane* worms *(amacimbi)*, onions, peppers, salt, and pumpkin. Mozambique's blending of Portuguese and indigenous cultures has been introduced. Maize porridge is called *nsima* or *xima* in Mozambique, closely followed in popularity by rice (combined with prawns or meat into a kind of *pilau*, called *chiru*). Cassava is made into *upshwa*, and cassava flour and ground peanuts are mixed together and cooked in *chiguinha*. In Mozambique *peri peri* chicken is called *Galinha a piri piri*, and cassava and coconut milk are both commonly cooked. Zambia is another landlocked country, and the stiff porridge to accompany sauces is called *nshima*, as it is in Malawi. Chicken stew and okra in peanut sauce are two typical dishes. Zambian beverages include *muukhoyo, tombwa*, and *kachasu*. When porridge is served at breakfast, it is generally made with twice the water that is used for lunch or dinner porridge. In both Zambia and Malawi, fish such as bream, hake, or the small dried *kapenta* are eaten—Malawians are said to eat twice as much fish as meat.

Many things have affected southern African meal patterns, from inter-regional movements to urbanization and population pressures. For example, the San and Khoi people, after being displaced from their traditional lands, have adopted corn-based meals. The Herrero, who traditionally ate milk products such as curds and butter, have now shifted their diets to include *mielie*, meat, and black beans. As wild game has become less available, people have substituted sheep and beef.

A special situation affecting southern African foodways and tastes is the influence of migrant work in the area. Historically, in order to earn money, men have been forced to sign contracts to work in places such as the gold or diamond mines of South Africa or Zimbabwe (known as Rhodesia during colonial times). The workers' barracks have traditionally excluded women and children, requiring men to leave their wives and families in the rural areas of their homelands, such as Swaziland Lesotho or South Africa. The foods they have been served in these communities have affected their tastes and habits, so that when they periodically return home to their sending communities, they begin to introduce different foods into those areas. In addition, the work structure plus the lack of wives at the mines to grow and prepare traditional foods for their men, have combined to change what meals are served and when.

Studies of food habits and food preferences of black South African men have found that traditionally most men ate two meals a day, meat was not part of the daily diet, and that the first, midmorning meal around 11 A.M. typically consisted of a porridge from a staple cereal such as corn or millet and a vegetable-based relish or a legume and vegetable sauce. The second typical meal of the day included the same dishes as the first meal but was more substantial, and a relish, meat-based gravy or substantial vegetable dish was served with the porridge.

It has been shown that there have been changes in both the distribution and composition of meals: today, there are likely to be three meals instead of two, and different meals on weekends. Along with the traditional porridge and relish, such as tomato and onion relish, some studies have found that now a soft porridge may be eaten with sugar or brown bread, jam, and tea. Lunch tends to be a stiff maize porridge with a relish of gravy, vegetables, or tomatoes, and supper is the main meal of the day when meat, if available, is served, or a vegetable stew, such as one containing cabbage. Meal patterns on Sunday have been found to be more extensive, ranging from bread, tea, porridge, and relish, to ready-to-eat cereal, bacon, eggs, and sausage. On Sundays, the main meal appears to have become the midday meal, and most men report eating meat and starch dishes (ranging from rice, potatoes, samp, or maize porridge to mealie rice), plus a variety of three or four vegetables and salads. In addition, desserts are now more likely to be served, popularly including jelly and custard or canned fruit with custard. Overall, it appears that rice and potatoes are becoming more popular as staple foods, along with increased consumption of brown bread. Vetkoek is also growing in popularity, and eating bread for lunch or snacks is becoming more common, especially for schoolchildren. Meat consumption is also on the rise, the order of preference being beef, chicken, pork, liver, ox head, goat, bacon, mutton, and venison. Fruit consumption has been found to be increasing, with oranges and apples the most popular. Unsalted porridge is usually still preferred, although salt tends to be used to flavor relishes. Many spices, such as curry powder, pepper, cinnamon, ginger, mustard, cayenne pepper, chili powder, nutmeg, and vinegar, are now frequently used, and there has been a noticeable increase in the preference for the sweet-and-sour taste, such as sweet-and-sour beetroot and a drink made from water, sugar, and vinegar.

Other Groups

Other representative ethnic groups in the region include Swazis, Ndebele, Venda, and the Batswana of Botswana. Swazis, who live in one of the last monarchies on the continent, favor pulses such as round beans and lentils, cooked with maize-meal to make *lusontfwana* and *tinhlumaya nemphuphu*, respectively. Peanuts are boiled and shelled, or added to stews, crushed, or ground and added to soups, or mixed with samp and beans. The Ndebele are a blend of three ethnic groups, and their basic diet blends foods from these groups: Zulu, Xhosa, and Swazi. *Chakalaka* is a traditional Ndebele salad of cabbage, onion, tomatoes, and carrots flavored with chili and curry powder, possibly with other vegetables and baked beans added, and eaten with porridge. Venda food tends to be simple but flavorful. *Dofhi* (peanut sauce) is often included as the basis of dishes, as are dried meat (*tshievho* or *biltong*), and *mukusule (morogo)*, which are eaten with porridge. Rooibos is grown in the part of South Africa where the Venda people are based, as are numerous tropical fruits, caraway seeds, and *mufhoho*, a grain similar to mustard seeds. *Mopane* worms are found there as well. The Batswana hold guests in high regard and have a well-known proverb that reflects this: *"Moeng goroga re je ka wena"* ("When guests arrive, we eat").[4] This Tswana saying is similar to the proverb that introduces the eastern Africa chapter. The diet includes maize porridge (known as *mosoko*, or *bogobe bating*), *legola* (grain sorghum), *sebube* (grain sorghum porridge cooked in sour milk), *ting* (fermented maize porridge), tripe *(lserobe)*, and pounded meat *(seswaa)*. *Mopane* worms *(phane)* are popular accompaniments, as are *morogo*, especially leaves of bean plants. Dried beans and legumes are boiled and seasoned with salt and pepper, possibly with onions and a little oil, and eaten.

Chakalaka Salad (Southern Africa)

3 Tbsp vegetable oil

1 onion, grated

2 cloves garlic, crushed

2 Tbsp fresh ginger, grated

1 green bell pepper, grated

3 green jalapeno or other chili peppers, seeds removed and chopped

2 tsp curry powder (or to taste)

3 medium carrots, grated

1 medium cauliflower, divided into florets

1 small can baked beans (optional)

salt and any type of pepper to taste

Use a hand grater or food processor to grate the onion and green pepper into a large bowl. Peel and crush the garlic and add it to the bowl. Peel and grate the ginger and add it. Carefully remove the seeds from the jalapeno peppers and chop them finely. (It is possible to use the tines of a fork to hold the peppers while chopping them to avoid getting the oil from the peppers on one's fingers.) Rinse the cauliflower, remove the core and any outside leaves, and break it into small florets, cutting away any excess stalks to free the florets. Rinse and peel the carrots, then grate them with a grater or food processor. Heat oil in a heavy skillet and sauté the onion and sweet and jalapeno peppers with 2 or more teaspoons of curry powder for 5 minutes on medium heat. Add the carrots and cauliflower, stirring well to mix them. Turn the heat to low, and cook the mixture until the vegetables are almost tender, about 10 to 15 minutes. Mix in the baked beans, salt, and pepper, and cook until heated through. Cool and refrigerate. This side salad keeps for several days in the refrigerator. If a less sweet version is desired, omit the baked beans.

Sifting pounded nuts. Used with permission of Tafelberg Publishers.

Beverages

The research cited found all black southern African groups to rate fresh milk a preferred food, along with sour milk, *maghew*, and buttermilk. Fruit juices and carbonated drinks were also popular. Tea seems to have replaced *maghew* as a nonalcoholic beverage for social occasions. Some taboos have weakened or disappeared, such as those of some ethnic groups on eggs (most black ethnic groups, specifically for females of childbearing age, boys and young men) or fish (specifically North Sotho, Tswanna-Sotho, and Zulus). Fish and chips, tinned fish, and sardines are some of the ways in which fish are now commonly eaten. Most groups report eating snacks of dried fruit and peanuts, as well as eating cakes and biscuits. However, the traditional idea of Zulus that vegetables are "food for women" and men do not eat pumpkin still exists.

EATING OUT

The reality of migrant workers leaving their rural communities to find work lends a new twist to the concept of eating out. Instead of going to a restaurant in the Western sense, for decades many wage-earning black southern African men have been eating away from their homes on a daily basis. For example, almost half of Lesotho's total male labor force works in the South African industrial sector, and most of those men work in the mining industry, with more than one-third of the households in Lesotho relying on wages sent home as their family's main source of income.

Not only are the mines and caterers providing meals to these men, but roadside vendors offer snacks to them and travelers. Street food includes takeaway snacks such as grilled meat, deep-fried cassava or other chips, roasted corncobs, peanuts, cookies, cakes, a kind of doughnut, or boiled eggs. The next level is food (or *tea*) stalls, where lunchtime meals of rice or the cornmeal-based starch *mieliepap* (or *nsima, nshima,* etc.) are available, along with relish or stew side dishes. The same places provide morning meals of tea with or without milk and bread but are closed in the evenings.

In addition to being exposed to different diets in the migrant money economy, men have traditionally tended to socialize while drinking beer. Despite the growth of the wine industry in South Africa, beer can be considered the national drink of the region and beer-drinking a major avenue of socializing. Such drinking may take place in people's homes or in bars. Traditionally, however, the informal bars, known as *shebeens* in South Africa or *pungwe* in Zimbabwe, are rough "men only" beer-drinking centers and have also not crossed color or class lines. In this they differ from the pubs or bars familiar in Europe or the United States. Beer is drunk as an everyday kind of beverage, with varying degrees of alcoholic content. It is also an important part of ceremonial functions and is brewed from things such as corn, sorghum, or millet. Some regional names of local beers include *umqombothi*, *mageu* (or *maghew*), *amabele*, *amazimba*, and *luvhele*, made with the same ingredients used for porridges. The beers tend to be thick-textured and bitter-sweet. Commercially brewed lagers are increasing in popularity.

A second way of thinking about eating out is to take the words literally and talk about eating outside. A distinctive social tradition in the region is the southern African version of the barbeque, the *braai* or *braaivleis*. Although originally an Afrikaans tradition, the *braai* has transcended its origins to become a time-honored tradition, for white South African males a rite of passage, and an overall symbol of the region's casual, outdoor lifestyle. Literally, *braai* means grilled and *braaivleis* means grilled meat. The word *braai* can be used as a verb (to grill: for example, "please *braai* the meat"), as a noun (a grill: for example, "let's buy a new *braai*"), or the social event itself (a *braai*: for example, "you're invited to a *braai*"). Classic *braais* include meat cooked over hot coals on an open fire, often alongside stews or sauces cooked in *potjiekos*. A typical menu would include *boerwors*, steaks or *sosaties*, *mieliepap*, and a tomato and onion gravy, possibly followed by *melktert*. Other dishes might include salads and various sauces, fish or chicken, and foil-wrapped potatoes or other vegetables.

Braais can be held anywhere from the kraal to the bush, from a beach to a back yard, from a restaurant to a park. They usually include family and friends and generous amounts of beer. It is one of the few times that men will be found cooking, and the tradition, especially passed down from the (white) father to son, includes carefully building a fire, the men standing around the grill, drinking beer and talking while they work. The women congregate, too, as they prepare the supporting salads and socialize. Men traditionally do the actual grilling of the well-done meat. The process of preparation and socializing is integral to the experience and can take many hours, possibly lasting well into the night.

Nando's

Southern Africa has made its contribution to fast food restaurants through a global chain now found on five continents. During post-colonial wars in Mozambique and Angola of the 1970s and 1980s, a number of former Portuguese colonists fled those countries, many resettling in South Africa and opening small family restaurants. One of these, in a suburb of

Johannesburg, was called "Chickenland." A Portuguese immigrant named
Fernando Duarte took his friend Robbie Brozin to Chickenland in 1987 to
taste the restaurant's fiery version of *peri peri* chicken. The dish captivated
the men, who proceeded to buy the restaurant, eliminate all the other
dishes, and rename the restaurant "Nando's Chickenland." The recipe for
their sauce is a tightly kept secret, except for an acknowledgement that
the African bird's eye chili is its main ingredient. The company is now the
world's largest consumer of the African bird's eye chili and cultivates this
pepper on its own farms to supply its customers. The Nando's restaurant
chain is now global, and in Africa franchises are in Angola, Bostwana,
Ghana, Kenya, Lesotho, Malawi, Mozambique, Namibia, Senegal, South
Africa, Swaziland, Tanzania, Uganda, Zambia, and Zimbabwe.

SPECIAL OCCASIONS

The *braai* has fostered a sense of national identity in southern Africa.
It is a festive time when families and friends can come together to enjoy
each other's company and have a good time.

Other community special times include weddings, holy days, funerals, births and birthdays, rites of passage such as initiations, and festivals
marking the rhythm of nature.

Malay and Dutch communities have established numerous traditions,
such as serving yellow rice as part of a meal after a funeral. Malay descendants are predominantly Muslim and do not drink alcohol. They observe
Muslim holy days, fast, and follow other dietary restrictions. However,
Islamic law does not dictate the specific foods that can be eaten at a feast.
Among the Cape Malays, on the fifteenth night of Ramadan a thick, spicy
milk pudding called *boeber* is served to celebrate the middle of Ramadan.
Lebaran, the local name for the *Eid-ul-fitr*, which begins the day after the
end of Ramadan, is especially marked by feasting on pies, puddings, *kerries*
(curries), *bredies*, *geelrys*, *pastei*, kabobs, and so forth. Other Cape Malay
celebrations include naming ceremonies the seventh day after a child is
born, when a feast called the *doopmaal* takes place. There are different
words to refer to gatherings at which substantial hot food and meats are
served (*merang*) and those at which lighter refreshments are served such
as cakes and sandwiches (*moulud*). Funeral feasts (and this term extends
to other feasts, although not weddings) are called *gaja* or *gajaat*. The eating utensils among this group include fingers for solid foods and spoons for
soups and soft puddings, or rice. Knives are not usually necessary as meat
is pre-cut. Forks are not generally used.

One of the most memorable days in the life of a Malay woman is her wedding day. Traditionally, food has been garnished spectacularly for the bride, and elaborate rituals and foods are associated with this day. The bridegroom eats a special feast at his parents' home with invited guests, featuring *buriyani* and other meat dishes, followed by various milk puddings. He traditionally sends two large baskets of food called "bride's baskets" to his bride. This food is carefully and lovingly prepared and garnished, and tends to be brightly colored. One basket contains hot meat dishes, rice, and condiments, and the other, the dessert, particularly a baked custard. A bouquet of fresh flowers tied with satin ribbons is included in one of the baskets. Male and female guests are seated in separate rooms at all of the various wedding feasts.

The funeral *(kefiyat)* also has specific requirements, in particular that food should not be cooked in a house as long as there is a corpse there. Orthodox families observe this requirement, and food, including the traditional *wortelbredie* (*wortel* means carrot) must be prepared at a neighbor's house or outside in the yard. It is considered essential to provide a proper feast to appropriately honor the deceased, and people would rather go into debt than be accused of failing to do so.

In contrast, hunter-gatherer groups like the !Kung have traditionally not held feasts, which require a food surplus. Their lifestyle of sharing food among all community members probably inhibited the stockpiling of food for planned special occasions.

Among Bantu-speaking groups in southern Africa, an important rite of passage for males or females has been ceremonies marking the transition from adolescence to adulthood. Classically, for boys, this has often involved painful circumcision, but more than the physical change, it marks a change in social status. It involved a variety of elements, such as a time of seclusion, perhaps with a cohort of other young men, perhaps by themselves in the bush, and often included hazing to toughen them up, as well as instruction in the ways of manhood. At the end of the time, the newly initiated men would return to the community, their old clothes or blankets burned, and the huts where they had stayed also destroyed. Among the Xhosas, traditionally at the beginning of the process an animal is slaughtered, the boys eat a ritual meal, take off their clothes, and each put on a new blanket. Then they are taken to a river to be circumcised. Following this, they are smeared with mud and remain in seclusion for about three months. At the end of the time, a huge feast is prepared for them, they receive new clothes and names, and are welcomed back into the community as men. While this Xhosa *umgidi* tradition is being modified in contemporary times, the element of slaughtering sheep, cows, and goats to feast on when the young men are welcomed back into the community as men remains.

There are also "first fruit" festivals, such as *Incwala* (or *Ncwala*), a sacred ceremony in which the king of Swaziland gives his people permission to eat the first crops of the new year. It takes place over several days although it begins weeks earlier when wise men *(bemanti)* travel, some to the Lebombo Mountains to gather plants, others to collect water from Swazi rivers, and still others cross the mountains to the Indian Ocean (where their ancestors are from) to skim foam from the waves. At the appointed time the king goes into retreat. When the moon is full, young men harvest branches of a small tree called *lusekwane* and begin walking to the royal kraal located at Lobamba. They get there at dawn and build a *kraal* with their branches, sing special songs, and wait for the *bemanti* to arrive with the plants, water, and foam they have collected. A bull is sacrificed on the third day, and on the fourth day, at the pleading of his subjects, the king emerges and dances. He eats a pumpkin as a sign that his subjects can now eat the new year's crops. Two days later all the huts in the *kraal* and items used in the ceremony are ritually burned, and rain is expected to fall in response.

Ginger Beer (All of Sub-Saharan Africa)

4–8 oz ginger root (1/4 to 1/2 pound, depending on how strong you want it)

2 cups boiling water

2 cups cold water

1/2–3/4 cup sugar

2 Tbsp lime (or lemon) juice

6 cloves

a small piece of cinnamon stick (about 1/4 of a short stick) (optional)

Peel ginger root with a vegetable peeler, and grate it into a 2-qt. glass bowl or dish. Set the dish on top of a folded towel to keep it steady. Pound and mash the ginger well with a potato masher or wooden spoon, then pour 2 cups of boiling water over it, and let it sit for at least 2 hours. Line a strainer or colander with a cheesecloth that has been folded several times and place it over another glass bowl. Slowly pour the ginger-water mixture through the strainer. Squeeze, twist, and press the cloth to remove most of the liquid. Discard the ginger in the cloth. Add 2 cups cold water to the liquid in the bowl and up to 3/4 cup sugar, stirring to dissolve it. Add the lime or lemon juice, cloves, and cinnamon, and let sit at least an hour before removing the spices. Carefully pour the ginger beer into a pitcher, leaving most of the white sediment in the bottom of the bowl. Store the pitcher, covered, in the refrigerator.

Variations: increase or decrease the ginger or sugar, replace the cloves and cinnamon with fresh pineapple chunks (including the peel), and add it with the original grated ginger. Some versions use yeast or cream of tartar.

Serve the ginger beer chilled over ice cubes, diluted to taste with water, seltzer water, or even ginger ale. Use about 1/2 cup ginger beer per serving.

DIET AND HEALTH

San Diet and Biopiracy

The traditional diet of the San people was about 80 percent vegetable, eaten fresh, and they consumed 23 of 85 plant species that they knew to be edible in their environment and 17 of 55 edible animal species. The San had indigenous knowledge of the useful properties of many wild plants.

It appears that individuals in the group received enough protein, vitamins, and minerals in their diets, although the number of calories was only about 2,140 kcal per person per day during an average day. Unlike many African children, their young showed no sign of childhood malnutrition.

A growing concern in many parts of the developing world, including sub-Saharan Africa, is biopiracy, or the situation in which plants or their genetic materials are essentially stolen from the original users and appropriated by people from developed countries. At issue is the conflict between the rights of indigenous peoples and Western intellectual property rules. An example is the Hoodia cactus. For many years the San have cut off pieces of this bitter plant to carry with them on hunting trips into the Kalahari desert. They did not eat while they were hunting, but brought the meat back with them to share among everyone, so while they were hunting they relied on the Hoodia slices to keep them alert and prevent them from feeling hungry and thirsty. In the 1960s, the Council for Scientific and Industrial Research of South Africa (CSIR) began researching the Hoodia with the cooperation of the San. In 1996 CSIR patented it, and in 1997 licensed rights to it to Phytopharm, a company based in the United Kingdom. Hoodia is attractive to the obesity-plagued Western world because it promises an anti-obesity drug without any of the side effects of current treatments. The active ingredient, called P57, was isolated, and Phytopharm subsequently sold rights to the pharmaceutical giant, Pfizer. In July of 2001, a Pfizer spokesperson in the United Kingdom linked Hoodia to the San but said they were extinct. The San responded

Mini *ukhamba*, a traditional
Zulu herb container. Courtesy
of the author.

forcefully, and in November of 2001 the South African San Council,
representing the Khomani, !Kung, and Khwe peoples (found not only in
South Africa but also in Namibia, Botswana, Zambia, and Angola) signed
a compensation agreement with the San people.

Other examples of contested indigenous African plants or genetic materials include the Kinde Zulu cowpea; teff, a grain from Ethiopia; *brazzeire*,
from a plant in Gabon, a protein said to be 500 times sweeter than sugar;
thaumatin, another West African natural sweetener; and genetic material
from a West African cocoa plant.

A South African company, Phyto Nova, is said to be researching the
medicinal properties of another plant, *Sutherlandia Frutescens*, from the
sub-species Microphylla, known to San people as *insisa*, "the one that dis-
pels darkness," to Zulu *sangomas* (traditional healers) as *unwele*, to Tswana
people as *mukakana*, *phetola* in North Sotho, and *lerumo* in Lamadi, and to
Afrikaners as *kankerbossie* or "cancer bush."

Food Taboos

Bantu-speaking communities have varied social and cultural structures
and requirements. Among them, when an animal has been killed (tra-

ditionally by spears and/or arrows), there are often rules as to who gets what part of the animal. Men tend to eat more meat than women. The person who slaughters the meat is supposed to get certain parts, and there are parts women are not allowed to eat, such as a goat's head. In parts of Zimbabwe, meat from a porcupine is to be handed over to the chief. If people have a totem, such as a tortoise, lion, or leopard, they do not eat the meat of that animal, or it is said their teeth will fall out. Some parts of the animal are supposed to impart the quality of the animal to the person, such as a leopard's heart giving a man a brave heart.

As discussed earlier in this chapter, there have often been taboos on eating eggs, related to a concern about female sterility and the negative connotations of eggs being excreted, but these prohibitions are weakening.

Protein-Energy Malnutrition, Anemia, Goiter, Vitamin A Deficiency

The generalized food-supply crisis of sub-Saharan Africa extends over much of southern Africa. Some causes of famine and food shortages have already been touched upon in other chapters but are beyond the scope of this book to discuss in depth. High levels of poverty and food insecurity affect the health of many people. Protein-energy malnutrition (PEM) is the most common and serious diet-related health concern and is said to be especially correlated with a maize-based diet. While people suffering from mild or moderate PEM are not starving, the syndrome causes serious stunting of growth in children. When other illnesses or crises strike, the combination can quickly become lethal. Niacin deficiency is similarly linked to maize-based diets.

Anemia, particularly iron-deficiency anemia, is often a problem, especially for women. It can result from an inability to absorb folic acid found mainly in green leafy vegetables rather than failure to consume enough of it. The inability to metabolize the folic acid may occur because of internal parasites from malaria, hookworm, or roundworm.

Goiter is caused by iodine deficiency and occurs partly because of the geological reality that the soil lacks iodine, which means that the plants also lack it. Eating large amounts of cassava and cabbage may contribute to susceptibility to goiter. However, goiters are usually temporary and not especially dangerous. They are most likely to develop in premenopausal women whose thyroids are stressed with the pressures of bearing and nursing children and monthly menstruation.

Vitamin A deficiency, which can lead to blindness, is sometimes a problem in dry areas such as the Luapula Valley in Zambia, although it is almost completely absent from humid tropical places where there are year-round sources of vitamin A and beta-carotene.

Chili Peppers and Health

There are numerous health claims ascribed to chilies: as a good source of vitamin C, as well as sources of vitamin A and calcium; as causing the brain to release endorphins into the bloodstream (endorphins create a sense of well-being and are what causes the so-called runner's high); as boosting the body's metabolism thus causing calories to be burned faster (Japanese research suggests that five teaspoons of chopped chilies boost metabolism by 30 percent during a meal); as aiding in digestion, working as a stimulant; possibly protecting the gastric lining; and as easing symptoms of rheumatism, arthritis, headaches, shingles, and burns. Capsaicin oil is found in cough and cold mixtures, as well as used in ointments not only for rheumatism, but also for skin conditions. One of the six tastes identified by the Ayurveda, the Hindu wisdom regarding health and diet, is pungent, and includes garlic, chilies, and onion. India is said to be the largest cultivator of chilies in the world, and the Indian influence in bringing chili peppers into the diet in southern Africa has already been explained.

AIDS and Diet

The major health concern in the region is associated with the human immunodeficiency virus (HIV), which leads to acquired immune deficiency syndrome (AIDS), a fatal disease. It is contracted from exposure to blood, blood products, or body fluids, and is endemic in Africa, but especially in southern Africa where it is the leading cause of death for young adults and adults. AIDS may be spread via sexual intercourse, but it is also transmitted from blood transfusions of tainted blood, such as for malaria, hemorrhaging in childbirth, or traffic accidents, or infected needles for injections. Statistics from 2002 cite 38.8 percent of the population aged 15 to 49 years as infected with HIV/AIDS in Botswana, 31 percent in Lesotho, 23 percent in Namibia, 20 percent in South Africa, 33 percent in Swaziland, 22 percent in Zambia, and 34 percent in Zimbabwe.[5] These numbers translate into incredible suffering and have huge implications for diet. AIDS has spread rapidly in this region of the world for numerous reasons, including poverty, natural disasters, a history of exploitation, including the low status and vulnerability of women and related cultural practices and taboos, combined with a lack of education about sexually transmitted diseases. For example, in some places it is believed that one cure for AIDS is to have intercourse with a young virgin, and six times as many girls as boys of the same age are infected. Also, migrant workers are often away from their wives and may have intercourse with promiscuous women or prostitutes, then return home as carriers to possibly multiple wives in polygamous households. These women may contract AIDS, sometimes passing it on to their unborn children or nursing babies through their milk.

The implications for the health and diet of southern Africa are far-reaching. The people who are most likely to die are productive workers, either farmers, laborers, or parents. Most people in Africa die within a couple of years of contracting the disease, and this places unbearable pressures on their families: their labor is lost, they require extra care while they are sick, families need to spend more money on food and medicine at the very time that their incomes or resources are decreasing, and families have extended family to care for as they adopt children or wives of deceased relatives. In 2002 it was estimated that there were 400,000 AIDS orphans in Malawi, with more than half a million children in Zimbabwe having lost at least one parent to AIDS. The cost of numerous funerals with the expected feasting and signs of respect place additional heavy burdens on poor families of widows, elderly grandparents, or young children. Increasing desperation may also drive young women into prostitution or exploitative relationships to earn money, which further fuels the crisis.

There is another connection between diet and health. Individuals with HIV/AIDS may often live for years in developed countries where they can obtain nutritious diets. A diet rich in antioxidants is recommended to strengthen people's resistance to the progress of the disease. It is estimated that people living with HIV have higher than normal nutritional requirements of up to 50 percent more protein and up to 15 percent more calories. Where people are poor and already overworked and undernourished, as in many places in sub-Saharan Africa, the disease becomes even more deadly. These are some of the issues that governments in sub-Saharan Africa are currently struggling with. Not only are people unable to afford antiretroviral medicines, they may not be able to afford a nutritional diet.

NOTES

1. Intuitively, this proverb suggests that one should not destroy the very thing that helps one survive (i.e., tough food cooked in a pot will be softened for those

who are unable to chew it). However, the meaning goes deeper than that. According to one writer, the proverb is best understood in the context of a story from Malawi about a community and an old woman. Corn (maize) is a staple food in much of sub-Saharan Africa and is eaten fresh (or green) on the cobs, dried and ground into flour to make a thick starch eaten with a sauce or relish, or the whole dried kernels are fried. This fried version is difficult to chew and requires strong teeth. According to the story, before metal pots became common, one community had a single clay pot for cooking, and it belonged to an old woman. When the corn was fresh in the fields, everyone borrowed her pot to cook the corn, which she also ate, and everyone lived happily together. As the season passed, the corn dried on the cobs in the field, and the other community members (who were younger and had teeth) continued to borrow the old woman's pot to fry their maize, but she was unable to eat it with them. In a jealous fit she broke the pot to make them suffer. The woman became very hungry, and when the people came and found the pot broken, one boy announced they had some fresh corn for her, "But now how are you going to cook it?" Thus, the proverb is about how jealousy and greed end up hurting the jealous or greedy person himself or herself. It is a warning to those who have something that can help another but refused to share it with others. See also: http://www.afriprov.org/resources/explain.htm.

2. Dorinda Hafner, *A Taste of Africa* (Berkeley, Calif.: Ten Speed Press, 1993), p. 95.

3. Dorah Sitole, *True Love Magazine, Cooking from Cape to Cairo* (Capetown, South Africa: Tafelberg Publishers, 1999), p. 62.

4. *Ibid.*, p. 28.

5. Patrick Dixon, "The Extent of the AIDS Nightmare: Latest AIDS facts and HIV Statistics—Africa AIDS Crisis," in his book *The Truth About AIDS* (Kingsway, 2002), p. 90. http://www.globalchange.com/ttaa/contents.htm.

3

Eastern Africa

Mgeni njoo, mwenyeji apone.
Let the guest come so that the host / hostess may benefit (get well.)[1]

—Swahili, Luya, and Haya proverb

INTRODUCTION

The Horn of Africa and East Africa

Discussing East African food and culture is a bit like the three blind men describing an elephant—it all depends on what part of the creature one is touching at the moment. Two of the most common ways of thinking about eastern Africa are geographical and political. People outside of Africa often divide the eastern region of Africa into two parts: the "Horn of Africa" and "East Africa." Usually included in the Horn of Africa are the countries of Ethiopia, Eritrea, Djibouti, and Somalia, but the Food and Agriculture Organization (FAO) also adds Sudan, Kenya, and Uganda. Since the 1970s the term *East Africa* has commonly referred to Kenya, Tanzania, and Uganda. This was largely a political choice since all three countries were British colonies and held common services such as railways, airlines, ports, and telecommunications systems. Although that regional cooperation disintegrated in 1977, there have been attempts to revive it. Still others include in East Africa the two countries that border the east and central regions: Rwanda and Burundi.

Eritrea and Ethiopia (the Abyssinia of ancient times) are closely aligned politically and culturally, and Ethiopia attempted to assimilate Eritrea during the twentieth century, leading to years of war until Eritrea won its freedom in 1991. Similarly, there is a long history of interaction between Ethiopia and Somalia, and many people living in the Ogaden region of eastern Ethiopia consider themselves Somali. Tiny Djibouti is basically a city-state and has close cultural ties to Somalia and economic ties to Ethiopia. About half its population is made up of the Issas, who are linked to Somalia, and the Afars, who have links with Eritrea and Ethiopia. This book takes a broad view of eastern Africa and will include all of the countries named except Burundi and Rwanda, which are included in the central Africa chapter.

Eastern Africa is geographically quite diverse. Bounded on the east by the Red Sea and the Indian Ocean, three-quarters of the region is either arid or semiarid, especially the northern half of Sudan and much of the other Horn of Africa countries. However, the two most notable physical features are its fertile highlands and its Great Rift Valley, with two southward-reaching arms dividing them, creating troughs and swells over parallel fault lines. The troughs create valleys containing a number of lakes, which has earned it the name Great Lakes region. The highlands, or swells, contain extinct volcanoes that form some of the highest mountain peaks in Africa, such as Mount Kilimanjaro and Mount Kenya. The lakes include Lake Turkana, Lake Victoria, and Lake Tanganyika. This vast depression, or rift, begins in the Middle East and extends all the way southward to Mozambique in the southeast.

It was around places such as Lake Turkana that some of the earliest evidence of human ancestors (*homo habilis* and *homo erectus*) has been uncovered, dating back to around 1.8 million years ago. Thus, East Africa is often considered the cradle of civilization.

The most familiar positive image of sub-Saharan Africa held by Westerners is derived from East Africa. This is the part of Africa that is home to spectacular wildlife and breathtaking scenery. Photographic safaris and related tourism remain important industries, especially in Kenya and Tanzania.

As was the case with the Sahara Desert, many places in East Africa that are today semidesert were once filled with lush vegetation and wildlife. In parts of present-day Kenya, archaeological evidence of stone age tool-making has been dated to 238,000 B.C.E. Probably these tools—axes, cleavers, scrapers, and knives—were used to dig and hunt for food, especially antelopes, giraffes, and other animals that were drawn to the water at the lakeshores.

The highlands are generally cooler than the lowlands and receive higher rainfall than other areas, and it is in this area that most of the crops are produced. The drier lowlands lend themselves more to pastoralism and rearing animals. Crops and animal production together account for about 90 percent of East African employment.

There is also great ethnic variation in the region. Language families again help put this diversity in perspective. The population in 2002 was estimated to be about 190 million people living in roughly 2.3 million square miles and speaking languages from five major language families (see Chapter 1). However, these five families encompass more than 500 linguistically distinct communities. In addition, many people today living in this region have Arabic, Indian, or European origins. The *lingua franca* of East Africa and the official language of Tanzania and Kenya is Swahili, also known as Kiswahili. This is a Bantu language, but many words in it draw heavily from Arabic, and it incorporates words from other languages such as English. For hundreds of years it has been the main language of trade and commerce in the region, as well as parts of central Africa. The generic name Swahili has also become the name given to the local African people who have spent the last several centuries trading, mixing, and intermarrying with the Muslim, Arabic, and other, immigrants.

HISTORICAL OVERVIEW

Early History: Khoisan, Cushites, Bantu, and Nilotes

The region has experienced a great deal of migration of a variety of peoples throughout its history. The earliest people living in the interior may have been Khoisan (a.k.a. San, Bushmen) speakers who lived in the savanna, forest, and lakeshores perhaps 5,000 years ago (the same people introduced in Chapter 2 on southern Africa). These hunters and gatherers used spears, snares, and poisoned arrows to hunt both large and small game (rabbits, dik-diks, buffalo, giraffes, elephants, etc.) while also gathering wild foods such as fruits, nuts, tubers, honey, grasshoppers, caterpillars, termites, eggs, and birds. Today there remain only tiny remnants of these original inhabitants.

Later migrants into much of the area included southern Cushitic speakers from the Ethiopian highlands around 2000 B.C.E. who were primarily nomadic pastoralists, but who also are thought to have introduced the finger millet they had domesticated in Ethiopia. A second wave of eastern Cushites most likely followed about 1,000 years later and settled in central

Kenya. It is believed that cattle were introduced into Ethiopia from North Africa around 3000–2000 B.C.E. and that the Cushites brought them with them. It is also believed that this group produced the first camel herders in Africa and probably introduced camels into the area. Bantu-speaking agriculturalists came from the south and east, and Nilotic-speakers (or Nilo-Saharan) came from the northwest. There was a lot of migration and jostling, especially between 500 B.C.E. and 500 C.E. Bantu speakers included the Kikuyu, Meru, Gusii (or Kisii), Embu, Akamba, Luyha, and Myikinda in Kenya; the Sukuma, Nyamwezi, Makende, Haya, Zaramo, Pane, and Chagga in Tanzania; and the Buganda and Busoga in Uganda. The Nilotic-speaking migrants included the Maasai and Samburu in Kenya and Tanzania; the Turkana, Pokot, Luo, and Kalenyim in Kenya; and the Langa, Acholi, Teso, and Karamajong in Uganda.

Some of the Cushitic-speaking migrants seem to have settled near areas with more water, such as the upland area or slopes of places such as Mount Kenya and Mount Kilimanjaro, but some of them may have introduced camels into Egypt and been able, with the help of their camels, to travel deserts. Thus, the Afar and Somali were able to live in arid and semiarid areas from Djibouti to the Tana River in Kenya.

Near the same time, a small number of agriculturists, the Nilotic-speaking peoples cultivating sorghum and raising livestock, moved into what is today Uganda, perhaps as far south at the Zambezi River valley. Then, probably between 2,000 and 3,000 years ago, Bantu-speaking migrants who had traveled eastward through the equatorial rainforests arrived in the area, too. The Bantu speakers incorporated central Sudanic grain-farming and livestock-rearing techniques to their yam-based agriculture and were able to take over most of East Africa's cultivable lands. By the 1500s their systems ran the spectrum from intensive irrigation to shifting cultivation.

The lands of eastern Africa where crops could not be grown, ranging from semiarid to desert, became the realm of herding peoples. The arid northeast was taken over by Cushitic-speaking Somali and Oromo who emphasized camels, while cattle-oriented Nilotes claimed the grassland and savanna of the interior plateaus. Thus, the people living in southern Somalia developed farming while the northerners developed routes for moving their herds and families from one watering hole to the next.

The social and political organization included a few centralized kingdoms in the fertile areas whose rulers inherited their authority and that were socially stratified and economically diversified, as well as many chiefdoms that were more egalitarian and decentralized.

Early Kingdoms

There is a common Western stereotype of isolated, provincial African groups living a primitive existence with little contact with outsiders. Two important early East African kingdoms caution against such a simplistic view. The first is the Nubian kingdom of Cush that emerged along the Nile in northeastern Sudan in the early 2nd millennium B.C.E. and continued to about 350 C.E. It was a commercial and cultural center that linked Mediterranean and Middle Eastern civilizations with (black) African civilizations to its south. Cush conquered Egypt in the mid-eighth century before Assyrians gained control. It is remembered for its stone pyramids at the iron-making center of Merowe. As noted in Chapter 1, metal technology allowed productivity in agriculture to greatly advance.

A second kingdom, Axum (or Aksum), in northern Ethiopia, rose to power in the fourth century C.E. as Cush's power declined and was eventually eclipsed. Axum was a Semitic kingdom that flourished from about 300–700 C.E. and was most powerful in the fourth century under King Ezana who successfully led a military expedition against Cush. He was also the first Axumite king to convert to Christianity, and the Amharic state of Ethiopia and the Ethiopian Coptic church has its roots in this history. An important historical landmark is found in the rock churches at Lalibela. The strict Orthodox Church that evolved, with numerous fast days and dietary restrictions, would influence the food culture of the entire region.

Along with the finger millet originally from Ethiopia, one of the earliest and most important imported foods in the East African diet was bananas (and plantains). They may have traveled south from Egypt more than 2,000 years ago, possibly having been introduced into Egypt via trade with India, but more likely Malaysians and Polynesians who sailed to Madagascar and the southeastern coast of Africa brought them. Many believe that Indonesian immigrants reached Madagascar during the first millennium and carried with them new foodstuffs, especially bananas.

The Swahili Coast

While migrations were going on in the interior, along the coast of the Red Sea and Indian Ocean other major historical events were taking place that influenced the food and culture of the region. These involved Arab and Persian (present-day Iran) traders and the expansion of Islam into the area. From around 700 Muslims from the Arabian peninsula and Persians

Dhows along the Swahili coast. Adapted by J. Susan Cole Stone with permission from Tafelberg Publishers.

began interacting with the people and sailing boats called dhows to the coast to trade their glass beads, glassware, ironware, textiles, wheat, and wine for gold, ivory, tortoise shell, rhino horn, and, most importantly, slaves. The infamous Indian Ocean slave trade has received less coverage in the West than the trans-Atlantic slave trade, but it is estimated that from roughly 700 to 1911 about 14 million Africans were enslaved and subjected to extremely harsh conditions. One source estimates that this included 9.6 million women and 4.4 million men. Many of these were women who were destined to join harems as concubines; others were young boys who were castrated to become eunuchs, if they survived the brutal process. Due to the lucrative trading, wealthy, urbanized, cosmopolitan port city-states were established along the coast from Somalia to Mozambique. These included Kilwa, Malindi, Mombasa, Mogadishu, and Dar es Salaam, and islands such as Zanizibar (famous for its clove plantations) and Lamu.

A good number of the Arab traders and merchants intermarried with the Africans, and the profitable trade expanded across the Indian Ocean to India and China, bringing into the area foods, spices, religious taboos, and cooking techniques that would also influence the diet.

It was during this era that one of the earliest accounts of the food and culture of the area was written by the medieval travel writer Ibn Battuta, an Islamic scholar from Tangier in North Africa during a 1331 trip to the east coast, including Mombasa and Kilwa. Ibn Battuta found the city of Zeila ("a people of the blacks," 40 km east of the present-day Djibouti border), whose "camels and sheep are famed for their fatness," disgusting:

(Zeila) is a big city and has a great market but it is the dirtiest, most desolate and smelliest town in the world. The reason for its stink is the quantity of fish and the blood of the camels they butcher in its alleyways. When we arrived there, we preferred to pass the night on the sea, though it was rough. We did not spend the night in the town because of its squalor.[2]

However, Battuta commented favorably on a meal served to him by the sultan of Maqdashaw (Mogadishu in present-day Somalia): betel leaves with areca nuts, followed by rice cooked with ghee (clarified butter) and topped with chicken, meat, fish, and vegetables, green banana cooked in fresh milk (which may have actually been coconut milk), accompanied by side dishes of sour milk with pickled lemon, pickled and salted chilies, green ginger, and mangoes.[3]

Perhaps the earliest written account of the East African coast is found in *The Periplus of the Erythraean Sea: Travel and Trade in the Indian Ocean by a Merchant of the First Century*. It describes the Arab and Roman-Graeco merchants who were trading with Lamu and refers to the city of Meroe and the Axumites.

European Colonizers

The influence of the Portuguese abounds throughout eastern Africa, as in all other regions. As was noted earlier, during the mid-to-late 1400s the Portuguese had traveled southward along the western side of Africa and up the eastern coast. Explorer Vasco da Gama rounded the Cape of Good Hope at the southern tip of Africa in 1497 and started traveling northward. He and his crew enjoyed the hospitality of a sultan at Malindi (Mozambique) who provided him with a pilot who knew the route to India. The Portuguese returned in 1502, this time to conquer, and fought the Arabs who monopolized trade. Despite unsuccessful attempts by the Ottoman Turks to regain control, East Africans were subjected to a couple of hundred years of harsh colonial rule before the Portuguese were finally defeated and left in 1720. The major Portuguese contribution to the food of the area included the introduction of numerous new world foods, including cassava, chili peppers, corn, peanuts, the sweet potato, and probably tomatoes. The sweet potato is said to have spread from Africa to Europe, then on to the Americas and Asia. After the Portuguese left, the area reverted to Arab control under the Omani Dynasties. However, the earlier wealth and prosperity never were regained.

In the nineteenth century European powers became interested in East Africa and planned to occupy it. The Omani of the time moved to the island of Zanzibar, began laying out clove plantations, and in 1832 moved his court there. Zanzibar's clove trade became legendary—the island became known as the spice island during the 1800s and exported its cloves globally.

When the sultan left, Britain and Germany rushed to the mainland, and by the mid-1800s an agreement was reached in which Germans received Tanganyika (present-day Tanzania), while the British took Kenya and Uganda. This was the era of European explorers, and the famous exchange of remarks between United States newsman Henry Stanley and British explorer David Livingston ("Dr. Livingstone, I presume") took place when they met at Ujiji on Lake Tanganyika. European powers carved up the region according to their own political fortunes. After World War I, Tanganyika was mandated to the British. The French and Italians were also present in the area, and Ethiopia had its own designs on territory. Somalia was divided into British, French, and Italian *Somaliland*. Britain took over Italian Somaliland and administered it from 1941–1950. In 1950 Italian Somaliland was returned to Italy as a U.N. Trust Territory for 10 years. By 1977 Ethiopia and Somalia were at war.

Landlocked Ethiopia, which shared an eastern border with Somalia, also desired to control Eritrea, especially to gain access to the coast. Ethiopia itself was never colonized although Italy occupied it briefly and claimed Eritrea as a protectorate. In the first half of the nineteenth century, both Egypt and Abyssinia (Ethiopia) tried to gain control of Eritrea. The English established a consulate in Massawa in 1849 but did not want a colony there. The French established themselves further south in Djibouti, so it was the Italians who actually colonized Eritrea, joining the "scramble for Africa" late, in the 1880s. Until 1941, the Italians planted cotton, vegetable crops, and orchards, and established a biscuit factory, salt and potash mines, and vineyards and wineries. In the World War II era, the British captured Eritrea in 1941 and retained control until the early 1950s.

The various colonizers left indelible marks on the cultures with which they interacted. For example, in the 1940s British soldiers wanted beer, which was not available in Eritrea, so the Melotti winery agreed to brew it if the British military would provide the ingredients. The beer, made with imported ingredients, became popular with Europeans in the area, and its popularity eventually spread to Eritreans and Ethiopians, until it is now as popular as local alcoholic drinks. Italians also brought pasta, pastries, pizza, *fritatti, capretto,* crème caramel and *Macedonia di futta,* fruits, and vegetables still eaten in Asmara, the capital city.

There is a marked, and ancient, Asian influence in East Africa. As described, during the heyday of the Swahili coast, Indian traders used to come to the coast of East Africa to ply their wares, although they rarely stayed to settle. Later, at the turn of the nineteenth century, the British set out to construct a Mombasa-Uganda railway and imported around 32,000 indentured laborers from the Gujarat state in West India and the Punjab. Many of these workers stayed, given British encouragement to migrate there after World War II. While the Indians tended to isolate themselves from and look down on the Africans, their spices and foods, from curries to samosas to chapati, were still to exert an influence on the region. It was most likely Malaysian immigrants who introduced plantains and bananas into eastern Africa.

Chapati (East Africa)

3 1/2 cups whole wheat flour or unbleached white flour, or a combination

1/2 tsp salt

1/2 cup vegetable oil or shortening

1 1/2 cups warm water

1 Tbsp melted butter, margarine, ghee, or vegetable oil

Sift the flour and salt together into a bowl. If using shortening, rub it in with your fingertips until well mixed before proceeding. If using oil, mix it with half the water (3/4 cup), make a well in the center of the flour and dump in the water/oil (or water alone if using shortening), then stir well with a sturdy mixing spoon. Gradually add the remaining water, stirring continuously to get a soft but firm dough. Knead the dough a few minutes in the bowl, dusting your hands with flour if necessary. Cut or break the dough into 8 equal parts and shape each portion into a ball. Dust a flat surface and rolling pin with a little flour and roll out each ball into a very thin circle (about 1/8 inch or 2 mm thick). If using butter, margarine or ghee, melt it in a microwave oven. Use a pastry brush (or your fingers) to lightly coat the top of each of the dough circles. Starting at the outside, roll each circle up into a stick shape, then coil each into a pinwheel. Roll out each of the pinwheels into circles as above, about 1/8 inch thick. Lightly coat a griddle or frying pan with oil and heat to medium. Cook each chapati for a few minutes on each side until brown. If desired, use a folded dish towel or several paper towels to firmly press down on each chapati while it cooks (this pushes the air bubbles to the top).

Note: It is also possible to omit the steps after rolling out the circles the first time, and fry them directly.

Eat immediately, either as part of a meal, or as a snack with butter or dusted with sugar.

MAJOR FOODS AND INGREDIENTS

The major foods of eastern Africa include those native to various areas as well as foods introduced into the area from other parts of Africa and from around the world. This section focuses on some of the important indigenous foods and those adopted into the diet. It will also mention other protein sources before touching on beverages and *khat* (also *kat* or *qat*), a mild stimulant that is especially important in Muslim countries.

The Ethiopian highlands were the source of a number of plants, some of which remain isolated and particular to the region, some of which have traveled far from there. Three important ones are: coffee, *ensete*, and millet.

Coffee *(Coffee Arabica)*

A major contribution to the global food basket most probably originated in Ethiopia. Either the Ethiopian province of Kaffa in Ethiopia's southwestern highlands or the plateaus of central Ethiopia is likely the original home of the coffee plant, which was discovered growing wild around 600 C.E. It is believed to have been taken from there to Yemen, where it was cultivated by Arabs and traveled throughout the world. Today, coffee is Ethiopia's most important export. Some people believe that the coffee beans were brought to Arabia from Ethiopia by Sudanese slaves who chewed the fresh coffee berries during the trip to help them survive. Some Ethiopians in parts of Kaffa and Sidamo, two of the main coffee-producing regions, still mix ground coffee beans with ghee to give it a buttery flavor.

Coffee's stimulating property has also linked it with religion: monks in Ethiopia may have chewed the beans for centuries before they were ever brewed as a hot beverage. A popular legend contends that an Abyssinian goatherd named Kaldi who lived around 850 B.C.E. noticed his goats became unusually frisky (skipping, rearing, and bleating) after eating berries growing on nearby bushes. He sampled some, found them invigorating, and took a few home to show his wife, who suggested he share this blessing from heaven with the monks. According to the legend, they initially rejected his offering and threw the berries containing the beans in the fire, thus roasting them and leading to a new discovery.

Coffee beans were first prized for their medicinal and healing properties. Interestingly, the coffee bean traveled from Ethiopia, to Arabia, to Constantinople, to Europe, to England, to South America, and beyond. In the late 1800s the beans returned to East Africa when the British laid the foundations of Kenya and Tanzania's coffee industries by introducing Brazilian plants on their plantations there.

Ensete

Ensete, or *musa ensete*, the "false" banana (*Ensete ventricosum*) of the family *Musacae*, is a plant indigenous to Ethiopia and has been cultivated heavily in the gardens of the western Gurage and others in southwest Ethiopia. There it has been a staple crop even though, unlike its relatives the banana or plantain trees, it bears no edible fruit. Its starchy stem and leaf midribs have traditionally been harvested, fermented in the ground for weeks or months, then cooked as a kind of bread or a porridge. *Ensete* is thought to be indigenous to eastern Africa and to have originated in the lowland areas located between Uganda and Tanzania, around the Ruwenzori, Mt. Meru, Mt. Kivu, and the Kordofan mountains in the Sudan. In the Ethiopian highlands the plant has been seen only as a famine food, but in other parts of the country as recently as the late 1970s it was still central to the diet. One of the drawbacks of *ensete* is its low protein content.

Millet and Sorghum

These cereal grains were introduced in Chapter 1 on West Africa. Several types of millet exist, including pearl and finger millets, each with numerous varieties. Finger millet prefers a wetter and cooler climate than pearl millet. Despite the mystery surrounding the history of early cereals, it is thought that finger millet is probably the oldest known domesticated tropical African cereal. A version of it was likely grown at Axum in Ethiopia by the first century. Many Ethiopian food crops, such as *ensete* and teff, did not move far from the place they originated, but finger millet is one that did, spreading throughout parts of Africa, India, and Indonesia. About 2.5 million acres, or more than a million hectares, of millet are planted in Africa each year, and it is an important food crop in East African Uganda and Ethiopia, as well as Malawi, Zambia, and Zimbabwe in southern Africa. In an observation of one Ugandan ethnic group that could be extended to others, one anthropologist stated:

For a staunch Adhola person finger millet surpasses all others as a staple, as well as being used to brew the best beer. It is the traditional food of Padhola of strong and wise men and women. . . . Only *kwon* [millet bread] made from finger millet provides the bulk and solidity essential to a good food.[4]

Probably one of the better known exotic grains of sub-Saharan Africa is a type of millet from Ethiopia known as teff, or tef (*Eragrostis tef*). The name comes from the Greek words *eros* or love and *agrostis* or grass," which combine to mean, literally, *lovegrass*. Until very recently, this cereal grass grew only in Ethiopia and mostly in the western region. Teff is the most common ingredient in the spongy flat bread known as *injera* (or *enjera*). Teff is central to Ethiopia and Eritrea's cultural identities, as well as traditionally a centerpiece of people's diets. Although it is a labor-intensive crop to cultivate and process, teff reportedly has double or triple the iron of wheat, barley, or sorghum, as well as high concentrations of calcium, potassium, and other important minerals relative to other comparable grains. It is 14 percent protein, 3 percent fat, and 81 percent complex carbohydrate. In addition, it is claimed that it is the only grain to have a symbiotic yeast right in it.

Other Important Foods

Many of the foods discussed in earlier chapters are also crucial to East African cuisine. In addition to the important East African diffusion of Asian bananas, sugar cane, and cocoyams, the Americas supplied maize, chilis, cassava, peanuts, tomatoes, sweet potatoes, kidney beans, and potatoes, while Europeans notably introduced leafy vegetables such as kales and cabbages.

Corn (Maize)

Portuguese traders carried corn to eastern Africa in the 1500s, and Arab traders circulated it around the Mediterranean and North Africa. During the next hundred years corn traveled from the West Indies to the Gold Coast (Ghana) where, by the 1700s, it was used as a cheap food for provisioning slaves. By the end of the sixteenth century, maize was reported in the interior of Africa (the Lake Chad region of Nigeria) where it appears to have gradually replaced traditional food plants in western and central regions, especially the Congo, Benin, and western Nigeria. (However, another new world product, cassava, later replaced corn in southern parts of Congo and Tanzania, partly due to its hardier nature, which made it less vulnerable to drought and locusts.)

Migrant workers became used to eating corn in colonial mines or work camps or as emergency rations and developed a taste for it. Also, twentieth-century agricultural policies and the influence of agricultural extension workers coupled with the relatively low cost of producing corn helped increase its popularity. In eastern and southern Africa maize has traditionally first been pounded before being boiled into a thick porridge. In contrast, in the West African country of Ghana the dried corn kernels are generally soaked and dehulled before being ground, fermented, and cooked.

Corn can also be used for snacks. In Somalia, fresh corn (*galeey*) is fried in sesame oil to make popcorn (*salol*), which is frequently served with coffee to men as they chew *khat*. Tender corn cobs (called "green") are roasted or grilled, eaten with butter and salt, or boiled whole, or the kernels are removed and sautéed in margarine or boiled fresh or after drying them.

At any rate, by the end of the 1800s maize had established itself as a major African crop. In the last quarter of the twentieth century it overtook sorghum as the most important cereal grain in East Africa.

Other starches include sweet potatoes, cocoyams (taro), potatoes, arrowroot, and yams. Rice (*wali* in Swahili, *brees* in Somali) is most commonly eaten in Ethiopian, Asian, and Muslim communities, often flavored with coconut milk. *Pilau*, a kind of spicy rice and meat dish, is popular for special group occasions throughout the region, especially along the coast, and may be accompanied by spicy stews, chapati, or eaten alone. Western potatoes are used widely in fast-food fare to provide British "chips" or "French fries" that are often served with pork or beef sausages.

In Ethiopia, with more than 200 fast days a year when the use of animal products are prohibited or limited, a largely vegetarian diet has evolved, but poultry, lamb, beef, and fish are also eaten. Many parts of East Africa depend on livestock herding, and milk products are more prevalent there than in much of Africa where the tsetse fly has prevented cattle from thriving.

Fruits

Fruits, as in other parts of sub-Saharan Africa, are most often eaten as snacks and sometimes viewed as more appropriate for children than adults. Fruits include banana, papaya, citrus fruits (oranges, lemons, limes), melons, guava, passion fruit, custard apple, avocado pear, and mango. Traditional fruits that grow wild are largely unknown in the West, with the possible exception of baobab (*Adansonia digitata*) and tamarind. Others include wild custard apple, *saba, carissa, dialium, flacourtia* (Indian plum), *marula, vangueria, vitex, and jujube*. The versatile baobab was introduced in Chapter 1. The pulp of its fruit has a cream color and a sour-to-sweet taste that can be eaten several different ways: raw, as a sauce, or the seeds can be colored and coated with sugar and sold as candy. Sugar cane may be chewed raw as a snack, or made into beer.

Khat

Strictly speaking, the stimulant *khat* is not a food, but it is an important part of socializing in many parts of East Africa, particularly among Muslim populations that prohibit alcoholic beverages, such as in Djibouti. It serves a purpose reminiscent of the kola nuts of West Africa. Khat (also *kat* or *qat*) is also known as Abyssinian tea or *miraa*. The bark from fresh young shoots of the tree is peeled off and chewed. *Khat* also plays an important role during wedding ceremonies among the Somali and Boran of Kenya and Ethiopia.

Milk Products

Milk and spiced ghee are often integral to dishes. Butter contains oil, solids, and water. The clarifying process evaporates the water and separates the oil from the solids. This "butter oil" needs no refrigeration and keeps well for long periods without turning rancid. In addition, types of fermented or sour milk are eaten. Pastoralists, especially in southern Sudan, put milk from camels, cows, goats, or even sheep, into gourds or wooden containers, and churn it to make butter and sour milk. Different flavorings are added, either by burning sticks in the containers, such as the African olive (*Olea europeaea* ssp. *Africana* or *oloirien* in Maasai), which also disinfects them, or adding spices or herbs (e.g., in Somalia, a kind of basil, *Ocimum americanum*). Milk may be sweetened with sugar and eaten with porridge or ugali, or alternatively it may be mixed with blood. Nomadic tribes in Sudan prepare cheese by pouring camel milk into a skin bag fastened to the saddle of a camel, which is then allowed to ferment and is churned by the movement of the camel. Coconut milk is another popular flavoring, especially along the coast.

Mushrooms

In some parts of Ethiopia mushrooms are not eaten and a mushroom is referred to as "the hyena's umbrella," but in other places wild mushrooms are a delicacy collected in the wild by women or men.

Protein Sources

Protein sources include legumes, pulses (such as kidney beans, hyacinth or lablab beans, cowpeas, chickpeas, lentils, peanuts, and Bambara groundnuts), and milk products. Protein is also included in the diet in the form of meat, fish, poultry, and insects. Fresh blood, usually from a cow or a goat, is an important source of nutrients among pastoral peoples and may be mixed with milk. A special cut is made, often in the jugular vein, so that the animal does not bleed to death, and the blood is often mixed with milk. The Somali recommend fresh blood from a goat (*diik*) be given to women after childbirth.

Kuku na Mala (Chicken in Yogurt) (East Africa)

1 chicken or 2–3 lbs pieces, skin removed and cut into serving pieces (discard giblets and liver) (leave the bone in or cut the chicken from the bones, or use boneless chicken)

2 cloves garlic; one peeled and crushed, one peeled but whole

2 cups plain full-cream yogurt (if available), buttermilk, or sour milk (or *maziwa lala*)

1 medium onion, chopped

1 Tbsp curry powder

2 Tbsp coarsely chopped cashew nuts

1 bunch coriander leaves, chopped (if desired, keep a few Tbsp for garnish)

1 Tbsp cumin

butter or margarine for frying

salt and any type pepper to taste

Mix the crushed garlic clove with the yogurt and pour over the chicken pieces, stirring to coat well. Allow to marinate, covered, in a glass or ceramic bowl in the refrigerator for at least 2 hours. Sauté the onion and whole, peeled garlic clove in the butter or margarine over medium heat for several minutes. Add the chopped cashew nuts and all the spices, and cook 5 minutes longer. Stir in the chicken and marinade. Cover and simmer, stirring occasionally, until the chicken is tender and the sauce is smooth, about 30 minutes depending on size of chicken pieces. Serve with rice.

Eggs, and sometimes wild birds, are also eaten. Meats may be from the more common domesticated goat, lamb, beef, camel, or donkey, or wild game such as eland, impala, wildebeest, or zebra, or even ostrich or crocodile. Current laws prohibit hunting many types of wild game, but farms to raise them commercially have been established, often to provide meat for the tourist market. Meat is often free-range and therefore leaner and tougher than its Western counterparts. As in other parts of sub-Saharan

Africa, poultry, especially chickens, are raised as food to be served to special guests.

Fish is more commonly eaten along the coast or in areas with lakes and large rivers, with tilapia being the most popular, along with the Nile perch and a small sardine-like fish that is often dried. Along the Indian Ocean, prawns, crayfish, or lobster are prepared. Pastoral nomadic people tend to eat more meat. Termites, locusts, and caterpillars are seasonal treats in many places. For example, in parts of Kenya children pick flying white ants out of the air after a rain, filling pails, and eating them the way American children might berries. The rest are fried in ghee and enjoyed by men and children.

Seasonings

Salt is the single most important seasoning used in cooking. Historically, salt has been obtained from traders as well as made as a filtrate of ashes made after burning plants such as banana peels, bean leaves, or water reeds. Salt may be added to stews, starches, meats, or coffee.

Spices are often used more sparingly in the interior of East African countries such as Uganda and Tanzania. It is generally agreed that Ethiopia has the most complex use of seasonings in the eastern region, followed by the coastal areas. Besides variations in seasonings between the coastal cities and the interior, there are differences between regions and countries, but often in the Horn of Africa countries a variety of seasonings are used, such as those in curry, which is a mixture of sweet and savory spices such as allspice, cayenne, cinnamon, cloves, coriander, cumin, fenugreek, ginger, nutmeg, and black pepper.

Mushroom and Onion Curry (Eastern Africa)

1 lb fresh mushrooms, any type

2 onions; one peeled and minced, one peeled and thinly sliced

1–2 cloves garlic, peeled and crushed

hot red pepper to taste (if fresh, seed and chop first*, or use dried ground)

2 Tbsp vegetable oil or margarine

1 Tbsp lime or lemon juice

1/2 tsp turmeric powder

salt to taste

Clean the mushrooms by gently rinsing and wiping them lightly with a paper towel. Trim the ends slightly. If they are small, just cut the tip of the stem off, if they are large, cut them into quarters or thick slices after trimming the stem. Mince one onion and the garlic. Add the turmeric and red pepper and mix the mushrooms with the spices, chopped onions, and garlic. Heat the oil (or margarine) in a pan over medium heat, and add the combined mushroom mixture and the sliced onion. Sauté over medium heat for about 10 minutes, stirring often. Add the lemon (or lime) juice and salt to taste, beginning with 1/2 teaspoon. Stir and adjust other seasonings to taste.

*Remember to use extreme caution if working with fresh chili peppers. See the notes in the *Mbanga* Soup recipe.

Variation: Vegetables are often seasoned with curry powder or similar seasonings. For example, instead of using mushrooms, wash and chop a head of cauliflower, double the oil to 4 Tbsp, chop the onion (not mince), slice 3 tomatoes, omit the lime or lemon juice and add 1/2 cup water, and replace the turmeric powder and red pepper with a teaspoon (or more) of curry powder to make fried cauliflower (*Bilingani la Kukaanga*). First heat the oil and brown the onions, then add the cauliflower, curry powder, tomatoes and salt to taste and fry together for 2 or 3 minutes, then add about 1/2 cup water, cover and simmer on low heat until the cauliflower is tender and most of the liquid absorbed. Serve with rice or chapati.

A signature seasoning of Ethiopia and Eritrea goes by the Amharic name *berberé*, a sophisticated and complicated mixture of pungent spices, most notably hot red pepper. It is the fundamental seasoning for dishes, and the quality of a woman's *berbere* is said to be one of the most important considerations in choosing a wife. The seasoning may be prepared in large batches using up to 15 pounds of peppers and 5 pounds of garlic, a process consuming several days during which ingredients are dried, roasted, pounded, and ground. However, once the mixture is prepared it will keep for months, or even longer if oil is added to make the spice paste known as *da'lik*.

Vegetables

Most African people use green leaves, such as cassava, pumpkin leaves, or cabbage, to produce sauces or stews to eat with their heavy, filling starches at mealtimes. Cooked greens are a common element in sub-Saharan African cuisine. Collards or kale are especially popular in eastern Africa. They go by the Swahili name of *sukumawiki* (or *sukuma wiki*). That is also the name of a popular gravy or stew made from them in Kenya, often eaten with ugali. *Sukumawiki* literally means "push the week" and refers to the fact that the kale (or another green such as spinach or Swiss chard), which can grow wild, is inexpensive and easily available, so a sauce made from it can stretch the family budget until the end of the week. Collards and kale leaves are nutritious members of the cabbage family, and good sources of calcium, phosphorous, iron, potassium, vitamin A, and vitamin C. Onions, tomatoes, pumpkins, eggplants, and okra (called lady fingers) are also popular vegetables.

Sukumawiki ("Push the Week" Greens) (East Africa)

1–2 bunches of fresh kale (if unavailable, substitute Swiss chard, collards, or spinach) finely chopped (if substituting frozen greens, first defrost and drain them)

2 onions, chopped or thinly sliced

3 or 4 tomatoes, blanched, peeled and chopped (OR substitute canned tomatoes, OR 2–4 Tbsp tomato paste)

2 Tbsp vegetable oil

1–2 cloves garlic, crushed (optional)

2 tsp coriander powder (OR 1 heaping Tbsp finely minced fresh coriander leaves) (optional)

1 sweet green bell pepper, chopped (optional)

1/2 lb any leftover meat or poultry cooked or raw (optional), cut into small pieces

salt and red or black pepper to taste

Wash the kale and finely chop the leaves, including the center stalk. Set aside. If using raw meat, cut it into small pieces and brown it in the 2 Tbsp vegetable oil on medium heat. When it is browned and nearly cooked, add the onion (and garlic, coriander, and green pepper if using). If using cooked meat, add it when the onions are browned. If using fresh tomatoes, peel first (drop them into boiling water for a minute and then cold water to loosen the skins), then chop them. Add the tomatoes or tomato paste and stir into the onions (and meat, if using). Stir in the greens, and mix well. Allow it to simmer for about 15 minutes, or until the leaves are cooked, and the sauce thickened. Stir in salt and pepper to taste.

Variation: This is a leftover standby, and open to innumerable variations depending on what is on hand. For example, it could also include a couple of chopped carrots or chopped cabbage cooked with the kale.

This would traditionally be served in Kenya with *ugali* or chapatis (see recipe). If desired, substitute the recipe for *bidia* or serve with rice or boiled plantains.

Wheat and Barley

Unlike the western or central part of the continent, wheat and barley can be successfully grown in parts of East Africa, particularly in the drier highlands of Ethiopia and Kenya. Popular wheat-based foods include various breads, ranging from Indian chapati and Western-style loaves, to cakes, the deep-fried stuffed turnovers known as *samosas* (or *sambusas*), and a doughnut called *mandazi* (or *mahamri*, coconut doughnuts, or *kaimaiti*, sweet doughnuts). Barley may be used in porridge.

Beverages

Fruit and other juices are not particularly popular in some East African cultures, although this is not true of all places, such as Somalia. As in many non-Muslim parts of the continent below the Sahara, beer is the beverage of choice, prepared from a variety of ingredients.

Tea can be flavored using lemon grass, ginger, lemon, mint, or honey. It is often served British style or as Indian-style chai flavored with spices, milk, and sugar. Coffee is drunk primarily in Ethiopia and Eritrea and sometimes in Muslim coastal communities.

COOKING

Division of Labor

There is a tradition of a strong division of labor in eastern African society. As in other parts of sub-Saharan Africa, cooking has historically been a woman's domain, with kitchens off limits to men: women cook and serve; men dine. That work remains largely labor intensive. The accepted norm is for a woman to marry and bear children. Because polygamy is practiced in many parts of sub-Saharan Africa, especially in Muslim areas, a woman may cook primarily for herself and her children, with the husband rotating eating his meal among the different wives, a process that does not always lead to smooth domestic relations.

In addition to preparing and serving food, women are often the ones who tend to family gardens, procure firewood and water for cooking, and even market produce to earn a little cash.

It is common in pastoral families to have a division of labor between boys and girls, too. Among pastoral peoples such as the Maasai, men (and boys) are usually responsible for the herding and watering of the animals, women (and girls) for the milking and food-processing tasks.

Much of the diet of nomadic peoples comes from their livestock in the form of milk, blood, and meat. The traditional diet for young Maasai males was composed almost entirely of these three elements, whereas women, children, and older men have been expected to supplement their diets with agricultural products such as corn and beans. Traditionally, land was held communally, with wealth determined by the number of cattle owned (each family branded their cattle). The cattle provided not only meat and milk, but also hides for clothing, and storage containers, and dung for fuel for kitchen fires.

The exception to the female monopoly of food preparation might be roasting meat. Traditionally, as in parts of southern Africa, outdoor roasting of meat may be shared with males, or even a male prerogative as is reportedly the case among the Iteso of Kenya and Uganda, where "only women can cook a starch, and it must be cooked inside the cooking-house on the women's fireplace constructed with three stones. Men, on the other hand, can cook meat, but only outside and only by roasting."[5] This social division of labor has been explained by contrasting the concepts of inside and outside, nature and culture. Thus, women are traditionally connected with cooking pots, the home, and domesticity (inside), while men are associated with nature, the larger world, and political life (outside).

In many parts of eastern Africa, the main meal structure includes a starch of some sort with a side dish of a sauce or soup. The primary traditional cooking technique remains boiling or frying over a fire made from firewood or charcoal and a three-stone hearth, perhaps over a shallow pit. Breakfast may be leftovers or porridge. However, contemporary social changes continue to modify traditions.

Ethiopia and Eritrea

Ethiopia's national staple is *injera* (or *enjera*). *Injera* is also popular in Eritrea, and a version is called *canjeero* in Somalia. The equivalent of rice in Japan or tortillas in Mexico, *injera* is a kind of flat pancake most commonly made out of teff, a special grade of millet with a small gray grain. The pounded grain is usually fermented for several days to make a sour dough, then cooked on a covered griddle. *Injera* can also be made from sorghum or wheat. The batter may be poured in a spiral fashion, starting on the outside, then covered and the edges sealed with a damp rag. Like a pancake, each *injera* cooks quickly. Traditionally, an Ethiopian woman might be seen in the round straw-thatched hut called a *tukul* making her family's three-day supply (around 25 at a time) over a eucalyptus wood fire. *Injera* serves as both a plate and a utensil. Sauces/stews are ladled on top of it, and additional pieces of the bread may be served alongside it. Small pieces of the *injera* are torn off and used to scoop up the stew. The stews are called *wat* (also *watt* or *we't*) and people often call the national dish of Ethiopia, *doro wat*, a spicy chicken stew. For the stew, the chicken is cut into 12 parts, and hard-boiled

Making injera in Ethiopia.
© TRIP/B. Seed.

eggs are immersed in the spicy gravy that accompanies it. There are also less spicy stews called *alicha* (or *alecha*). Traditionally, proper *wats* were always cooked in earthenware pots that were made by skilled potters and fired for impermeability.

Chicken and beef are the most common meat or poultry sources for the stews, but there are fish *wats* as well. Given the many fast days in Ethiopia and the strict influence of the Ethiopian Orthodox church, vegetarian *wats* have also been developed using vegetables such as garbanzo beans (also called chick-peas), lentils, onions, and beans in a complex blend of seasonings. A well-known fasting dish is *yeshimbra assa*, or "chick-pea-flour fish," a dish that combines chopped onions, *berberé*, oil, *wat* spices, chick-pea flour, and salt to make small cakes shaped like fish that are fried in oil.

Injera is traditionally served on a *mesob*—a covered circular basket table woven from grasses dyed red, green, blue, and yellow and waterproofed with aloe, generally made by housewives for their families.

Hospitality in Eritrea and Ethiopia, as in many sub-Saharan African countries, is a serious duty, and it may sometimes take the form of pressuring guests to eat more. To honor a special guest, or to express friendship, the host or hostess may wrap a piece of *injera* around a choice piece of meat and pop it directly into the guest's mouth.

Doro Wat (Spicy Chicken Stew) with *Injera* (Ethiopian Flat Bread) (East Africa)

This *wat*, or stew, is often called the national dish of Ethiopia. It is traditionally served literally on a large slightly sour spongy crepe called *injera,* with folded *injera* served alongside it. Ethiopians or Eritreans would have all the ingredients necessary for the meal on hand, from *berberé* (a unique fiery seasoning in a paste or powder form) and *niter kibbeh* (clarified spiced butter) to teff, but for Western kitchens and pantries adjustments must be made. Making the sourdough starter and preparing the *injera* is usually a 2- or 3-day procedure, but this modified version captures the spirit of the dish.

6 eggs

2 to 3 lbs chicken thighs or drumsticks, skin removed

juice from 1 lemon (2–3 Tbsp)

1 tsp salt

2 large onions, chopped

1 Tbsp garlic, minced or press (4–5 cloves)

1 heaping tsp fresh grated ginger (or 1/2 tsp dried ground ginger)

2 Tbsp butter or margarine (or ghee or *niter kibbeh*)

1 tsp black pepper (freshly ground if possible)

3 small chicken bouillon cubes (or 1 1/2 large cubes)

1/8 tsp ground nutmeg

1/3 tsp ground cardamom

1/4 tsp fenugreek, crushed or ground

1/4 cup *berberé* (or "make-do" *berberé:* 1 tsp ground ginger, 1 tsp ground cayenne pepper, 2 Tbsp plus 2 tsp paprika, 1/4 tsp ground cloves, 1/2 tsp ground cinnamon. Note: If a spicier berberé is preferred, substitute a teaspoon or more of the cayenne pepper for the paprika.)

2 Tbsp paprika

2 Tbsp tomato paste

1 cup water

Place 6 eggs in a saucepan, cover with water, and bring to a boil. Lower heat and simmer until done, about 10 minutes. Remove, cool, peel, and set aside. Remove the skin of about 6 chicken thighs and 6 drumsticks (cut the pieces in half to make about 24 pieces total, if desired), and place them into a bowl. Prick each chicken piece with a fork several times. Squeeze the juice from one lemon into a bowl and remove any seeds. Sprinkle the juice over the chicken pieces, along with 1/2 to 1 teaspoon salt, stirring the chicken to evenly distribute the juice and salt. Set aside to marinate for about 30 minutes while preparing the vegetables and spices.

Onion, garlic, and ginger: Chop 2 large onions by hand or in a food processor and put in a large bowl. Press 4 or 5 cloves of peeled garlic to get about 1 tablespoon, and add to bowl along with 1 heaping teaspoon of peeled grated fresh ginger (or 1/2 teaspoon dried ground ginger).

Prepare the first group of dry spices on a small plate or in a small bowl: mix together 1/8 teaspoon ground nutmeg, 1/4 teaspoon ground cardamom, and 1/4 teaspoon crushed fenugreek (often found as *methi* seeds in Indian food sections of grocery stores). In a second small bowl prepare a batch of "make-do" *berberé*. (Note: detailed instructions on preparing this important and unique Ethiopian seasoning is beyond the scope of this book but may be found in many African cookbooks or on the Internet.) Heat a large, heavy skillet on medium heat, melt the butter or margarine (or ghee or *niter kibbeh*), then add the onions, ginger, and garlic and cook for about 5 minutes, stirring occasionally until the onions are soft but not browned. Take care not to burn the butter on too high a heat. Add both plates of spices and 2 additional tablespoons of paprika, stirring well to mix. Crumble the bouillon cubes and sprinkle into the pan, and add the tomato paste and a cup of water to the pan and mix thoroughly. Heat, stirring occasionally, until the sauce is bubbly. Add the chicken to the frying pan, stirring and turning the pieces to coat all sides. Lower the heat to simmer, cover the pan, and cook until the chicken is cooked, 15 to 30 minutes, depending on the size of the chicken pieces. After 10 or 15 minutes, make small slits in the eggs so that the yolk shows, and add them gently to the stew. Replace the cover and let the stew continue to simmer. Check occasionally to make sure there is enough water, and add a little more if necessary to keep it from scorching. However, the sauce should be quite thick, like heavy cream. When the chicken is fully cooked, add the black pepper and remove the pan from the heat.

To serve: In Ethiopia this would always be eaten with *injera*, but it also can be eaten with rice or pita bread. See the recipe below for directions on how to serve with *injera*.

Injera

1 1/2 cups all-purpose flour

1/4 cup whole wheat flour

1/4 cup cornmeal (preferably stoneground or *masa harina*)

3/4 tsp salt

2 1/4 tsp baking powder

1 1/2 tsp active dry yeast

1 3/4 cups warm water

Sift the flours, salt, and baking powder into a large bowl. Stir in the yeast, then the warm water, and allow it to sit covered in a warm place for about an hour to rise. It can be left for up to 6 hours. When ready to cook the *injera*, measure 2 cups of the batter into a blender container. Add about 2/3 cup of water and pulse for a few seconds several times until the batter is smooth and thin. Heat a nonstick (or well-seasoned cast iron) skillet over medium heat until a drop of water bounces when sprinkled on it. For a 10-inch pan pour 1/4–1/3 cup batter into the pan all at once, then tilt and rotate the pan quickly to cover the bottom with a thin even coating, as for crepes. Use a spatula if necessary to help spread the batter. Cook only on one side, until the air bubbles appear and the entire pancake/crepe is dry but not browned on the underneath. If overcooked, the *injera* will become brittle and not remain soft and pliable. If undercooked, the *injera* will taste doughy and raw. Continue the process until all the dough is used up. As the *injera* cook, stack them up and cover with a clean cloth or paper towels to keep them from drying out. They may also be kept warm in a low oven or reheated briefly, covered with a damp paper towel, in the microwave.

Variations: A meat version of this stew with *injera* would be called *sik sik wat* or *beg wat*. Substitute 2 pounds of stewing beef or lamb for the chicken (and modify the type of bouillon cubes) and omit the eggs. For a vegetarian version, substitute 2 pounds of small zucchini, halved and quartered. Cooking time may be slightly increased for the meat, but greatly decreased for the zucchini. Milder stews are called *alechas*, and vegetable *alechas* or side vegetables such as braised cabbage would likely be served alongside the *doro wat*.

To serve: Place one *injera* on each plate with the smooth side facing the plate, ladle a little of the stew on it, including an egg, and serve additional injera folded into quarters on the side or on a serving dish. Alternatively, overlap injera on a serving platter moving from the center to the outside, ending with the injera covering the edges of the platter. The doro wat may be served in the center of the platter or in a bowl. To eat the stew, tear off a piece of the bread and use it to scoop up some of the *wat*. Etiquette requires that your fingers should not touch the stew or your mouth during this process. This recipe will serve about 4 people. If other stews or side dishes are served and extra *injera* is desired, the recipe can easily be doubled.

Kenya, Tanzania, and Uganda

Moving from the Horn of Africa to Kenya, a typical non-nomadic East African household, such as a Kikuyu kitchen, is described next. The Kikuyu (or Gikuyu) are today the largest and most powerful ethnic group in Kenya. They are a Bantu-speaking people (whose language is called Gikuyu or Kikuyu), who once lived in the fertile highland areas between

Mount Kenya and Nairobi, the capital city. Before the Europeans came, they raised crops such as beans, sorghum, millet, peas, and yams. However, the colonial powers like the British recognized how valuable the land was and displaced the Kikuyu to establish their own houses and plantations, thus creating a class of wage laborers living in overcrowded conditions and working for them.

Traditionally, cohorts of Kikuyu boys and girls are organized into generation sets that stay together and at different ages hold or are subject to the authority of others.

Important traditional and contemporary equipment (including Swahili names for them) for cooking in much of East Africa include

- a mortar and pestle (*kinu*): both a small stone one used for crushing herbs, garlic, and spices and a large wooden one for pounding grains such as maize for *muthokoi*. Modern kitchens likely replace some of these with ceramic or stainless steel mortars and pestles, garlic presses, electric blender, electric grain mills, or they buy pre-ground spices or flour.
- a charcoal brazier (*jiko*): used for everything from boiling, frying, and grilling to roasting corn. Modern versions include gas and electric cookers and barbecue grills.
- a wooden vermicelli maker (*kinu cha tambi*): from the coast, replaced by ready-made pastas.
- a coconut grater (*mbuzi*): a portable, folding carved wooden stool containing a serrated steel blade. One sits on the stool and shreds the white flesh of the coconut using the blade. The grated coconut was traditionally used to make coconut milk, but modern methods include using a blender or juice extractor, or buying already desiccated coconut.
- gourds or calabashes (*kibuyu*): these containers, made by hollowing out and removing the seeds from a kind of squash, are used for churning milk into cooking ghee by rocking it back and forth. Water can also be carried in them, and *ugi* (a kind of porridge) or beer fermented in them. Plastic, glass, or other nonreactive containers such as bowls or jugs are replacing them. A half calabash is also called *kibuyu* and is used as a dish for foods, especially porridge and soups. Modern equivalents include any plate or bowl.
- a wooden paddle (*mwiko*): a *mwiko* is stronger and heavier than a wooden spoon, and has a flat blade at the end for more efficient stirring of *ugali* or stew. They come in many sizes, from a small one for family meals to a large commercial size that can turn *ugali* for as many as 50 people.
- a wooden blender for soup (*chombo cha kupigapiga*): replaced by a wire whisk or electric blender in modern homes.

- a strainer *(kifumbu)*: traditionally palm leaves were woven together into a cylindrical cone that could be squeezed to extract milk from grated coconut, but now muslin cloth or a nylon sieve may be used.
- a grindstone for spices *(jiwe la kusaga dawa)*: similar to the small stone mortar and pestle *kinu* described above.
- a wooden spoon *(mkamshi* or *jijiko)*: in a variety of shapes and sizes.
- a clay pot for cooling water, with a spigot at the bottom, and a lid on top for pouring in the water *(mrunfi)*: this would be replaced by a refrigerator in a modern home.
- a clay cooking pot *(chungu)*: regular saucepans, a crock pot, or a pressure cooker now can replace these.
- an aluminum pan *(sufuria)*: any saucepan, frying pan, or deep fat fryer can now be used.
- a grindstone for grain *(jiwe la kupazia)*: grain can now be purchased as flour, or taken to grain mills.
- a woven palm basket *(kitanga)*: traditionally used to collect flour.
- a chapati pan of heavy iron *(karai)*: a heavy flat pan used for frying chapati.
- a winnowing basket *(kiteo)*: becoming less important as flour is pre-milled.
- a ladle *(upawa)*: made from a coconut shell with a wooden handle attached. It is used to stir and serve soup but can now be replaced by stainless steel or nonstick ladles.[6]

In addition, historically, a woman (or a child) might use a 4- or 5-gallon drum suspended by a rope across her forehead to fetch water, or she might carry water on her head in a calabash. A stone cooking hearth was used in addition to the *jiko*. Since ovens were not a part of the traditional kitchen in many parts of East Africa, dough tended to be fried or deep-fried as when making chapati, *mandazi*, *kaimati*, or samosas.

The diets of nomadic people of East Africa, such as in southern Sudan or Somalia, are richer in milk and milk products, meat, and blood (called *labee* in Somalia). Bones are sometimes used to make a bone soup. This topic will be discussed more in the next section.

Wali wa Nazi (Coconut Rice) (East Africa)

Wali is the Swahili word for cooked rice and *nazi* for coconut. This dish is popular in coastal areas of eastern Africa, although it is also eaten in other parts of the continent. A version is easy to make in a rice cooker.

2 cups rice (basmati, jasmine, or long grain)

1 can coconut milk (no sugar)*, plus enough water to make 4 cups

1/2 tsp salt

Add all ingredients to rice cooker, stir, cover, and cook until rice is tender.

*Canned coconut milk is convenient, but it may be made from scratch by cracking open a coconut and draining out the liquid inside. (Set that liquid, the coconut water, aside to pour over fruit salads or chill and drink as a beverage.) Remove the white meat inside and grate it into a bowl. Take another bowl and line it with a cheesecloth, draping the edges of the cloth over the rim of the bowl. Pour a cup of boiling water over the coconut and let it steep until the water is cool enough to touch. Then, gather up the cloth and squeeze and twist it to remove most of the liquid. This is the first pressing of the coconut milk, and it is the richest. Pour the milk into a separate bowl and repeat the process two more times, to get 3 cups of coconut milk. Add 1 cup of water to make the liquid for cooking the rice. Coconut milk may also be made by replacing the fresh grated coconut with dried, grated, unsweetened coconut.

Variation: Coconut rice can be cooked on a stovetop in a heavy pot. To make a richer version, first chop an onion and sauté it with a few tablespoons of margarine or peanut or other oil, then add the rice and sauté it briefly before stirring in the coconut milk/water. Bring the pot to a boil, covered, then lower the heat and cook until the rice is done, about 20 minutes. Stir the rice once or twice to make sure it is not sticking, and add a little more water if necessary. To make a less rich version of coconut rice, increase the rice to 3 cups and the water to 6 cups.

Serve with any curry, chapati, sour milk (*maziwa lala*), or yogurt.

TYPICAL MEALS

As described for the Iteso in Kenya, in general in eastern Africa people do not feel they have eaten unless they have eaten their particular region's staple food. In several languages, the word for food also refers to the staple starch dish: The word *irio* is Gikuyu for food and is also the generic name of a staple dish described here. Its equivalent among the Kikamba is *isyo*, the Luo equivalent is *nyoyo*, and the Swahili equivalent is *chakula*. A popular type of *irio* is *githeri*, a dish made from fresh or dried beans, corn, potatoes, and various seasonings, such as, onions, garlic, coriander leaves, tomatoes, salt, and ghee, which may be mashed together or fried before mixing them into the mixture. Another version of *irio* is the Kikuyu *mataha*, which includes salt, mashed peas and beans, green corn, green (cooking) bananas, and potatoes. It may also include pumpkin leaves or other greens. If it is fried, onions, cooking fat, and curry may be included.

The Adhola of southeastern Uganda use the word *chiemo* to refer to staple foods such as finger millet, which are filling, and call the relishes, including the sauces that accompany *chiemo*, *fufa*.

It has been suggested that stable agrarian societies organize their eating around a core-fringe pattern, in which a starchy *core* or carbohydrate food is complemented by a *fringe* of foods that make the core more palatable and appetizing. These fringe foods would be the relishes in East African cooking. While a third legume component to the meal pattern has been added, the idea of core-fringe foods has been applied to African societies. However, it is important not to oversimplify the relationship of different foods. For example, among the Gurage, "Ensete can be served as the centerpiece, the staple, or the trimming, according to the hour of meal-taking, or when eating serves a function other than a strictly nutritional one."[7] In Uganda among the Adhola the cow pea plant provides numerous dishes, one of which, *maigra*, "is primarily a relish, but ... is so sustaining that it may also be eaten by itself as *chiemo*."[8] Certainly the dichotomy cannot be applied to nomadic or primarily pastoral societies, either.

Often people traditionally begin their day with a small meal of porridge (also called gruel) or cassava, although bread and tea are becoming more common in urban areas. As described here, however, during certain times of year such as Ramadan, the meal pattern varies. The main meal of the day is usually eaten in the afternoon or evening.

An important traditional breakfast food in East Africa is porridge, called *uji* in Swahili. It can be made from a variety of ingredients, and its consistency varies from thin to thick. This has always been a good source of easily digestible food and water for children and nursing mothers. One of the social changes in the region is that the less nutritional tea is displacing porridge.

Ugali has been called the most important food in East Africa. It holds the place of honor that *fufu* or rice does in much of western Africa. It is a stiff starch made from white or yellow cornmeal, finger or bulrush millet, or red or white sorghum, with cassava flour sometimes added.

Ugali is known by many names other than its Swahili one and comes with many variations in texture, taste, and ingredients. A version in southern Sudan is called *asida*. It is called *posho* in western Uganda, and in northeast Uganda and the nearby northwest border of Kenya a soft version called *atapa* or *atap* is popular. *Ugali* is a bland foil to diverse foods, including fermented milk, grilled meat, beans or peanuts, cooked green vegetables, and chicken or fish made into stews, sauces, or gravies. It is eaten by breaking a small piece off with the thumb and first two fingers of the right hand, then scooping up some of the accompanying stew or vegetables.

In other places such as among the Baganda of Uganda, bananas are the main starch and are prepared with innumerable variations. Banana plants continue yielding for many years and produce year-round, which makes them a reliable crop, especially in times of famine. A special type of banana that must be cooked and is green when it is ripe is called *matoke*, and this is also the name for a popular dish in which it is mashed, for example with meat (*matoke n'yama*) or with fish (*matoke ngege*). The bananas may be steamed in banana leaves before mashing them and are enjoyed with a peanut sauce. When cassava is prepared the same way as *matoke* it is known as *mogo*. Bananas can be served in other forms as well. In Tanzania, a popular wedding cake is made from mashed beans and bananas, perhaps washed down with some locally brewed *dengelwa* (sugar cane beer). In Arusha, cooked corn and rice are mixed with sour milk. A dry, mashed mixture of corn and beans with smoked, nearly ripe bananas, that can keep for several days is called *mangararu* by the Meru of northern Tanzania or *makukura* in Swahili. Fermented bananas are also used to make beer.

Somali nomads dry camel meat in the sun before frying it in small pieces in oil, then covering it with camel ghee (a clarified butter made from camel's milk) to make a portable long-lasting meat that will keep for months. In the Sudan, meat is generally dried after slaughtering it, along with the layer of stomach fat and the internal organs, which are pulverized. Ethiopians cut meat into long strips and coat it with a spicy powdered hot pepper mix before drying it. This meat is known as *quanta* and may be used in spicy stews eaten with *injera*.

Cleanliness is an important value, and one's hands must be carefully washed, often at the table, before eating. Hands may be the eating utensils, especially when the food is provided in a common bowl. Rules of etiquette may also include eating only in *your* part of the bowl and who is allowed to eat meat or fish. Traditionally, children and/or women may eat separately from the adult men.

Westerners often think that women are strongly disadvantaged in households where they must do the cooking and serving. However, women have found ways to use that power to their advantage by, for example, refusing to cook for a husband who has earned their displeasure.

Mataha (Mashed Potatoes with Corn and Peas) (East Africa)

This is an adapted version of a popular Kikuyu dish from Kenya.

5 medium potatoes

2 cups of fresh or frozen green peas (or substitute cooked or canned kidney or small red beans)

2 cups of white (if available) corn or hominy (Note: if using dried corn or hominy, soak the corn overnight before using, or substitute 2 cups canned corn or hominy)

2 Tbsp vegetable oil

salt to taste

Peel and cut 5 medium potatoes into several pieces, and cover with water in a pot with a little salt (optional). Bring the water to a boil, and cook until done, then drain. Cook the corn and peas separately, and drain. Mash the potatoes well in the pot or in a mixing bowl using an electric mixer or a potato masher. Add a little milk and/or butter if desired to the potatoes and continue mashing until all lumps are gone. Mix together the mashed potatoes, corn, and peas. Add salt to taste.

Variation: To make fried *mataha*, heat 2 Tbsp oil in a frying pan and cook the mixture over medium heat until it is heated through. If desired, add a teaspoon of curry powder and a tablespoon of chopped onion to the oil and sauté for a few minutes before adding the mashed potatoes and vegetables.

To serve: The mixture should be somewhat dense and firm. Pile the potato mixture into a mound on a platter, make a well or nest in the center, and fill it with stew.

EATING OUT

Nyama Choma (Grilled Meat)

Africans tend to be quite sociable. Among the Iteso of Kenya, the proper traditional greeting is "An'ajon?" which means, loosely translated, "At whose house is beer being drunk today?"[9] That would probably be a nutritious local beer brewed from finger millet. Among non-Muslims, beer drinking and socializing while eating roasted meat is a favorite pastime. Muslims are more likely to drink coffee or tea with their meat, which may also be eaten with *ugali*.

A scene that plays itself out repeatedly in East Africa is groups of friends socializing together, often while drinking beer or tea or coffee, and eating meat roasted over a wood or charcoal fire, or *nyama choma* as it is known in Swahili. This might be either at someone's home or in an informal restaurant.

Beer is an important beverage in sub-Saharan Africa, associated with socializing rather than drinking alone to become intoxicated. In Sudan, sorghum is used to make *merissaan* (opaque beer) or *assaliya* or *um-bilbila* (clear beer). Wines may be made from dates (*sherbot, nebit,* and *dakkai*) or honey (*duma*). The famous amber-colored mead from Ethiopia is *tej* (or *t'ej*), which is made from fermented honey and the boiled stems of a tree called *esho* (*Rhamnus prinioides*) and is traditionally served in special long-necked bottles after meals. Other wines include *mnazi* or *pombe ya mnazi*, a kind of palm wine made from coconut palms. There are also various locally distilled alcoholic beverages made from fermented grain or banana, but these can be dangerous.

East African communal casual gatherings vary from the Western individualized social habit of eating out formally in restaurants as a leisure activity. Snacking and various "fast foods" abound along with other inexpensive places for working people to eat. While orthodox Christians, Muslims, or Jews do not eat pork, it is largely consumed as a "fast food." Snack foods sold at kiosks or by roadside vendors include corn, as well as foods that reflect Indian influences, such as *samosas* or *mandazi*.

The experience of eating at another's home is a common one: either dropping in around dinnertime (men especially might show up at an important man's house around the time of the main meal) or to observe a time of community celebration or solidarity: marriages, birth days (literally, days celebrating the recent birth of a child, not the annual celebration known in the West), holy days, funerals, harvest days, or initiations. Hospitality is an important value among East Africans, and the cooking lends itself to sharing, as the proverb at the beginning of this chapter suggests. Such gatherings would take place seasonally: pastoralists such as the Maasai celebrate weddings, encourage courting, and undertake initiation rites during the rainy season, the time of abundance.

Men eating at a food stall in Dar Es Salaam, Tanzania.
© TRIP/F. Good.

Similarly, in agriculturally based societies, these activities would be most pronounced at the close of the harvest season.

Many times Christians and Muslims refuse to eat meat together, largely because of dietary restrictions. Muslims, in particular, are required to eat only meat that is certified as *halaal* (that is, food that is lawful and permissible to eat according to Islamic dietary law). This is true, even though, for example, in Ethiopia both Christians and Muslims bless the animal "in the Name of the Father" before they kill it.

SPECIAL OCCASIONS

There is a deep African spirituality, whether it is expressed in worship of God or gods, or in respect for the elders or ancestors, or in understandings of the spiritual forces in the world. There is also often a profound connection to one's homeland. As Jomo Kenyatta (the *Gikuyu*, or *Kikuyu*), first president of Kenya, has written: "Communion with the spirits is perpetuated through contact with the soil in which the ancestors of the tribe lie buried."[10] Even urbanized people today often feel a special bond to their homelands and travel back to them on important holidays or for special events such as funerals or naming ceremonies. Pregnant women often travel from urban areas to their homelands so that their children are born there. Even where social change is occurring and traditions are weakening, respect for the ancestors and spirits requires adherence to food taboos and requirements. Thus, even though peanuts, a cash crop introduced into southeastern Uganda, replaced sesame in daily use, people continue to prepare the small sesame seed cakes ritually provided as food offerings to the spirits.

As in other cultures, the major rites of passage throughout life, from birth through puberty, marriage, and death, are accompanied by special rituals and often ceremonial or party foods. Seasonal times of harvest or rich pastureland are often interconnected to holy days or initiation ceremonies or weddings—times when feasting and parties most often take place.

There are also food taboos, such as in some places a prohibition against women and children eating chicken and eggs. In western Kenya, traditionally only the male head of a family could eat the tail part of the chicken, and the Kamba of Kenya served a gizzard to the most important person in a group of visitors. Conversely, the Luhyia never shared the gizzard, for it was believed that if two people shared it, they would always be in disagreement.

Family eating Easter meal around a *mesob*, Gondar, Ethiopia.
© TRIP/B. Seed.

In parts of Uganda the growth of cowpeas has been associated with well-being and fertility, and a special dish was eaten after the birth of a woman's first son and first daughter. In southern Sudan, a certain type of *ugali* made from sorghum has been served at weddings and special rituals surrounding a woman's first menstruation. Eating specific foods, or refraining from eating, are observed by various religious groups. Orthodox Christians in Ethiopia are said to abstain from any animal products 208 days of the year, including Lent and most Wednesdays and Fridays. During fasting times, most orthodox do not touch food or water until 3 p.m. While children under 13 years old are technically exempt, they like to test themselves.

The act of fasting, or *Saum* (or *Sawm*), is one of the five pillars of Islam, and Muslims believe that through self-denial, they exercise their will and sharpen their minds. The large Muslim population found in eastern Africa takes fasting seriously. While many people fast regularly throughout the year, Ramadan is the most important month in their calendar. The second chapter of the Muslim holy book, the Quran (Koran), prescribes fasting throughout this ninth month of the Islamic lunar calendar (which varies from year to year), and from dawn to sunset no eating or drinking are allowed. The fasting continues for around 30 days. Children who have reached puberty and adults are expected to engage in this fast, whereas children are encouraged to fast at least half a day. In Somalia *afur* or breakfast (literally "break fast") is observed, and every day at sunset families gather together and eat foods such as dates, *bur*, and *sambusi*, after which people may go to the mosque or other place of prayer for *Tarawih*. Muslims are also allowed to eat *Suhur* food, which refers to food eaten between midnight and near dawn. The *Suhur* meal is important because it fortifies people for the day of fasting ahead, and they leisurely eat a substantial meal of corn or rice over an hour or two. The celebration at the end of Ramadan is called *Eid-ul-fitr*, and is a joyous occasion with feasting.

Secularization after World War II, along with Marxist influences, the growth of urbanization, and Western influences, have all led to a weakening of tradition and the power of religion in places such as Ethiopia and Eritrea. Loss of respect for fasts is said to be responsible for a popular Ethiopian dish called *shifinfin* ("hush hush" or "wrap up") so-named because people ordered it in whispers, and it arrived at the table in a deep bowl hiding succulent meat *alicha'we't* secretly buried under layers of *injera*.

Burundo (nowadays *qur't*) is choice raw meat served at the end of banquets or other special occasions such as contemporary weddings in Ethiopia. No one is certain how it originated. Perhaps soldiers first ate it when kings banned lighting fires during military expeditions. In places such as Ethiopia, people still prefer fresh meat to refrigerated or frozen meat. Traditionally, people would buy a whole cow to kill and divide, and meat was not sold in shops. This led to the practice of preserving extra meat by drying it, for example to make *qwan'ta* for *wats*, traveling, or as a snack for visitors.

In other parts of East Africa outside influence is seen in the preference for tea as a morning or snack-time beverage, or before or after meals. Preparation techniques commonly call for boiling water, then adding tea leaves, milk, and spices to make *chai ya maziwa*. The Maragoli and Taita of Kenya are said to value tea highly.

Coffee is most popular in Ethiopia, Eritrea, Sudan, and Somalia, where it is an important aspect of hospitality and social interaction. In earlier times coffee drinking was limited to Oromos and Muslims, and the Christian clergy condemned it as a Muslim drink. By the 1880s Menelik (the Emperor) drank it, and it became popular to a wider audience. Originally, the coffee was flavored with salt, butter, or spices. The beans were roasted, ground in wooden mortars, then mixed with butter and honey and made into small balls that were boiled in a pot. Italians introduced sugar as a popular flavoring in the 1930s, and Ethiopians adopted it enthusiastically.

In Ethiopia, coffee drinking is a highly developed art and ceremony and for hundreds of years has been a popular event and pastime. The red coffee berries must be properly dried in the sun and husked, washed, and dried before the beans are roasted over coals to a dark brown color, then pounded/ground to powder with a wooden pestle.

In a typical scenario, the woman in charge of a coffee ceremony begins preparations by spreading fresh-cut grass on the house's hard mud floor. She builds up a fire by blowing or fanning the coals in her stove, likely made from an oil drum. As the water in the pot on the drum comes to a boil, she adds the coffee powder and tops the pot with sisal strands to retain heat while allowing the steam to escape.

The aroma of the brewing coffee permeates the air as the household and any guests gather silently, enjoying the smells and anticipating the up-coming coffee drinking. Sometimes incense is burned. Clean tiny coffee cups *(siniwoch)* are ceremonially rinsed and placed on a special wooden tray with four legs, then the scalding hot coffee is poured, and the tray is passed around. There is a saying that *"ye bunna sibatu, mefajetu"* ("the pleasure of coffee is in its burning sensation").[11]

The first round of leisurely sipping and visiting is called *abol*. Hot water is added to the coffee in the pot, and the guests put their cups back on the tray for them to be filled again for the second round, the *huletegna*. The process is repeated a third time, the *bareka* (blessing), when God is asked to bless the house and make it prosperous.

Another major social event is a wedding, and cakes are important whether they are made from wheat flour or another flour, such as corn flour. These cakes may look unfamiliar to Westerners, such as when the dough is mashed into balls, wrapped in banana leaves, and steamed.

Another happy occasion in much of eastern Africa is the naming of a newborn. In many Christian, Muslim, or traditional homes, once the baby has lived for about a week, a special celebration is held at which the child receives his or her name. This festive occasion is accompanied by feasting and may include, as at weddings or other large gatherings, a rice *pilau*.

DIET AND HEALTH

Food Insecurity

The media image of East Africa has been strongly influenced by pictures of starving children in drought-stricken Ethiopia or Somalia, of children in refugee camps, and more recently, of orphaned children and women and men dying of AIDS. At the other extreme is the safari-influenced tourist image of the awe-inspiring Africa with gracious colonial-style houses and tastes of exotic wild game. Both images hold seeds of truth, but both are distractions.

Certainly, food insecurity is endemic to much of East Africa and poses a crisis situation. Per capita food production has declined from the early 1970s through the 1990s and has been associated with famines in the Sahel and Ethiopia. In late 2000, the FAO reported that in the Horn of Africa alone around 70 million people live with chronic food insecurity and are often threatened by famine. The root causes of this insecurity are beyond the scope of this book but include drought and natural disasters, along with armed conflict, poverty, and a population that has doubled since 1974. About 99 percent of the cultivable land is not irrigated. These are issues that must be addressed before the area can hope to be freed from the problems of mal- or under-nourishment.

The major health and diet-related issues are the same as those that have been discussed in other chapters. The most widespread and serious issue is protein-energy malnutrition or kwashiorkor, but pellagra (largely niacin deficiency), also historically associated with maize diets, is also a concern. Other problems include vitamin A deficiency, rickets, scurvy, and anemia.

It has been argued that if its foods are eaten in traditional amounts and combinations, the East African diet is ideally balanced and healthful. The basis for this claim is that traditional rural agrarian diets are low in meat and fat and high in vegetables and fiber. In addition, some studies conclude that Maasai and Samburu tribes have historically had very healthy lifestyles and diets and have had practically no incidences of hypertension, heart disease, cancers, and so on. Although the Maasai traditionally eat some meat and drink blood, with milk and animal fat as their only sources of protein (animal fat making up 60 percent of their energy intake), they suffer less heart trouble than do Westerners, largely because they combine the animal products with antioxidant herbs.

The key words here are "right amounts and combinations" and "balance." However, East Africans are often not able to eat what they want when they want it.

East African governments are attempting to address some of the nutritional deficiencies by researching new strains of higher protein or vitamin-rich varieties of traditional crops. For example, a new type of corn, QPM, or quality protein maize (also known as *nalongo*, the twin), has been developed in Kenya. In addition, an improved type of orange-fleshed sweet potato is being introduced with a higher beta-carotene content that will help combat vitamin A deficiency.

Pastoral Lifestyle and Drought

There are special needs of pastoral peoples in the arid and semiarid parts of East Africa, such as the Maasai of Kenya and Tanzania or the Turkana of Kenya, who are particularly susceptible to lack of rainfall. They need to be mobile to move their goats, sheep, camels, horses, donkeys, and cattle around to find grazing lands. However, their nomadic way of life is often not supported by governments unsympathetic to the specific needs of their lifestyle and who make policies restricting their ability to move their herds freely especially across national or regional boundaries, or force pastoral people onto less desirable land. Drought can weaken their animals and make them more susceptible to disease, plus overgrazing of the animals can lead to soil erosion. Also, when people are hungry and lack water, their resistance to disease is lowered, and they are more susceptible to death from malaria, respiratory infections, and diarrheal diseases. Thus, drought can also have debilitating effects on agricultural families who depend upon rainfall for their crops.

A study of health among the Turkana in Kenya discusses a number of health differences between nomads and more sedentary peoples, including problems related to a diet rich in milk and proximity to animals.[12]

AIDS and Diet

AIDS has had devastating effects on this region, as in other parts of the continent. The link between diet and combating AIDS was introduced in Chapter 2, where the concern that over-emphasis on antiretroviral drugs, which are expensive and beyond the reach of many Sub-Saharan Africans, needs to be corrected and modified with a recognition of the importance of a healthy diet in the lives of AIDS sufferers, especially as many of the drugs are highly toxic when not combined with a healthy diet. Places such as the Kenya Medical Research Institute (KEMRI) are actively attempting to develop healthy, affordable diets targeted at HIV/AIDS patients.

NOTES

1. The idea that a guest bestows blessing on the home he or she enters is a common idea in eastern (and central) African proverbs. Besides Swahili, it is found in the Haya and Luyia languages and in countries including Somalia, Kenya, Tanzania, and Uganda. Several interrelated levels of meaning are attrib-

uted to the proverb: (1) There is generally a big meal to welcome a guest, perhaps involving killing a chicken or goat, so a guest's arrival is associated with special food and a break from normal everyday chores; (2) guests often bring gifts for the host/hostess/family members, such as meat or bananas, or things like new seeds or medicine that can literally heal the recipients; (3) the guest often brings news of relatives and friends, an important aspect of the social support network that keeps families and communities strong. See http://www.afriprov.org/resources/explain.htm#mar1999.

2. Said Hamdun and Noël King, *Ibn Battuta in Black Africa* (Princeton, N.J.: Markus Wiener Publishers, 1994), p. 15.

3. Ibid., pp. 17–18.

4. Anne Sharman, "Food and Recipes in Padhola," in *The Anthropologists' Cookbook*, ed. Jessica Kuper (New York: Universe Books, 1977), pp. 107–8.

5. Ivan Karp and Patricia Karp, "Social Aspects of Iteso Cookery," in *The Anthropologists' Cookbook*, ed. Jessica Kuper (New York: Universe Books, 1977), p. 103.

6. This information was culled from Rosanne Guggisberg and traditional sources (recipes) and Elaine Mwango, comp., *Cooking with an African Flavour* (Nairobi: Mount Kenya Sundries, 1933), p. 2.

7. William and Dorothy Shack, "Cooking in the Garden of Ensete," in *The Anthropologists' Cookbook*, ed. Jessica Kuper (New York: Universe Books, 1977), p. 80.

8. Sharman, "Food and Recipes in Padhola," p. 109.

9. Karp and Karp, "Social Aspects of Iteso Cookery," p. 101.

10. Jomo Kenyatta, *Facing Mount Kenya* (London: Heinemann, 1979), p. 21.

11. Daniel J. Mesfin, ed. *Exotic Ethiopian Cooking: Society, Culture, Hospitality and Traditions*. Rev. extended ed. (Falls Church, Va: Ethiopian Cookbook Enterprises, 1993), p. xxix.

12. Simon Harragin, "Health and Healthcare Provision in North West Turkana, Kenya." Overseas Development Institute, Pastoral Development Network, paper 36c, July 1994. Available as PDF file from http://www.odi.org.uk/pdn/papers/index1.html.

4

Central Africa

Si ton ventre n'est pas plein, interroge ta main.
If your belly is not full, ask your hand.[1]

INTRODUCTION

Central Africa is often called the heart of Africa. Also known as Equatorial Africa or Middle Africa, it is the region most closely associated with the image of the *Dark Continent.*

Water is the lifeblood pumping through this heart. Central Africa is dominated by tropical rain forests, estimated to be about 8 percent of the continent's surface. These forests are bounded on the west by the Atlantic Ocean, on the east by the Rift Valley, and on the north and south by savannah grasslands. They depend upon heavy rainfall as well as the Congo River Basin with its myriad lakes, creeks, rivers, and swamps. The Congo River is the fifth longest in the world, and second in Africa only to the Nile River. At more than 1.6 million square miles (4.1 million square kilometers), its watershed area is the world's second largest basin area and has the potential to provide one-sixth of the world's hydroelectric power. Many of the rivers in central Africa are unnaviagable from the sea and this fact, combined with the dense vegetation of the rain forests, has historically isolated and protected much of the interior from human settlement and expansion.

In reality, much of the darkness of this part of the world was in the eyes of the (European) beholders. The first Westerner to explore the Congo

River was the famous Anglo-American journalist and explorer Henry Stanley, who in 1876 and 1877 traveled more than 1,600 of its 2,718 miles. He was later hired by the Belgian king Leopold II to return, and between 1879 and 1884 he established 22 settlements on the Congo and its tributaries, thereby helping to establish the Congo Free State in 1885.[2] While less of a racist in his day than many, he did not realize how ruthless and greedy King Leopold would become, and Stanley popularized the image of "darkest Africa" in writings such as *Through the Dark Continent* (1878), *In Darkest Africa* (1890), and *My Dark Companions* (1893). Besides his ethnic use of the word *dark*, Stanley probably experienced a great deal of time far from sunlight during the months he spent deep within the Ituri rain forest, as well as the emotional darkness of seeing starvation, sickness, and death attack the men with him.

Images of light and darkness are also associated with the poetry of Rudyard Kipling, as in his 1899 poem "The White Man's Burden." The theme was picked up in the United States in events such as the 1901 Pan-American exposition in Buffalo, New York, where the food and culture sections of the fair exhibited "Darkest Africa," followed in 1902 by Joseph Conrad's novel *Heart of Darkness*, set in the Congo. Although the Western world cheered Conrad's book as an indictment of the evils of imperialism, Africans such as writer Chinua Achebe were deeply offended by the use of Africa in a stereotypic way as a backdrop for white, Western characters. This deeply rooted image of central Africa was revisited and revised in Barbara Kingsolver's novel *The Poisonwood Bible* (1998).

To understand the food and culture of central Africa, one must become familiar with its precolonial as well as colonial past, in particular the migration of Bantu and non-Bantu populations, the history of the ancient Kingdom of the Kongo, and Portuguese, French, and Belgian involvement in the region's history, especially the slave trade.

The list of countries composing central Africa is, as in all the regions, somewhat variable, because border countries can often be placed in neighboring regions. Overall, the Congo River dominates the geography, and two of the region's countries take their names from it: The Democratic Republic of the Congo (or DRC, formerly Zaire, which is said to be another name for the Congo River) and Congo. The other countries included here are Cameroon, Equatorial Guinea, the Central African Republic (CAR), Gabon, Angola, Burundi, and Rwanda. *Cameroon* comes from the Portuguese name for the Wouri River, which fifteenth-century explorers called "Rio de Camarões," or "The River of Prawns." Gabon's name is also linked to the Portuguese and water. It comes from the Portuguese word *gabao*, a coat with sleeves and a hood, a shape resembling the site of their early fifteenth-century explorations in the Como River estuary.

The equator slices directly through Gabon, the DRC, and the Congo, and the other countries are clustered near it. While much of the area lies within the tropical rain forest belt, two of the countries, Rwanda and Burundi (sometimes considered part of eastern Africa) are mountainous and hilly. Population densities vary from small, densely populated countries such as Burundi and Rwanda to large, less densely populated countries such as the DRC. The DRC is roughly four times the size of France, or a little less than one-quarter the size of the United States, and the third most populated country in sub-Saharan Africa after Nigeria and Ethiopia.

Equatorial Guinea is the only Spanish-speaking country in all of sub-Saharan Africa. Apart from Equatorial Guinea and a small part of Cameroon, where English is spoken, in central Africa French is the language spoken by educated people. This shared language base is one of the colonial heritages. The CAR, Congo, and Gabon, along with Chad, were part of what was known as the French Equatorial Africa Empire. Cameroon was originally a German colony that was later jointly administered by France and Britain. The DRC (called the Belgian Congo before it was Zaire) was a Belgian colony, as were Rwanda and Burundi.

The country boundaries as set up by the colonial powers often displayed ignorance about or indifference to the geographical distribution of local ethnic groups. Thus, for example, northerners in Gabon have family connections in Cameroon and Equatorial Guinea, and families from southeast Gabon have relatives in the DRC.

HISTORICAL OVERVIEW

Early History: Pygmies and Nilosaharans

Besides central Africa's varied microenvironments that range from hills and mountains to tropical rainforests and savannah grasslands, the region encompasses diverse lifestyles. Although one of the more urbanized regions of sub-Saharan Africa, its now endangered but extensive rain forests have long been home to indigenous forest peoples popularly referred to in the West as pygmies. The English term emphasizes the short stature of the peoples and has a faintly negative connotation. Ancient Egyptians knew about them and called them "people of the trees," or the "dancers of the gods." Some scholars and writers use more neutral, but less precise, terms such as "forest peoples" or "forest foragers." While the African pygmy groups in central Africa speak more than 10 distinct languages and are found in parts of the DRC, Congo, the CAR, Cameroon, and Gabon, their total numbers are estimated to have dwindled to 150,000 to 300,000.

There is great variation in their hunting techniques, settlement patterns, food preferences, gender roles, barter arrangements, and dependency on peoples outside the forest. Probably the largest and most well-known groups are the Efe, Mbuti, Baka, Aka, and Twa (or Tswa). The Efe and Mbuti are from the Ituri Forest in the eastern Congo-DRC basin, while the Baka and Aka are from the western Congo-DRC basin. The Twa are from the high regions surrounding Lake Kivu. Although small in numbers, and with distinct culinary practices and preferences, these hunters and foragers have influenced the food culture of the region by providing food to others outside the forests.

The earliest agriculturalists to arrive in central Africa are believed to have been Nilosaharan speakers who moved near but not into the equatorial rain forests. They stayed in the adjoining savanna areas to cultivate sorghums and tend domesticated animals such as sheep, goats, and cows. Another group of agriculturalists, based in the highlands of the Cameroon, were early cultivators of yam and oil palm who began expanding around 5,000 years ago, moving east to settle in the lands along the Congo river watershed (as well as the Nile River watershed). These farmers moved up to the northern edges of the forest.

Bantu Migrations

As early as 4,000 years ago, western-migrating, iron-working, Bantu-speaking agriculturalists from a branch of the Niger-Congo moved into the actual rain forests to begin food cultivation. They most probably came south from Nigeria's Cross River valley through Cameroon into the rain forests of west-central Africa. By the third century these peoples had spread throughout the rain forests. In addition to farming, they were skilled river fishermen, gradually spreading along the rivers. After entering the forests in the south they followed other northward-flowing rivers to the east. By about 2,000 years ago there was a line of Bantu-speaking villages based on fishing and farming, with forest hunter-gatherers who lived deeper in the forests circling around them.

The Bantu migrations and expansion were mostly based on peaceful assimilation rather than military conquest. The Bantu speakers interacted with the peoples along the way and demonstrated flexibility in mixing and matching languages as well as political, social, economic, and technological aspects with these neighbors in a pragmatic way.

There are hundreds of Bantu-speaking ethnic groups in central Africa today. Major ones include Kongo, Mongo, Luba, Bwaka, Kwango, Lulua, Kasai, Douala, Hutu, and Baganda. While there are estimated to be between 200 and 250 African languages in the DRC alone, among its approximately 58 million people, almost half of the population come from four ethnic groups: the Mongo, Luba, Kongo (all Bantu-speaking people), and the Mangbetu-Azande (from the Hamitic language family). Lingala is the *lingua franca* trade language of the DRC.

A common contribution of Bantu-speaking groups to the names of dishes is the use of *echo* words, also called *reduplication*, to name them, such as *fufu, sakasaka, dongo-dongo, jammu-jammu,* and *coupé-coupé.*

Kingdom of the Kongo

By the 1300s one of the Bantu-speaking peoples from the north, the Kongo (or Bakongo) established a powerful kingdom on the southern bank of the Congo River. By the 1480s when Portuguese explorer Diogo Cão became the first recorded European explorer to visit the river, he found the king (or *manikongo*), Nzinga Nkuwu, friendly and interested in becoming a trading partner. Cordial relations began, with an emissary sent to Portugal and missionaries, artisans, and explorers welcomed into the Kongo. However, beginning around the middle of the 1500s Portugal became primarily interested in exploiting Kongo for slaves for its sugar plantations in Brazil and Fernando Po.

The Kingdom of the Kongo may have initially supplied slaves from raiding borders at Loango to the north, Ndongo to the south (present-day Angola), and Mbangala further inland. By the 1550s most of the slaves were traveling across the Atlantic to Brazil and the Spanish Caribbean.

Other wealth from the Kingdom of the Kongo came from mineral resources such as the copper of Bembe and the Mbanza Kongo iron. In addition, by the first half of the 1800s Arab traders were active in the trade for ivory and slaves from the Kongo.

Portugal gradually took control of the Kingdom of Kongo and established its rule in Luanda to the south. By 1665 the Kongolese kingdom began disintegrating, and the kingship was dissolved in the 1700s. By the 1800s the area became part of Portugal's Angola colony, and Mbanza Kongo (the capital) was renamed São Salvador. Later, under King Leopold of Belgium, the central Africa colony was called Congo Free State after the dissolved kingdom. The French colony to the north of the Congo River was also named Congo. However, these and the present-day Congo countries extend far beyond the original kingdom.

MAJOR FOODS AND INGREDIENTS

Apart from the foods eaten by the forest hunter-foragers, the foods of central Africa use largely the same ingredients as those in western and/ or eastern Africa, although with generally simpler preparation methods. In central Africa they are commonly referred to by their French names in addition to their local names. Peanuts are known as *arachides*, and palm butter from the red oil palm is known as *sauce graine* or *noix de palme*. A version of chicken in palmnut sauce, sometimes called the national dish of Gabon, is *Poulet Nyembwe* (or *Gnemboue*). The linguistic roots of some names of foods and dishes further illustrate the global migration of central African foods. For example, the word for peanut in Kimbundu, a Bantu language of Angola, is *nguba*, from which the American term *goober* is derived. Similarly, palm oil is known as *dendê* oil in Brazil, from the oil palm's name in Quimbundo, a language spoken in Angola. Green leaves, which are both gathered wild and grown in farms, are *feuilles*. The popular cassava *(manihot utilissima)* leaves are *feuilles de manioc*. While cassava was observed cultivated in the region in 1611, originally only the leaves were eaten. It was said to be the Portuguese who, having introduced cassava into their southern and central African colonies, imposed consumption of the tubers on the people and taught Angolans the complex processing techniques for making the coarse flour known as *gari* that they had learned from their Brazilian colonies.

Other greens include okra, pumpkin, sorrel, sweet potato, cocoyam or taro, bitterleaf, and *ndolé* leaves (*Vernonia amygdalina*). A green leaf that grows wild is *gnetum africannum* (also *okok, koko,* or *eru*). The fruits or pods as well as the leaves of okra (*ngumbo*) are eaten, as is the case with pumpkins and other melons, sweet potatoes and cocoyams or taro. In addition, *cucurbitaceae*, seeds from gourds and melons, pumpkins, and squashes, are often dried and ground to be used as flour to thicken soups and stews (e.g., *egusi* melon seeds and wild mango, or *mangue sauvage*). Starches besides cassava include corn, sorghum, and millet. As in West Africa, red palm oil, *elaeis guineensis*, is characteristic of the region's cuisine. In some groups it is closely identified (along with beans) as a symbol of fertility. As in western Africa, palm oil is an important component of

Shredding leaves (*feuilles*) for cooking. Courtesy of
Doug Himes.

the diet, providing energy and lipids, calcium, phosphorus, and vitamin
A. Beans (*haricots*) are also widely eaten.

In countries in east-central Africa such as Rwanda or Burundi, sweet potatoes are a staple of the cuisine. They may be eaten a variety of ways, from
boiled in their skins and mashed, to roasted. Bananas and plantains (the
"potatoes of the air") are also eaten. The plantains were first introduced
on the east coast of Africa from the 500s. By the 1400s they had diffused
throughout the region. These cooking bananas may be steamed, boiled, or
roasted in a manner similarly to the *matoke* or *matooke* of Uganda.

Tomatoes, onions, peppers, and salt (including *sel indigene*, salt that is
made locally from the ashes of leaves or bark as well as imported), are
important seasonings. The mineral *sel gemme* (mineral salt) is known as
kanwa in Cameroon. It is used, among other things, to soften *ndolé* leaves,
meat, stockfish, and beans.

Yams and rice are also eaten, although less often than cassava or corn.
Meats, fish, and fowl are all part of the diet, both wild and domesticated.
These include chicken or guinea fowl, goats, game, or bushmeat (*viande
de brousse*), including antelope, buffalo, elephant (now often outlawed),
crocodile, hippopotamus, and sometimes snake, monkey, and bird. Kola
nuts are sold. Bouillon cubes such as the ubiquitous Maggi cubes are prized
seasonings for soups, stews, and sauces. They come in a wide variety of
flavors, from beef to chicken to shrimp.

Rwandan Beef Stew with Sweet Potatoes (Central Africa)

1 lb stewing beef, cubed

1 onion, chopped

3 Tbsp vegetable oil

3 small green cooking bananas or 2 medium green plantains (or substitute regular green bananas)

juice of 1 lemon (about 3 Tbsp)

1/4 cup tomato sauce

1/4 tsp ground sage

1 cup water

salt and cayenne pepper to taste (about 1/2 to 1 tsp salt and 1/2 tsp or more red pepper)

4 medium sweet potatoes, unpeeled

3 Tbsp butter or margarine

Peel the plantains or bananas (see the recipe for green plantain chips for directions on peeling a green plantain), cut into pieces, and sprinkle with lemon juice. Peel and chop the onion, then cut the meat into cubes. Heat the oil in the pan and fry the meat and onions until the meat is browned and the onions golden. Add the plantains or bananas, and cook them for 5 minutes, stirring constantly. Add the tomato sauce, sage, salt and red pepper to taste, and 1 cup water. Lower the heat, cover the pan, and simmer until the meat is tender. Depending on the size of the cubes and the toughness of the meat, this may be 30 minutes to an hour. Check and stir occasionally, and add more water if necessary.

While the stew cooks, rinse but do not peel the sweet potatoes and put into a pot with enough water to cover them and a little salt, if desired. Bring the water to a boil, lower it and cook them until tender, around 30 minutes. When cooked, drain them and remove the skins. Mash them with a potato masher or electric mixer, and season with the butter or margarine, salt and black or white pepper to taste, and serve with the stew.

Some leaves, such as *ndolé* leaves, are bitter, and require chopping and cooking repeatedly in fresh water, then squeezing to get rid of the bitter taste. People judge *ndolé* dishes by the degree of bitterness in them, how many leaves are used, and what other ingredients were added, such as ground peanuts or ground or pounded meat or fish.

The hunter-gatherers (formerly known as pygmies) who live in the equatorial rain forests have been very influenced by the urbanization and growth in agriculture in the region. One of the biggest changes is the adoption of many of the foods of farmers, such as cassava, as well as rice,

Shop in Gabon run by a West African immigrant. Courtesy of Doug Himes.

beans, peanuts, and tomatoes. They will often trade food gathered from the forest, especially prized bushmeat, for salt or staple foods and necessities on which they have come to rely. Besides necessities such as cooking utensils, they also trade to acquire prestige foods such as rice or red wine. Women especially work part-time in farmers' fields near the forest to earn cash for some of the things they cannot obtain in the forest.

In addition to hunting, forest people gather wild foods including berries; fruits; nutrient-rich insects such as caterpillars, beetles, ant larvae, and pupae termites; weevil larvae; snails; leaves; mushrooms; nuts; honey; and roots. Although introduced fruit bushes and trees are said to be underutilized, they are cultivated by farmers and range from *patchuilu*, orange and lemon, pawpaw *(Carica papaya)*, and breadfruit *(Artocarpus utilis,* from Oceania) to plum tree *(Dacryodes edulis)*, coconut *(Cocos nucifera)*, and mango *(Mangifera indica)*. Oil in their diets comes mainly from palm oil, ground wild seeds and nuts, and animal fat.

African Palm Weevil *(Rhychophorus Phoenicis)*

One tropical food that is unfamiliar to Westerners but considered a delicacy in central Africa, such as the *mopane* worms of southern Africa, is the African palm weevil, or *rhychophorus phoenicis*. Enjoyed in tropical forest areas throughout the world, from the Amazon, Borneo, and Papua, to the central region of Africa, these fatty, thumb-sized larvae are highly prized and reportedly have their highest economic value in Cameroon in urban areas such as Yaoundé and Douala. The larvae are collected by skilled harvesters who spend hours in waist-high muddy water braving insect bites and snakes to remove the larvae from trunks of *Raphia* palms that grow close together in swampy lowlands.

Bushmeat Markets

A major road constructed in the early 1930s that passes through the Ituri Forest between Kisangani and eastern DRC led to the development of a lucrative meat market for bushmeat *(viande de brousse)*. Truckers and others on the road could buy the valuable meat at low prices and transport it to eastern DRC or Kisangani, and by the late 1950s and early 1960s the trade was thriving. In the CAR a decent road network also enabled the Aka to develop meat markets in the larger towns, although the Aka in interior parts of northeast Congo were not able to do so.

Cameroon, often considered the most accessible and developed part of central Africa (and sometimes included as part of western Africa), is near other West African cities and the Douala seaport. People in surrounding areas have cash from crops such as coffee or cocoa or hardwood exports and live near the forests so they are able to buy highly valued game meat from the Baka. Estimates place the bushmeat harvest in central Africa at more than 2 million tons a year. There is concern that population growth, the new roads, and logging practices that destroy habitat, combined with increased urban demand for bushmeat, may lead to the extinction of some central African wildlife.

It was noted in 2003 that the world's largest frog, the giant *Conraua goliath*, found only in the isolated rain forests of Cameroon and Equatorial Guinea, is rapidly disappearing. In the 1960s it was assumed that the survival of the frogs was guaranteed. That is no longer the case. Rivers are growing toxic due to use of illegal agrochemicals, and there has also been inexorable hunting of the frogs, which are considered delicious, and "pure, associated with clean-water spirits and good for pregnant women."[3]

COOKING

Serving and Social Relationships

Getting, preparing, and serving food are all steps in a process that varies from place to place. As is the norm for the rest of sub-Saharan Africa, preparing and serving food is predominantly a female affair. Food provisioning, however, varies. Among the forest hunter-foragers, men in general do the bulk of the hunting. Hunting has long been a symbol of manhood. Some net hunting groups such as the Mbuti and Aka traditionally rely more heavily on meat in their diets than others such as the Efe and Baka. It is essentially the men who have done the spear or bow hunting and collecting of honey, with women fishing and gathering fruits and tubers. Net hunting focuses only on small to medium-sized ungulates (animals with hooves) such as duikers, antelopes, or chevrotain. The division of labor, such as in net hunting, is often flexible. For example, Mbuti women chase the game into the net while the men kill the meat after it is trapped, whereas the Aka reverse the process.

Gender division of labor, as well as dependency on villages for food and other goods, also varies according to group. Some anthropologists consider bow hunting less efficient than net hunting and think that forest groups who rely on bow hunting tend to stay closer to villages where they have access to other sources of food from farmers. Others argue the opposite: when women participate in net hunting, they are no longer available to collect vegetables and fruits so they rely more on trade with farmers.

However, all hunter-forager forest groups have growing contact and interaction, including intermarriage, with their farmer neighbors and villages. They appear to be in danger of becoming, such as the aboriginal San

Girls returning from the farm.
Courtesy of Doug Himes.

and Khoi of southern Africa, a marginalized impoverished class providing labor for other ethnic groups.

Alcoholic beverages, especially palm or banana wine, play a major role in the life of many central African societies. For example, among the Ngbaka and Ngando in the CAR, an important traditional activity for adult men has been collecting the sap of the oil palm every day at dawn and before sunset. This palm wine is consumed the same day, with the quality of each man's palm wine the matter of much discussion and debate.

For forest peoples in Rwanda and Burundi, banana beer (*la bière de banane*) plays a similar role to palm wine. Among the BaTwa a variety of banana called *l'igikashi*, described as tasting like green olives, is put into the ground to ripen for five or six days, until the banana turns yellow. The bananas are then peeled, mixed, and allowed to ferment in a hollowed-out tree trunk. Flavorings are added, such as *aiguilles*, and the mild version of the beer is served to women and children. A stronger version is served to the men.

Equipment and Utensils

Among the forest hunter-foragers, mobility is essential, and therefore permanent possessions, including cooking equipment, have traditionally been kept to a minimum. Drying racks for preserving food are important both in hunting camps and in homes. For example, among the Mvae in southern Cameroon, after trapping and butchering animals such as duikers, the catch would be smoked for a few days over a large rack. Besides bushmeat, fish and seeds of fruits such as *Irvingia gabonesis* have been dried or smoked and stored on racks over the fireplace. In the tropical rain forest environments few foods were stored in the Western sense. While kernels from *Irvingia gabonesis* were made into loaves that could be kept above a smoking rack for several days, other forms of storage have been less formal. Food such as wild yam tubers can be harvested and stored in the ground at the same place they grow, and cassava tubers (in the ground) or plantains are a "living store" that can be harvested year round as needed. However, farmers in central Africa who cultivate yams other than wild yams and cocoyams have stored them in granaries made of branches and tree bark.

Among nonurban people living near the forest areas, kitchens are usually located away from the house and have several fireplaces for cooking as well as a smoking rack. Shelves and cupboards serve as a larder and as storage for kitchen utensils. Increasingly, mass-produced items are replacing traditional handmade cooking utensils.

Pounding is an essential component of food preparation. The ubiquitous mortar and pestle is also found in this region, frequently made from a tree limb and a hollowed-out tree trunk. For women in countries such as southern Cameroon, Congo, and northeastern Gabon, the time-consuming tasks of harvesting, processing, and preparing cassava tubers is one of their most important jobs. Research in southern Cameroon found that traditionally housewives processed cassava into cassava sticks twice a week, and making enough of the sticks for a family of five took an entire day.[4]

The basic meal pattern in central Africa is similar to that of western Africa: a main starchy food accompanied by a relish, stew, or sauce. Traditionally, breakfast might simply be leftovers from the previous day, and snacks would be eaten during the day, with a larger meal taken in the early afternoon.

Apart from cooking in pots, a major cooking technique involves using heat-resistant leaves to cook food, either by wrapping a starchy food and boiling or steaming it in a leaf envelope, or by wrapping meat or fish and cooking it directly on the embers of a fire. As is the case in other parts of Africa, leaves, such as the commonly used *marantaceae* (banana leaves), impart a delicate flavor to the food as it cooks. Cooking in leaves has an ancient history and probably preceded cooking in iron, and perhaps even

Cassava sticks (*bâtons de manioc*) are a popular central African food. Courtesy of Doug Himes.

clay, cooking pots. It is economical, mobile, practical, and very efficient, for the biodegradable leaves used can also double as disposable plates or bowls.

Until about 100 years ago the Bantu-speaking Woyo of the DRC incorporated art into their daily life by carving proverbial symbols (*taampha*) with advice for maintaining a successful marriage into the wooden lids that covered their ceramic serving pots. Traditionally, men ate with other men, but their wives served them their food. If there had been a disagreement between the husband and wife, she covered the pot with a lid specially decorated to make the disagreement public so that others could help to mediate and settle it. For example, a lid might warn against the folly of fighting within the family by showing two goats tied to a central projection or two birds sharing a single bug. Conversely, a man might air his complaints by choosing a special lid to cover his empty dish.

A woman received her lids from her mother and grandmother upon marrying, or commissioned them from local carvers as the need arose. A man's parents could also provide him with lids. For example, one Woyo pot lid's seven pictographs and their meaning is described in detail, including the need to distinguish the true value of things, to not idly talk about intimate family affairs, for the husband to give the wife the information (tools) she needs, to reinforce the role of the man as the ruler of the home, and the woman's ability to leave and return to her family (this one symbolized by a bird caught in a hunter's trap only by its tail feathers).[5]

Culinary Images and Family Relationships

Chapter 1 introduced the frequent use of culinary metaphors for cooking, family, and sexual relationships in western Africa. This pattern is found in many societies in sub-Saharan Africa, eastern and central as well as western. These metaphors include describing sex as *hot*, referring to the womb as a *hearth* or *cooking pot*, calling sperm, blood, and ova *ingredients*, describing the gestation time for a fetus as *cooking and stirring the pot*, and the actual birth process as *serving a meal*. For example, among the Bangangte of the grasslands of Cameroon, sex is hot just like really good music, a great joke, or a mouth-watering meal is. Also, when a man impregnates a woman, he cooks her, and together the man and woman measure, mix, and cook the ingredients to make a child. Until the child is born and becomes a *fresh person* the fetus is referred to as if he or she is food being cooked.

In a similar way, culinary imagery and metaphors are used to describe marriage and sexual relationships, which are intertwined. Among the

Bangangte marriage is known as *na nda*, which literally translates to "to cook inside." A wife is a woman who cooks inside her house and her kitchen. Traditionally (although this is changing with the arrival of a cash economy) only unmarried women were supposed to cook outside, where anyone could smell the aromas of their cooking food. After marriage a woman was relegated to cooking inside the kitchen her husband built her. He alone was allowed to smell the smells from her cooking pot, and it was originally next to the hearth that their children were delivered.

Certainly, social sharing of food exists side-by-side with this simplified metaphorical division and symbolism: not only would a woman share food with her husband and children, she would also share with co-wives, guests, relatives, and assorted social network groups in the community with whom she was involved.

TYPICAL MEALS

Central Africa is stereotyped as the sub-Saharan region with the least sophisticated cuisine. Certainly it is less represented in the culinary literature available. However, research among the Yassa and Mvae in southern Cameroon suggests that there is an elaborate gastronomy, with women identifying between 17 and 21 recipes they like to cook.

Groundnut Sauce with Pumpkin (or Okra, Eggplant, or Spinach) (Sub-Saharan Africa)

A characteristic of much of sub-Saharan African cooking is its flexible and forgiving nature. Cooking is still an oral, not written, tradition, and cooks improvise freely according to what ingredients are available. Classic groundnut (peanut) sauce (or soup or stew) falls well within that tradition.

3 Tbsp peanut or other vegetable oil

1 onion, peeled and finely chopped (about 1 cup)

1 large clove (or 2 medium cloves) of garlic, peeled and crushed in a garlic press or finely minced (optional)

2 cups chopped tomatoes (peeled if desired)

1 small can prepared pumpkin [Note: see vegetable variations listed below]

1/2 cup creamy natural-style peanut butter

2–3 cups water (or more, if desired)

salt and black, white, and/or cayenne pepper to taste

Prepare the tomatoes, if using fresh. Before chopping them, peel them, if desired. (To peel tomatoes drop them into a saucepan of boiling water for a minute, then into a bowl of cold water. The skins will split and slip off.) Peel and chop the onion. Heat a skillet on medium heat, add the 3 Tbsp oil, and sauté the chopped onion for a few minutes until it is translucent. Then add the chopped tomato and garlic, and continue cooking for another 5 minutes. Stir in the can of pumpkin. Stir the peanut butter with a cup or two of water until smooth and then stir it into the mixture on the stove. Lower the heat, cover the pan, and allow the sauce to simmer for about 15 minutes to allow the flavors to blend. Stir occasionally to make sure the sauce does not scorch, and add more water if necessary.

This sauce has endless variations. Fresh, leftover, dried, canned, or smoked fish, meat, hard-boiled eggs, or poultry may be added to it (first slice or cube any fresh meat or poultry and fry it with the onion). Stock, milk, or bouillon cubes may be added with or replace the water. A small can of tomato sauce may be substituted for the fresh tomatoes. If additional water is added to thin it, the sauce becomes a soup to be eaten in a bowl. Otherwise, it can be eaten on a plate with rice, a boiled or roasted or mashed starchy vegetable such as yam, potato, or cassava, or *matoke* or any of the versions of *fufu, ugali, putu,* and so on.

The traditional structure and organization of eating arrangements has varied among forest peoples. Among many, adult men would eat separately in a special meeting place. Dishes would be carried to them from their households, and shared among themselves informally, with seniority the basis for settling any differences over coveted bits of food. Sometimes only men of the same family would eat together. Traditionally, women and small children have often made up their own food consumption group, and until puberty older children have often received individual portions of the starch, but shared the relish. Adolescent boys and girls have often used independent dishes, while the elderly and physically and mentally sick ate alone. However, this scenario was not true among the Aka pygmies or the Ngbaka of the CAR, where the whole family traditionally eats as a group unless the community is hunting in a camp, when the men eat separately. Among the forest groups, children experience a great deal of freedom and are allowed to hunt and trap small animals such as snails, tortoises, or birds and cook and eat them as a snack together away from adults.

The 1960s saw the rise of the concept of the "cultural superfood," the staple food, along with fish and meat, that people want to eat at almost every meal. It is the food that makes a person feel full or satiated, and if it is not eaten there is a sense of something missing. In central Africa, this food would most likely be a starch in the form of yam or plantain, or cassava, such as *bâton de manioc.* However, this desire for the routine superfood is balanced against another need, that for novelty and variation.

As modernization occurs in central (and western) Africa, especially in urban areas and among the educated elites, daily routines and patterns have shifted. This is especially noticeable in the use of Western notions of time and meals to divide the day into breakfast, lunch, and dinner meals, as well as using the concept of light and heavy meals. In addition, it includes patterns of nuclear families eating and sharing together, along with increased incorporation of Western prepared foods and cooking techniques into diets, although blended with central African realities such as large families and the need for large cooking pots and traditional cookfires alongside modern gas or electric stoves. In one example, this process has been documented, along with the interrelationship between food consumption and modernity, among Cameroonians living in the provincial town of Bamenda.

Representative Dishes of Central Africa

Fufu

Central Africans also have their versions of *fufu*. *Fufu* may be the Lingala name in the DRC, the CAR, or Cameroon, but this thick starchy porridge to accompany stews, soups, and sauces is also known as *bidia* in the Tshiluba language of Kasai regions of DRC or in the CAR.

Bidia (White Cornmeal Porridge) (Central Africa)

This stiff fufu of the DRC is also known as bidia and may be made from corn flour alone, or cassava (tapioca or manioc) flour alone, or a combination of the two. It is the central African version of the starch known variously in other parts of Africa by such names as ugali, sadza, pap, putu, or nshima.

4 cups water (or 2 cups water and 2 cups milk)
2 1/2 cups white corn flour (preferably a fine white corn flour such as Indian Head or Hodgson Mill (substitute yellow corn meal if white is unavalable.)

Bring 2 cups of water to a boil in a heavy saucepan. Mix 1 1/2 cups of the corn flour with 2 cups of cold water (or milk), using your fingers or a fork to work the liquid into the flour to make a lump-free paste. Turn the heat under the saucepan to medium and pour the paste into the boiling water, stirring constantly with a sturdy wooden spoon to keep lumps from forming, or mashing any lumps that do form against the side of the pan to break them up, about 10 minutes. Gradually add a third of the reserved cup of corn flour, stirring vigorously to blend all of the cornmeal into the mixture. Repeat twice more until all of the cornmeal is used. Stir several minutes more until the porridge forms a ball and pulls away from the side of the pan. Moisten a large bowl and dump the bidia into it, pushing it down with a wooden spoon to mould it. Alternatively, wet your hands and shape the bidia into a ball in the bowl by pressing it against the sides of the bowl. Let it sit, covered, for 10 minutes up to an hour before eating. It will get stiffer as it sits.

This recipe serves 6. Eat the bidia with a relish, sauce, or stew. To eat, turn the bidia onto a serving platter. (It may also be sliced into individual portions if desired.) To eat in the traditional manner, first wash hands, then tear off a small portion of the porridge with your right hand, and indent it with your thumb (this becomes the equivalent of an edible spoon), then scoop up the stew or sauce, and place the entire morsel into your mouth.

The central African version of *fufu* differs from its western Africa relative. Unlike the pounded yam or fresh plantain and cassava *fufus* of Ghana, these *fufus* are made from dried cassava flour (*fufu de manioc*), dried processed cassava (*fufu gari*, a more Anglophone dish than Francophone), or maize flour (*fufu de maize*). This *fufu* is reminiscent of the *nsima* of Malawi and Zambia, or the *ugali* of Kenya and Tanzania.

Steamed or Grilled in Leaf Packets

The steaming or grilling of foods wrapped in leaves is an important cooking technique, and one used in other parts of sub-Saharan Africa. For Africans, especially those living outside of the continent, there is a modern tendency to use aluminum foil in place of the leaves, but the flavor is significantly altered. An example of a dish in this category is *kwanga*, soaked cassava tubers wrapped in leaf packets and steamed. The words *maboké* (pl.) or (*liboké*, sing.) or *ajomba* or *jomba* refer to this process, as in a meat packet (*liboké de viande*) or fish (*liboké de poisson*). In these dishes, ingredients such as onion, tomato, sometimes okra, or crushed peanuts seasoned with lemon juice or hot chili pepper are added to make a sauce, and the closed package is grilled over hot coals or steamed.

A popular dish among the Mvae is made by mixing pounded, cooked cassava, crushed peanuts, palm oil, and fresh-water shrimps with salt and chili pepper, then wrapping small packets in *Marantaceae* leaves and braising them. This dish is prized at picnics and hunting parties and is called "the witchcraft drum," because it is so tasty that people quarrel over it.

The Bangwa, a Bamileke-speaking group from the mountains that divide the plateau grasslands and the forest lands in Cameroon, along with other groups such as the Douala, enjoy a steamed bean pudding similar to Ghana's *tubani* or Nigeria's *moimoi*, called *koki*, or *ekoki* or *gateau de hari-*

cots. It is made by grinding skinned beans or cowpeas like black-eyed peas and then adding salt, palm oil, chili pepper, and tender inner cocoyam leaves (with their higher sugar and protein content than the more mature leaves). The pudding is then wrapped in sturdy, outer cocoyam leaves and boiled or steamed until it is cooked and solid. This pudding, with variations, is especially popular for special occasions such as dances, funeral feasts, or men's or women's meetings.

Other Cameroonian favorites include *miondo* or *bobolo* (fresh cassava soaked, fermented, and ground, then shaped into long thin loaves that are wrapped in leaves and tied with a long string wrapped gracefully round and round them, then steamed or braised). One person would probably eat about three miondo for a meal, along with an accompanying sauce or stew. When the cassava is seasoned with salt, oil, and hot pepper before it is steamed it is known as *mintumba* and is eaten by itself as a snack.

Another popular dish is *ekwang* (or *ikwang*) made from grated cocoyam with a little salt, a dash of palm oil, and also wrapped in leaves and steamed.

Ground melon seeds may be made into *munkon* or *nkondo ngon*, literally a "maiden cake," probably originally served at a woman's engagement or marriage. The ground, seasoned melon seeds are mixed with little pieces of meat or fish. A banana leaf is softened over the fire, then rolled into a tube and one end is fastened with string. The mixture is poured into the open end, which is then also tied, and the entire packet is steamed.

A central African dish closely related to West African stews is called *moambé* and likely includes meat or poultry, palm oil, onion, tomato, okra, garlic or sorrel leaves, and chili pepper. If pounded or ground peanuts are included with chicken the stew might be called *moambé nsusu*.

Soups include *mbanga* soup (palmnut soup) or *ndolé* soup (bitterleaf soup).

Mbanga Soup (Palmnut Soup) (Central/Western Africa)

Many variations of palmnut soup exist throughout central and western Africa. In Ghana, the Akan call the soup *abe nkwan*, in Cameroon it is known as *mbanga* soup, and it's known as *banga* soup in Nigeria. For Westerners the fresh or dried palmnuts central to the dish are not available, so canned cream of palm fruit must be used (see resources section for where to find it). This version combines both meat and seafood.

2 large onions, finely chopped

2 lbs stewing beef (or bottom round or chuck roast) or lamb, cut into chunks

1–2 lbs soup bones if meat is boneless (optional)

1 28-oz can of pureed tomatoes (or blanch, peel, and puree fresh tomatoes)

1 large can palmnut cream concentrate (*sauce graine*) (29-oz or 800 g)

1 lb fresh mushrooms (portabella or any other type) (optional)

6 oz smoked fish (mackerel, whiting, etc.*)

1 lb fresh shrimp with shells

3 king crab legs (optional)

1 10-oz package frozen chopped okra (optional)

1 medium eggplant, peeled and cubed (3 cups) (optional)

1 fresh chili pepper to taste, chopped fine or ground, OR ground red pepper to taste**

1 clove garlic, crushed (optional)

2–3 large beef or shrimp bouillon cubes, such as Maggi® (optional)

2 Tbsp dried shrimp or prawns, ground into powder (optional)

salt to taste

*If using smoked herring, make sure it is soaked in several changes of hot water to remove excess salt before adding to soup.

**Always use extreme caution when handling fresh hot chili peppers. Avoid excessive touching of the peppers directly, never touch your eyes or face after chopping peppers, and remember that most of the heat in chili peppers is in the membranes on the inside. It is sometimes recommended that people wear rubber gloves when handling peppers, if possible.

Chop the onion. Remove excess fat or gristle from the meat, and cut it into chunks. Then add the meat to a large heavy pot with 1/2 cup water and the rinsed soup bones, if using. Chop or grind the fresh pepper, and sprinkle it or the dried pepper over the meat. Crush the garlic and add to the pot. Crumble the bouillon cubes and add. Stir all with a wooden spoon, cover, and put the pot onto the fire over a medium-high heat to steam for about 15 minutes (or longer if the meat is tough). If using eggplant, peel and cube it, and put it into a small saucepan with about 2 cups of water. Bring the water to a boil, lower the heat to simmer, and cook, covered, around 10 minutes or until the cubes are soft. Remove the eggplant and puree in a blender, if available. Set aside. Open the can of tomato puree and add to the meat in the soup pot. Open the can of cream of palm fruits and pour or scoop it into the pot. Add 1 1/2 to 2 cans full of water to the soup (or about 4 to 6 cups, depending on how thick a soup is desired). Allow the soup to simmer while preparing the vegetables and fish. Clean the mushrooms (if using) by rinsing them, patting them dry with a paper towel, and trimming the ends of the stems. If they are small, add whole to the soup. If they are large, cut into halves, quarters, or slices. Rinse the smoked fish, remove and discard the bones and skin, and add the fish to the soup. Rinse and devein, but do not peel, the shrimp, and rinse the crab legs and add to the soup. Add the pureed eggplant, powdered dried shrimp, and frozen okra to the soup, and stir well. Cover and allow to cook for about 20 minutes for the flavors to blend and the okra to cook. As the palm oil rises to the top, skim it off with a spoon and save to use in cooking stews. Just before serving adjust the salt and red pepper to taste.

Variations: The soup may be simmered longer to thicken it, or less water added. Fresh or frozen greens such as kale or spinach may be cut or ground and added to it also. A very rich version includes both palmnut cream and peanut paste. The meat may be omitted and replaced with fresh fish (the fresh fish is not steamed first, and the cooking time is decreased).

Serve with a thick porridge such as *fufu*, or rice, rice balls, or boiled African yam slices.

Beer can be made from corn, millet, plantains, bananas, and sorghum. In the urban areas, tea and coffee have become popular beverages. Similarly, in urbanized areas, snacks are popular, purchased from roadside vendors strategically located on roads and transportation centers such as taxi and bus stations. These snacks range from hot *beignets* (similar to doughnuts, but unsweetened and perhaps made from corn flour) to fried plantain, from grilled meat kabobs (*brochettes*), grilled corn, or roasted peanuts to soft drinks, fresh sugar cane, or seasonal fruits. Porridges tend to be thinned with water for breakfasts, as well as for weaning infants and feeding convalescents.

Other dishes include *sakasaka, pondu* (cassava leaves, onion, and dried fish), and *saka-medesu* (cassava leaves and beans).

Cameroon's coast is famous for its seafood. After observing prawns in the River Wouri, the early Portuguese explorers proceeded to name the river, and then the entire country, after them. Grilled, carefully seasoned fish (*poisson braise*) is another specialty of the coast, and no feast or party is likely to be without examples of most of these dishes, from *ndolé*, to *koki*, to grilled fish. The fish are seasoned with the ubiquitous ginger, garlic, onion, and peppers, but also with special seasonings such as *mbongo tchobi*, from the bark of a tree, or the wood *ibind* used to make blackened fish, or a seed such as *pebi*.

EATING OUT

As in most of sub-Saharan Africa, the concept of eating out in central Africa differs from Western conceptions of restaurant special occasion meals.

Eating snacks from roadside vendors is one type of eating out. One consequence of the shift to a cash economy is that women need to find opportunities to earn money. Also, as men who used to hunt are less able to provide the traditional meat to their wives, women must purchase foods for their families. Thus, as mentioned, married women among the Bangangte who used to only cook inside their homes for their husbands and families, now prepare and sell food on roadsides and in the markets. It is literally called "cooking on the road." Popular street food in the cities includes spicy *brochettes* sometimes eaten on a skewer and sometimes in bread rolls with salad and dressing.

As in other parts of sub-Saharan Africa, people are sociable and, in the case of numerous forest peoples, have tended to congregate together regularly in one another's homes to drink palm wine and socialize. Western restaurant traditions are not a part of the cultural heritage of much of the region, although with urbanization and modernization, restaurants are found in cities that feature the cuisines of former colonial powers, although they cater to central African elites and expatriates. These restaurants tend to feature French or other European dishes. As in western or southern Africa, it is now common to find central African regional dishes taking their place proudly next to continental dishes. One reason may be that on the rare occasions that persons go out to eat, they wish to taste something exotic, like Western foods. It may also be the fascination and elevation of European things as somehow superior to things African, and it may be the cultural preference to honor guests with special, expensive foods related to the prestige factor intertwined with food as conspicuous consumption.

Outdoor restaurant in Libreville. Courtesy of Doug Himes.

Central African hotel restaurant. Courtesy of Doug
Himes.

Guest houses and hotels often have restaurants in or near the premises
to provide sit-down meals for travelers, and these restaurants likely include both local and foreign dishes on the menu.

SPECIAL OCCASIONS

Special occasions include holidays such as New Year's Day and Christmas, as well as births, christenings, weddings, engagements, funerals,
the end of mourning, initiation ceremonies for young people such as the
nkanda (or *mukanda*), and the end of the school year. In the past, there
were also special rituals involving food among men's and women's societies, such as the *indende* ceremony that is still observed among the Yassa.

An abundance of food is the rule at such gatherings. Traditionally this
might include palm wine (*vine de palme*) and, for example, cassava sticks
(*bâtons de manioc*), fish, and/or meat. Today people are likely to include
commercially produced beer, red wine, and spirits (hard liquor). Side-by-
side with local everyday foods, special occasions make demands on hosts
to provide prestige foods. For example, the ability to provide guests alcoholic drinks is viewed as a sign of economic affluence and masculinity,
and the more expensive the alcohol, the better. This preference places a
special hardship on the poor.

Hosts do not want to appear cheap so they will make every effort to
provide their guests with thick sauces or stews and succulent meats to
sustain or establish their socioeconomic status and meet expectations.
Certain imported foods are considered status foods. Along with red wine

and other commercial alcoholic beverages, these include rice, pasta, and tinned foods. Meat, and especially domestic animals, which are expensive, is highly prized. It is considered a sign of respect to offer guests rice even though it is not considered to provide the same feeling of satiation as cassava.

Besides ensuring one's status, there is also a desire to show respect to others, such as one's in-laws or an honored guest. Thus, the Mave, who are not fishermen, might offer fish or plantains, another special occasion food, to distinguished guests or in-laws.

Among many forest peoples, when a woman is engaged, or just after she marries, her relatives will come daily to scrutinize and discuss the quality of her fiancé or husband's palm wine: is it too sweet, bitter, or sour?

Two illustrative examples of festive occasions come from the Yassa of southern Cameroon: the engagement and *indende* ceremonies.[6]

A prospective bridegroom must make important offerings of food and drinks to his future in-laws, a process with three basic steps. First is the "knocking at the door," when he brings palmwine or red wine to the girl's father. Second, the "publishing of the banns," when both the paternal and maternal families of the future groom must give the fiancée's family two cartons of cigarettes, two wads of tobacco, and two bottles of whisky. In return, the woman's family prepares a banquet during which the brideprice is negotiated. Finally, "the bringing in" occurs, when the bride's mother receives gifts of prized foods such as drinks and meat to share among her family, plus other presents and money. The two families then feast together, after which the bride becomes an apprentice in her new family under the careful supervision of her mother-in-law. The main course of a wedding meal would probably include choice game, such as a roasted, smoked forest porcupine.

After his marriage, traditionally, the new son-in-law and mother-in-law must maintain a formal distance, neither eating in front of each other nor together. The bride could become intimate with her new mother-in-law, but not around food.

Among some of the forest hunter-gatherers, honey has served as an engagement gift from a man whereby he declares his love to his chosen bride. He would also give honey as a dowry to his perspective in-laws.

A representative special occasion dish among many central Africans is made from the *ndolé* leaves, with each group having its preferred variation. Ask a Cameroonian, for instance, to describe a special Sunday dish for a Douala family, and one will likely hear about one or more variations of making *ndolé*. The process for cooking the leaves invariably involves first washing them and removing the tough center stems, then boiling the leaves in water with *sel gemme* for a long time until they are soft. Next they are pressed in a sieve by one person as another repeatedly pours cold water over them and squeezes out the excess water. After they are cooked, other ingredients are added, such as beef, onions, tomatoes, peppers, and dried crayfish *(manjanga)*. Gourmet cooks know when the correct degree of bitterness is reached, as well as how to season the leaves. For example, they might briefly blanch some peanuts and grind them, making sure there are not too few or too many peanuts for the amount of ndolé leaves. The final dish may be lightly garnished with fresh, gently sautéed shrimp and a drizzle of heated oil.

In the *indende* ceremony, women spend a week gathering offerings of food and other special items, although if there are food shortages they may ask the men to help them. These include a crate of beer and a crate of carbonated drinks and two cooking pots each of rice, sugar, doughnuts, sweets, and cigarettes. Traditionally the ceremony included a ritual red soup-like concoction made of plantains, a dead fish from the beach, peanuts, cucumber seeds, palm oil, special greases, and the grated bark of the Paduk tree *(Pterocarpus soyauxii)*. The women paddled a dugout canoe to a sacred place and dropped the mixture into the water while singing to placate angry spirits and persuade them to restore abundance.

Two kinds of ripe banana juice enjoyed in Rwanda are known as *umutobe* or *urwangwa*. *Uurwangwa* is especially drunk by men during important discussions, or during ceremonies.

DIET AND HEALTH

This section addresses several questions: How well does the diet meet nutritional requirements, including geographic and seasonal variations? What is the role of "sweet" and "bitter" tastes? How does the principle of "sympathetic magic" influence food taboos and prescriptions? How do ideas about sorcery and witchcraft affect beliefs regarding the relationship of food to health and healing? How is the diet changing?

Nutritional Status and Illness

Much of central Africans' basic diet is high in carbohydrates, and PEM is an issue, with the potential for going from mild to severe when food is scarce. Still, the nutritional problems stem less from the diet than from other causes.

Health problems have been more likely to occur in the forest regions from infectious diseases facilitated by the growth of bacteria in the moist, humid, equatorial environment. This reality leads to epidemics of diseases such as measles, bronchitis, malaria, and diarrhea. Internal parasites aggravate the situation, leading to malnutrition and less healthy immune response systems. Insects transmit many diseases such as malaria, filariosis, and sleeping sickness. Other infectious diseases in the region include hepatitis B, which can lead to cirrhosis or liver cancer.

The roots and leaves of cassava contain cyanogenic glucosides, mainly linamarin, which can transform into hydocyanic acid. This acid can use up iodine stores and lead to goiter. Soils in countries such as the DRC also lack iodine, and thus, the plants do as well, adding to the prevalence of goiter especially among young women.

Anemia is another issue in the region. This can be from dietary deficiencies of iron or folic acid made worse by the environment. Poor sanitary conditions can lead to fecal contamination of the water, leading to intestinal parasites such as tapeworm, oral infections, or direct transmission through the skin, such as with hookworm or eelworm.

Although it appears not yet to have reached the rate in eastern or southern Africa, the spread of AIDS continues to pose problems to the health and well-being of central Africans.

Vision problems from vitamin A deficiency are rare in the humid tropical areas where there is no lack of vitamin A and beta-carotene, such as is found in palm oil. This contrasts to drier savannah areas. Seasonality of food availability is also less obvious in the tropical rain forest areas, although farmers use more energy when clearing fields, which may result in having a lower nutritional status at those times. Also, some forest foods, such as the oil palm fruit, caterpillars, game, fish, and honey, are subject to seasonal variation. Traditionally, however, forest peoples have an overall balanced diet.

Bitter and Sweet Tastes

People everywhere have definite ideas about what foods are good, in the sense of both tasty and healthy to eat, and those that are not.

Sweet and bitter tastes are two basic tastes that are important in central African cuisine. There is a careful attention to just the right degree of bitterness, whether it is in stews or relishes prepared from leaves, or in palm wine. The bitter taste in plants mainly comes from alkaloids, which are usually poisonous. As has been shown, bitter cassava, and some leaves, need to be carefully soaked or processed in several batches of water before cooking and eating, and perhaps this has contributed to a careful discrimination among bitter tastes. However, it should also be noted that many of the bitter tastes associated with toxicity are less of a problem within the forest than outside of it. For example, the wild yams that grow in the forest are not toxic, whereas those outside the forest are.

The diet has traditionally only included sweet tastes from fruits and berries eaten as snacks, rather than adding sugar to main dishes. Honey, eaten directly, has been a highly prized food, especially among the forest peoples. Men climb trees to gather it at the end of the dry season. It is highly valued and eaten without accompaniment, as a meal in itself. In contemporary urbanized central Africa, a taste for sweet foods, from ice cream to sweetened beverages such as soda or coffee, has developed.

Certain chemicals found in plants in central Africa are very sweet, such as Gabon's *brazzeire*, a protein said to be 500 times sweeter than sugar. Research in the central African equatorial rain forest has shown that children among the forest hunter-gatherers are very fond of the red fruit of a creeping plant (*liane*) (*Dioscoreophyllum cumminsii*). The white tuber from this same plant is edible raw or after cooking. The berries contain a tiny amount of a protein biochemists call monellin that, like *thaumatin*, mimics the taste of sugar.

Research among people in Cameroon living in the rain forest, compared with groups living outside it, shows that while all groups are highly sensitive to bitter tastes, those in the forests had far less sensitivity to sweet tastes. Some nutritionists believe that since many fruits and plants in the forest contain sugar, it has not been necessary for forest hunter-gatherers to develop the ability to discriminate among sweet tastes the same way it has been for bitter foods.

Sympathetic Magic, Food Taboos, and Prescriptions

Intrinsic to understanding people's ideas of healthy foods in central Africa is the principle of "sympathetic magic," whereby people take on the characteristics of the appearance or traits of the food itself. This is especially true of taboo and prescribed foods. Although these prohibitions and prescriptions are gradually dying out, some of them are still respected or at least remembered.

The preference for red wine, for example, is still strong. It is said to be appreciated not only because of its intoxicating quality, but because it gives a person blood and heats one up in the evenings.

Of course, some foods are prohibited for other reasons, such as someone having had a bad experience with it and deciding no one in the family will eat it again, or because it is a family totem, for religious reasons (people in the Christian Kimbanguist Church do not eat pork or monkey, or drink alcohol), or for good health reasons (such as, perhaps, pregnant women not eating salty or sugary foods). Another food, such as the breadfruit tree, might have negative associations as it does among the Yassa and Mvae, where it is considered fit to be only a famine food and a symbol of laziness and agricultural inefficiency.

The list of food taboos and prescriptions has traditionally been especially strong for pregnant women or new mothers, ranging from not eating the meat of a fish cut in half to bush meat found in the forest, or a pregnant animal. The reasoning behind the partially eaten game was that the bad influences outside the security of the village would mean that the baby would be born incomplete. While hunters especially enjoy wild game such as the tree pangolin or scaly anteater (*Manis tricuspis*) and the African palm civet (*Nandinia binotata*), pregnant women were forbidden to eat them because the anteater curls up, a position assumed harmful to giving birth. The civet has spotted skin, which it was thought would leave marks on the baby. Pregnant Mvae women were forbidden to eat meat from the three-fingered tree hyrax, a nocturnal animal that hides in a hollow tree during the day. People feared that their children would have only three fingers and an unsuccessful life. Similarly, eating elephant meat might give a child a wide mouth and a long nose.

On the other hand, women were encouraged to eat potto meat (*Perodicticus potto*) because the small animal has great grasping strength. Soon after childbirth, a Mvae mother might be given python meat or meat from a chimpanzee to strengthen her back to become like that of the powerful snake or to gain the sturdiness of the chimpanzee. Similarly, for the same reason, one of the python's (or the chimpanzee's) vertebrae was tied to the baby's waist.

According to custom, women in the Odzala region of the Congo Republic were afraid to eat gorilla meat in case it made their husbands as brutal as gorillas. Similarly, for example, virile young men in parts of Cameroon might be discouraged from eating food whose appearance suggested impotency, such as bushpig's tail, or *bâton de manioc* wrapped in the leaf of a Marantaceae with a soft petiole, or the old-looking, wrinkled flesh of the land tortoise that has a tail unable to stand erect.

In many tropical forest communities, traditionally only the elders and otherwise strong could eat meat of dangerous animals. For example, only Mvae elders were supposed to eat buffalo and elephant meat, and among the Yassa, respected elders were the only ones powerful enough to eat the meat of the Gabon viper (*Bitis gabonica*).

Sorcery

The rational Western approach to medicine and accidents, from germ theory to mental illness, has not traditionally held much credibility in central Africa. In a frequently hostile environment, people live with a close awareness of the spirit world and feel a continuity with their ancestors, as well as having strong values concerning communality and interconnectedness. One's ties to others, living as well as dead, influence perceptions of events and illnesses. Their etiology of disease often uses food metaphorically as a symbolic devouring of the victim by the sorcerer. For example, among one group in central Africa, a substance in the sorcerer's stomach (*evu*) enables the people to carry out evil deeds. The *evu* leaves his body at night to eat the victim. The Western idea of cause and effect is not accepted: an arm or leg is not broken by natural causes from the natural world; it is devoured in the supernatural world.

Similarly, if a child becomes sick, the cause may be divined to be one of the parents breaking a food avoidance rule, with the child needing to be treated according to the prescribed remedy.

Among the Banganté, sharing food has been historically viewed as fostering fertility and a sense of solidarity and harmony within the family. In contrast, traditionally there is another kind of eating that is evil and destructive. It revolves around the witchcraft of vampires (*ndum*) and evil witches' rotating credit societies. This bad kind of eating is called *fed*, the same word that their language uses to describe roasted snack foods, the way animals eat, and the way witches eat, and it is symbolized in sculptures featuring prominent, sharply filed teeth. In contrast to the communal, tranquil family meals, this kind of eating tears people apart. When witches engage in *fed*, the goat they rip apart with their pointy teeth is believed to be a sacrificed relative or another woman's fetus.

However, sharply filed teeth alone do not have a negative image in much of central Africa. In fact, for some pygmy groups, at the age of 13 or 14, as a rite of passage, adolescent boys file the enamel of their incisors to a sharp point to please and impress the girls.

Food is an important therapeutic part of treatment for illness. For example, in some rain forest groups it is used to treat spirit possession caused by *mindi* (spirits of the water or ancestors). Traditionally, a special medicine made of medicinal leaves and fruits is administered to all the participants: patients, drummers, and the public. A special drink from honey, egg, and pieces of *costus* stalk is made as an offering to calm and soothe the *mindi*, and the healer (*nganga*) drinks it.

Palm wine is an important component of all social events among many of the forest peoples, including healing. The communal consumption of the palm wine serves as a visible sign of solidarity between the patient and all the members of the social environment, once again demonstrating commensality within all elements of the community.

Another therapeutic dish in southern Cameroon that is used among the Yassa as a part of exorcisms of possessed patients, for victims of witchcraft, or those who have transgressed against prohibitions, is *mosuka*, made from meat or eggs, plantains, marrow seeds *(cucumeropsis manii)*, palm oil, and special medicinal plants.

NOTES

1. Sophie Ekoué, *Cuisine et Traditions: Recettes D'Afrique* (Paris: Cauris Editions, 2003), p. 80. This proverb introduces Ekoué's section on pygmy cooking. My interpretation is that the hunter-gatherers in central Africa would (at least in the past before deforestation) say that food is everywhere for the taking, so if you are hungry, all you need to do is reach out your hand and take it.

2. This *free* state did not mean *freedom*. Rather, it meant no longer tied to the Kongo (or Congo) Kingdom that ruled from the fifteenth to the seventeenth centuries.

3. Jennifer Holland Steinberg, Geographica: "Big Frog-Really Big," *National Geographic*, 203, no. 6.

4. Bryna M. Freyer, Curator, Smithsonian Institution, personal communication on Central African Woyo pot lids, July 2004.

5. Igor de Garine, "Organization of meals, food preferences and socio-economic aspects," in *Food and Nutrition in the African Rain Forest*, ed. C.M. Hladik, S. Bahuchet, and I. de Garine (Paris: Unesco/MAB, 1990), pp. 81–82.

Glossary

akara Yoruba name for West African cowpea fritter. Known as *akara,* *ackla, accra,* or *kose* in Ghana. Called *akkra* in Jamaica and *acaraje* in Brazil.

alicha (alecha) Ethiopian or Eritrean stew that is less spicy than a regular *wat.*

amarhewu Thin South African porridge made from slightly fermented cornmeal.

amasi Curdled milk (Xhosa).

Bantu Sub-branch of Niger-Kordofanian language family. Includes Zulu, Xhosa, and Swahili. *Ntu* means "a person" and refers to the language rather than an ethnic group.

baobab Ancient tree found growing throughout the savannas of sub-Saharan Africa, with massive trunk and distinctive branches, and serving multiple culinary, social, and environmental purposes.

bâton de manioc Cassava stick, a staple food in Cameroon, made from **cassava,** soaked and pounded, then steamed in banana leaves.

berberé Amharic name for a distinctive, hot, spicy seasoning of Ethiopia and Eritrea.

bidia Also called *fufu,* a staple accompaniment for a relish, sauce, or stew, in the Democratic Republic of the Congo in central Africa, made from either white corn flour or **cassava** flour, or a combination. Similar to *ugali, sadza, pap,* or *nsima* from eastern and southern Africa.

biltong Dried meat popular throughout southern Africa, made commonly from venison and often using coriander seeds.

bissap Beverage in western Africa, especially Senegal (also *jus de bissap or bissap rouge*) made from dried red hibiscus flowers, called *sorrel* or *roselle*, steeped in water, and sweetened and flavored.

bobotie Traditional South African ground meat loaf.

boerwors Afrikaans sausage now popular throughout South Africa.

bogobe See *pap*.

braii Southern African verb meaning "to grill," also used as a noun to refer to a grill or a barbeque get together.

bredie South African stew, often made with lamb.

cassava (manioc or yucca) Tropical root crop originating in the Americas and now a staple food in sub-Saharan Africa where both its leaves and tuber are eaten.

chai Indian-style tea flavored with spices, milk, and sugar drunk in eastern Africa.

chakalaka Ndebele salad of cabbage, onion, tomatoes, and carrots flavored with chili and curry powder and often eaten with porridge.

chibhako Shona word for a flat smoothing spoon used to shape and smooth the surface of *sadza*.

chiemo Word used in Uganda use to describe staple foods like millet.

chop bar Informal, semi-enclosed restaurant in western Africa. "Chop" is the pidgin English word for "to eat."

chungu Traditional Kenyan clay cooking pot.

cocoyam (taro) Root plant introduced into Africa from the Americas whose roots and leaves are eaten. There are four different roots called taro. The one commonly found in Africa is Xanthosoma taro.

cola (kola) West African seed kernels from a tree in the cocoa family containing stimulants like caffeine that are chewed and are important in social and ceremonial life in much of West Africa, especially in Muslim areas.

cowpea Type of legume that includes black-eyed peas.

diiw ñoor Wolof name for the ghee (clarified butter) known as *nebam sirme*.

egusi Type of melon seed native to Africa, used in West African cooking.

Eid-ul-fitr Called Lebaran by Cape Malay Moslems, the day after the end of Ramadan, the feast of the end of fasting.

eland Two types of African antelopes.

ensete Plant indigenous to eastern Africa called the "false banana" plant because it has no edible fruit but whose stem and leaf midribs can be used to make a kind of bread or porridge.

feuilles de manioc **Cassava** leaves.

fonio Hardy, tasty, nutritious West African cereal grain that is difficult and time-consuming to dehull.

fufu Name in many parts of western and central Africa for a stiff porridge made by cooking and pounding a variety of starches from root crops, or from cooking grains that have been made into flour.

gari (farine de manioc) Coarse flour made from dried grated fermented **cassava.**

githeri See *irio.*

griot West African storyteller/singer, usually male, who keeps alive the traditions and history of the people through oral performance.

halaal Food that is lawful to eat according to Islamic dietary laws.

harmattan During the winter, dry, dusty winds blow from the Sahara Desert toward the western coast of Africa. This wind is known as harmattan and the season as harmattan season.

Hhɔmɔwɔ festival Thanksgiving festival of the coastal Ga people of Ghana that "hoots at hunger."

impala Large brown African antelope, with the male having slender lyre-shaped horns.

Incwala **ceremony** Festival in Swaziland where the king grants the people permission to begin eating the new crops.

Indende **ceremony** Women's ceremony among the Yassa of southern Cameroon to ask the spirits to restore abundance, in which a ritual soup is carried in a canoe to a sacred place and deposited in the water as an offering.

injera (enjera) Distinctive fermented bread of Ethiopia, Eritrea, and Somalia generally made of teff and cooked into a kind of crepe. Stews and relishes are ladled on top of *injera* (called *canjeero* in Somalia), and additional *injera* are served folded or rolled alongside.

irio Gikuyu word for "food" and the generic name for a staple dish in Kenya such as *githeri,* made from fresh or dried beans, corn, and potatoes seasoned with onions, garlic, coriander leaves, salt, and ghee.

jiko Swahili name for a charcoal brazier.

jollof rice One-pot rice dish whose name is derived from the Wolof ethnic group, but that is eaten throughout West Africa where rice is available.

jomba (ajomba) Central African name for foods such as meats, poultry, or fish wrapped in leaf packets with other ingredients to make a sauce and steamed or roasted over a fire. Also called *maboke* (plural) or *libkoe* (singular) in the Congo River area.

kanwa Name in Cameroon for mineral salt, or *sel gemme.*

khat (kat or qat) Also known as "Abyssinian tea" or *miraa,* a narcotic found in the bark from fresh young shoots of a tree (*Catha edulis Forssk, Celastraceae*). Peeled off and most commonly chewed, it is a stimulant allowed under Islamic law and an important component of socializing throughout East Africa similar to that of cola in West Africa. *Khat* staves off hunger and fatigue and is said to act as an aphrodisiac.

kifumbu Traditional Kenyan strainer for coconut milk made from woven palm leaves.

koki (ekoki) Steamed bean pudding in Cameroon made from skinned cowpeas, salt, palm oil, chili pepper, and cocoyam leaves. Similar to Ghana's *tubani* or Nigeria's *moimoi.* Also called *gateau de haricots.*

kraal Southern African word to describe an enclosed area (corral) in which cattle are kept, or a collection of huts forming a community, usually surrounded by a wooden fence.

kudu African antelope.

kwashiorkor Severe malnutrition in infants and children resulting from a diet high in carbohydrate and low in protein.

maas (also *amasi/inkomasi*) Thick, naturally curdled milk eaten in southern Africa.

mafé West African dish of meat or poultry in a creamy peanut and tomato sauce, particularly from Senegal.

maghew South African beer.

mandazi (maandazi, mahamri, mamri) Fried, slightly sweet bread similar to a doughnut. Popular in Kenya and Tanzania, *mandazi* is eaten for breakfast with tea or coffee, as a snack, or with the main course for a lunch or dinner meal.

masala Mixture of spices with Indian origins used in Cape Malay and other southern African cooking.

matoke Popular type of cooking banana in Uganda that is green when ripe. *Matoke* is also the name for a popular dish in which the banana is mashed, for example with meat (*matoke n'yama*) or with fish (*matoke ngege*).

mbanga soup Palmnut soup in western and central Africa.

mbuzi Coconut grater used in Kenya.

mealie (mielie) Maize, or corn.

melegueta pepper Small African seed once a substitute for black peppercorns and used for seasoning food and as a medicine in Africa, in Europe during the 1400s, and to treat and prevent slave illnesses during the Middle Passage.

mesob Covered circular basket table in Ethiopia woven from grasses.

moambé Central African stew.

mopane worms Worms that drop from *mopane* trees in southern Africa, considered a delicacy.

morogo In southern Africa, the name for green leaves, often wild, as well as the sauce or stew made from them.

mugoti Shona name for a sturdy wooden stick used to stir **sadza** while it cooks.

mugwaku Shona name for a serving ladle for **sadza.**

musika Shona word for a wooden whisk used in making thin porridge.

mwiko Strong wooden paddle in Kenya used for stirring **ugali** or stew, with a flat blade.

ndolé Name in central Africa for a type of bitter green leaves, and also the name of a stew made using them.

nebam sirme Pulaar name for a West African form of ghee made from fresh milk.

Nkanda (Mukanda) ceremony Initiation ceremony for young people in central Africa.

nsima (nshima) See *pap.*

nyama choma Swahili words for meat roasted over an open fire.

ɔtɔ ceremonial dish made from hard-boiled eggs, mashed African yam, and palm oil in Ghana.

palmwine Beverage made from the sap of the oil palm tree in western and central Africa.

pap Dutch word used in South Africa to refer to porridge made from corn-meal or another staple grain. A crumbly version is called *putu* or *phutu* (in Zulu), or *umphokoqo* (Xhosa). In Zambia porridge is called *nhsima;* in Malawi, *nsima;* in Botswana, *bogobe;* and in Mozambique, xima.

peril peril Originally the name of the very hot birdseye (or birds' eye) chili pepper. *Peri peri* now refers to a spicy African condiment or marinade made with this or other chili peppers, especially for grilled chicken or prawns.

phutu See *pap.*

plantain Large relative of the banana, with a higher starch content, that must be cooked and can be eaten green, yellow, or black and yellow.

potjiekos Distinctive cast iron pots with three legs used in southern Africa to slowly cook stews over a fire.

pungwe Zimbabwe's equivalent to South Africa's **shabeen.**

putu See *pap.*

quanta Name in Ethiopia for long strips of meat coated with a spicy powdered chili pepper mix and dried.

rooibos Shrub grown in South Africa whose leaves are dried and used in cooking, especially brewed to make a red herbal tea high in vitamin C.

roti Flat, round bread originally from India, often eaten with curries in southern and eastern Africa.

sadza (soda) In Zimbabwe, the name for a porridge or dumpling commonly cooked from a flour from white field corn or a red millet flour and accompanied with a sauce, stew, or soup.

Sahel Semidesert border of the southern edge of the Sahara desert that travels from Mauritania to Chad in the west. Some definitions include countries through the Horn of Africa to Somalia in the east.

Samosa (vamoose) Deep-fried meat or vegetable-stuffed triangular pastry with Indian origins, eaten in southern and eastern Africa.

samp In southern Africa, dried corn that has been coarsely broken.

Saum Abstaining from food, drink, and sexual intercourse, such as the daylight fasting that takes place during Ramadan. Saum is one of the five pillars of Islam.

shambakodzi Traditional clay pot with thick sides used in Zimbabwe to cook **sadza.**

shebeen Traditionally, rough "men only" informal drinking bars patronized by black South Africans.

sorghum Ancient African cereal grain that is now the fourth most valuable cereal crop globally.

sossatie Marinated meat kebab grilled on skewers, popular in South Africa.

Suhur Pre-dawn meal, the food eaten between midnight and near dawn during Ramadan.

sukumawiki (sukuma wiki) Type of green used in Kenya to make stews, and also the name of the stew. In Swahili the word means "push the week."

taampha Symbols representing proverbs giving marriage advice carved on wooden pot lids among the Woyo of the Democratic Republic of the Congo.

teff (tef) Millet grown in Ethiopia and Eritrea, especially used for making **injera.**

tej Ethiopian mead made from fermented honey.

thiebou dienne (dien) **or** *cCeebu jën.* Classic Senegalese marinated fish and rice recipe.

ugali Swahili name for a stiff porridge often made from cornmeal, eaten in East Africa with other foods. Millet, sorghum, and **cassava** flour are also used. Other names for this staple include *posho* (Uganda), *atapa*, or *atap*.

umcweba (umcwayiba) Swazi word for **biltong.**

umngqusho Xhosa name for **samp** and beans.

umphokoqo Xhosa name for a crumbly version of **pap.**

upshwa Cassava version of **pap** from Mozambique.

wat (or watt or we't) Name for a spicy stew in parts of eastern Africa, especially Ethiopia and Eritrea.

xima Corn **pap** in Mozambique.

yassa Senegalese marinade/sauce emphasizing onion, mustard, and lemon and commonly featuring chicken (*poulet yassa*) or fish (*poisson yassa*).

Resource Guide

WEB SITES

Excellent links, recipes, and cultural/historical/literary information, plus a discussion board, *The Congo Cookbook*, http://www.geocities.com/congocookbook/.

Information about food from sub-Saharan Africa's most populous country, http://www.motherlandnigeria.com/food.html.

Links, a discussion board, and general information about the food culture of Africa, http://www.betumi.com.

Peace Corps World Wise Schools site. Provides resources for schools and teachers. http://www.peacecorps.gov/wws/guides/pc/index.html.

Source for African proverbs and their explanations, http://www.afriprov.org/index.htm.

Useful links for locating African film resources, http://www.columbia.edu/cu/lweb/indiv/africa/cuvl/video.html.

FILMS

An excellent and powerful film introduction to the African continent and its people and cultures is the Africa series shown on public television in 2001 available on CD (or videos) and produced by National Geographic. The eight segments include: "Savanna Homecoming," "Desert Odyssey," "Voices of the Forest," "Mountains of Faith," "Love in the Sahel," "Restless Waters," "Leopards of Zanzibar," and "Southern Treasures."

Another good resource, with an emphasis on the rich history of black Africa, is the 1999 PBS "Wonders of the African World" film series in which Harvard University's Henry Louis Gates, Jr. travels to "The Black Kingdoms of the Nile," "The Swahili Coast," "The Slave Kingdoms," and "The Holy Land."

Senegalese Ousmane Sembene, labeled the father of sub-Saharan African film, often explores daily life in his films, such as the 1992 *Guelwaar*, a satire of food aid and Moslem-Christian relations.

Bitter Melons is a 1966 30-minute videotape by John Marshall that shows the daily life of a small band of Gwi San of the Kalahari in Botswana.

Baobab: Portrait of a Tree is a 1983 30-minute color film by Benchmark Films that provides a close-up look at the intricate ecosystem of the ancient, massive African baobab and the life cycles of the birds, insects, and mammals intertwined with it. Inc (BENM).

In Danku the Soup is Sweeter is a 1993 color documentary filmed in northern Ghana, West Africa, showing a project by the Canadian International Development Agency in which two rural women were able to develop a small-scale business selling butter and soup door-to-door. Distributed by Filmakers Library.

LITERATURE

Achebe, Chinua. *Things Fall Apart*. London: Heinemann, 1978. A good introduction to Yoruba community life in traditional Nigerian society, with information about foods, culture, and festivals.

Dangarembga, Tsitsi. *Nervous Conditions*. New York: Seal Press, 2001. The story of a young girl's coming of age in Rhodesia (now Zimbabwe) in the 1960s. Food plays a central role in the story.

Kingsolver, Barbara. *The Poisonwood Bible*. New York: HarperCollins, 1998. Story of a white American missionary family in the Belgian Congo (now the Democratic Republic of the Congo) during the latter half of the twentieth century during a time of political and social upheaval.

Smith, Alexander McCall. *The No. 1 Ladies Detective Agency*. New York: Knopf Pub. Gp., 2003. The first book in the popular series about Mma Ramotswe and her detective agency in Botswana provides a very accessible introduction to contemporary food and culture in southern Africa.

van der Post, Laurens. *First Catch Your Eland*. New York: Morrow, 1978. Personal and passionate reminiscences on sub-Saharan African food and culture by a South African travel and culinary writer. An expansion of the material presented in his 1970 *African Cooking*.

RECOMMENDED COOKBOOKS

Hafner, Dorinda. *A Taste of Africa*. Berkeley, Calif.: Ten Speed Press, 1993.

Harris, Jessica. *The Africa Cookbook: Tastes of a Continent*. New York: Simon and Schuster, 1998.

Hultman, Tami, ed. *Africa News Cookbook: African Cooking for Western Kitchens*. New York: Penguin Books, 1986.

Inquai, Tebereh. *A Taste of Africa: The African Cookbook*. Trenton, N.J.: Africa World Press, 1998.

Jackson, Elizabeth A. *South of the Sahara*. Hollis, N.H.: Fantail, 1999.

Longacre, Doris Janzen. *More-with-Less Cookbook*. Scottdale, Pa.: Herald Press, 1976. Contains a number of authentic, easy to prepare African recipes adapted for Western kitchens.

Nabwire, Constance, and Bertha Vining Montgomery. *Cooking the African Way*. Minneapolis, Minn.: Lerner, 1988.

Olaore, Ola. *Traditional African Cooking*. London: Foulsham, 1990. Re-release of the 1980 book *The Best Kept Secrets of West and East African Cooking*.

Osseo-Asare, Fran. *A Good Soup Attracts Chairs: A First African Cookbook for American Kids*. Gretna: Pelican Publishing Company, 1993. Good introduction to African cooking for adults as well as young people. The original 1993 hardback version of the cookbook provides color illustrations. The black and white paperback edition is not recommended.

Rozin, Elisabeth. *Crossroads Cooking: The Meeting and Mating of Ethnic Cuisines—from Burma to Texas in 200 Recipes*. New York: Viking Penguin, 1999.

Schlabach, Joetta Handrich. *Extending the Table ... A World Community Cookbook*. Scottdale: Herald Press, 1991. A Mennonite cookbook with a number of recommended, authentic, easy-to-prepare African recipes.

van der Post, Laurens, and the editors of Time-Life Books. *African Cooking*. New York: Time-Life Books, 1970. This classic on the entire continent is somewhat dated and covers the cuisines unevenly, focusing heavily on white-dominated colonial heritages of Portuguese-speaking Africa, as well as East and South Africa, but the sections on Ethiopia and West Africa are well done. It was the first book in the United States to take sub-Saharan African cuisine seriously. Also, see the companion: *Recipes: African Cooking*. New York: Time-Life Books, 1970. Many libraries still have copies of this book.

Appendix

Weights and Measures Conversion Tables

Standard U.S. Unit	Metric Eequivalent
1/8 teaspoon	.5 milliliter (ml)
1/4 teaspoon	1 ml
1/2 teaspoon	2 ml
1 teaspoon	5 ml
1 tablespoon (3 teaspoons)	15 ml
1/8 cup (2 tablespoons)	30 ml
1/4 cup (4 tablespoons)	50 ml
1/3 cup (5 tablespoons)	75 ml
1/2 cup (8 tablespoons)	125 ml
1 cup (16 tablespoons)	250 ml
4 cups (1 quart)	1 liter
1 ounce (oz)	30 grams (g)
1 pound (lb)	500 g
2 pounds	1 kilogram (kg)
1/4 inch	.5 centimeter (cm)
1/2 inch	1 cm
1 inch	2.5 cm

This book uses standard U.S. measurements. However, it is important to note that "cup," "tablespoon," teaspoon," and "pint" are not equivalent in U.S. and British measuring systems (and the systems of many African countries that were British colonies), as the table below indicates.

U.S. Unit/Equivalent	British Unit/Equivalent
1 U.S. cup (8 oz)	5/6 English cup
10 oz	1 English cup
1 1/4 U.S. teaspoons	1 English teaspoon
1 1/4 U.S. tablespoons	1 English tablespoon
1 U.S. pint = 16 fluid oz	4/5 English pint
20 fluid oz	1 English pint

Selected Bibliography

GENERAL/ALL REGIONS

Amoah, J.E.K. *The Story of Cocoa, Coffee and Sheanut: Environmental Issues and Food Values*. Accra, Ghana: Jemre Enterprises, 2000.

Appiah, Kwame Anthony, and H.L. Gates, Jr., eds. *Africana: The Encyclopedia of the African and African American Experience*. New York: Basic Civitas Books/Perseus Books Group, 1999.

Catchpole, Brian, and I.A. Akinjogbin. *A History of West Africa in Maps and Diagrams*. London: Collins Educational, 1983.

Chapman, G.P., and K.M. Baker, eds. *The Changing Geography of Africa and the Middle East*. New York: Routledge, 1992.

Clark, J. Desmond. *The Prehistory of Africa*. New York: Praeger Publishers, 1970.

Cusack, Igor. "African Cuisines: Recipes for Nation-building." *Journal of African Cultural Studies* 13, no. 2 (December 2000): 207–25.

Dagan, Esther A. *The African Calabash: When Art Shares Nature's Gift*. Montreal: Galerie Amrad African Arts, 1988.

Davidson, Basil. *Africa, History of a Continent*. New York: Macmillan, 1966.

de Smidt, Portia. *The Africa Café Experience: Flavours of Africa*. Cape Town: Ampersand Press and Faraway Publishers, 2003.

DeWitt, Dave, and Nancy Gerlach. *The Whole Chile Pepper Book*. Boston, Mass.: Little, Brown, 1990.

Dyasi, Rebecca, comp. and Louise Crane, ed. *Good Tastes in Africa*. Urbana-Champaign, Ill.: Center for African Studies, African Outreach Series, No. 3, 1983.

Goody, Jack. *Cooking, Cuisine and Class: A Study in Comparative Sociology*. Cambridge: Cambridge University Press, 1982.

Hachten, Harva. *Best of Regional African Cooking*. New York: Hippocrene Books, 1998 (originally published by Atheneum, 1970).

Hafner, Dorinda. *A Taste of Africa*. Berkeley, Calif.: Ten Speed Press, 1993.

Inquai, Tebereh. *A Taste of Africa: The African Cookbook*. Trenton, N.J.: Africa World Press, Inc., 1998.

Katz, Solomon H., and William Woys Weaver, eds. *Encyclopedia of Food and Culture*. New York: Charles Scribner's Sons, 2002.

Kiple, Kenneth F., and Kriemhild Coneè Ornelas, eds. *The Cambridge World History of Food*, vols. 1 and 2. Cambridge: Cambridge University Press, 2000.

Kittler, P.G., and K.P. Sucher. *Food and Culture*, 3rd ed. Belmont, Calif.: Wadsworth/Thompson, 2001, pp. 175–97.

Kuper, Jessica, ed. *The Anthropologists' Cookbook*. New York: Universe Books, 1977.

National Research Council, Board on Science and Technology for International Development. *Lost Crops of Africa*, Vol. I. *Grains*. Washington, D.C.: National Academy Press, 1996.

Newman, James L. "V.E. 1. Africa South of the Sahara." In *The Cambridge World History of Food*, ed. Kenneth F. Kiple and Kriemhild Coneè Ornelas. Vol. 2. Cambridge: Cambridge University Press, 2000, pp. 1330–39.

Odartey, Bill (Bli Odaatey). *A Safari of African Cooking*. Detroit, Mich.: Broadside Press, second printing, 1987.

Shaw, T., P. Sinclair, B. Andah, and A. Okpolo, eds. *The Archaeology of Africa: Food, Metals and Towns*. New York: Routledge, 1995.

Sokolov, Raymond. *Why We Eat What We Eat: How the Encounter Between the New World and the Old Changed the Way Everyone on the Planet Eats*. New York: Simon and Schuster, 1991.

Stock, Robert. *Africa South of the Sahara: A Geographical Interpretation*. New York: The Guilford Press, 1995.

van der Post, Laurens, and the editors of Time-Life Books. *African Cooking*. New York: Time-Life Books, 1970 (also accompanying *Recipes: African Cooking*).

Viola, Herman J., and Carolyn Margolis. *Seeds of Change*. Washington, D.C.: Smithsonian Institution Press, 1991.

von Welanetz, Diana, and Paul von Welanetz. *The von Welanetz Guide to Ethnic Ingredients*. New York: Warner Books, 1982.

WESTERN AFRICA

Akrofi, C.A. *Twi Mmebusɛm: Twi Proverbs*. London: Macmillan, 1958.

Akyeampong, Emmanuel. *Drink, Power, and Cultural Change: A Social History of Alcohol in Ghana, c. 1800 to Recent Times*. Portsmouth, N.H.: Heinemann, 1996.

Allport, Susan. "Women Who Eat Dirt." *Gastronomica* 2, no. 2 (spring 2002): 28–37.

Andah, Bassey W. "Identifying Early Farming Traditions of West Africa." In *The Archaeology of Africa: Food, Metals and Towns*, ed. T. Shaw, P. Sinclair, B. Andah, and A. Okpolo. New York: Routledge, 1995.

Anthonio, H. O., and M. Isoun. *Nigerian Cookbook*. London: Macmillan, 1982.

Ayensu, Dinah Ameley. *The Art of West African Cooking*. Garden City, N.J.: Doubleday, 1972.

Bankole, S. A., and A. Adebanjo. "Mycotoxins in Food in West Africa: Current Situation and Possibilities of Controlling It." *African Journal of Biotechnology* 2, no. 9 (September 2003): 254–63.

Bascom, William. "Some Yoruba Ways with Yams." In *The Anthropologists' Cookbook*, ed. Jessica Kuper. New York: Universe Books, 1977.

Beckwirth, Carol. *Nomads of Niger*. New York: Harry N. Abrams, 1983.

Bromberger, Bronwen. "Nebam Sirme: Preserving Milk and Tradition." *Gastronomica* 4, no. 2 (spring 2004): 75–79.

Carney, Judith A. *Black Rice, The African Origins of Rice Cultivation in the Americas*. Cambridge, Mass.: Harvard University Press, 2001.

Cunningham, Anthony. "Bush Meat (Ghanaian Case)." In *Riches of the Forest: For Health, Life, and Spirit in Africa*, by the Center for International Forestry Research (CIFOR), 2004, pp. 5–8.

Dovlo, Florence E., Caroline E. Williams, and Laraba Zoaka. *Cowpeas: Home Preparation and Use in West Africa*. Ottawa: International Development Research Centre, 1984.

Gold Coast Medical and Education Departments. *Gold Coast Nutrition and Cookery*. London: Thomas Nelson and Sons, 1956.

Internet Ancient History Sourcebook. "The Periplus of the Erythraean Sea: Travel and Trade in the Indian Ocean by a Merchant of the First Century." http://www.fordham.edu/halsall/ancient/periplus.html.

Irvine, F. R. *Woody Plants of Ghana: With Special Reference to Their Uses*. London: Oxford University Press, 1961.

MacCormack, Carol P. "A Sauce from Sierra Leone." In *The Anthropologists' Cookbook*, ed. Jessica Kuper. New York: Universe Books, 1977.

Mensah, Patience, B. S. Drasan, T. J. Harrison, and A. M. Tomkins. "Fermented Cereal Gruels: Towards a Solution of the Weanling's Dilemma. *The United Nations University Press, Food and Nutrition Bulletin* 13, no. 1 (March 1991), pp. 50–57. http://www.unu.edu/unpress/food/8F13le/8F131E08.htm.

Nwapa, Flora. *Cassava Song and Rice Song*. Ogui-Enugu, Nigeria: Tana Press Ltd., 1986.

Nyaho, E. Chapman, E. Amarteifio, and J. Asare. *Ghana Recipe Book*. Accra-Tema: Ghana Publishing Corporation, 1970.

O'Laughlin, Bridget. "Mediation of Contradiction: Why Mbum Women Do Not Eat Chicken." In *Woman, Culture and Society*, ed. M. Rosaldo and L. Lamphere. Stanford, Calif.: Stanford University Press, 1974.

Piot, Charles. *Remotely Global: Village Modernity in West Africa*. Chicago: University of Chicago Press, 1999.

Sarpong, Peter. *Ghana in Retrospect: Some Aspects of Ghanaian Culture*. Accra-Tema: Ghana Publishing Company, 1974.

Sefa-Dedeh, S., Y. Kluvitse, and E. O. Afoakwa. "Influence of Fermentation and Cowpea Steaming on Some Quality Characteristics of Maize-Cowpea Blends." *African Journal of Science and Technology (AJST)*, Science and Engineering Series 2, no. 2, (December 2001), 71–80.

Spivey, Diane M. "West Africa." In *Encyclopedia of Food and Culture*, ed. Solomon H. Katz and William Woys Weaver. New York: Charles Scribner's Sons, 2002.

Wilson, Ellen Gibson. *A West African Cook Book*. New York: M. Evans and Company, 1971.

Yebuah, Oku, and Mate-kole, http://festivals.Projects.eun.org/Ghana/homowo. htm.

SOUTHERN AFRICA

Africa News Service. "Diet and Nutrition Key to AIDS Survival." LifeExtension foundation's *Daily News*, April 7, 2001. http://www.lef.org/newsarchive/nutrition/2001/04/07/an/.

Dempster, Carolyn. "Medicinal plant 'fights' Aids." *BBC News*. http://news.bbc. co.uk/1/hi/world/africa/1683259.stm.

Ellert, H. *The Material Culture of Zimbabwe*. Harare: Longman Zimbabwe, 1984.

Else, David, J. Connolly, M. Fitzpatrick, A. Murphy, and D. Swaney. *Southern Africa*. 2nd ed. Melbourne: Lonely Planet, 2000.

Etsabo, Diana, and Hydin Gethin. "KEMRI Seeks to Formulate Diet for HIV/AIDS Patients." *The East African Standard* (Nairobi), July 4, 2003. http://allafrica.com/stories/200307050070.html.

Flanagan, W., and J. Nichols. *Chillies*. Hout Bay, South Africa: Mbira Press, 2002.

Gerber, Hilda. "Malay Fare at Religious Festivals." In *Traditional Cookery of the Cape Malay*, ed. Hilda Gerber. Cape Town: A. A. Balkema, 1954 (reprinted in 1978), pp. 13–33.

———. "Daily Fare and Family Celebrations." In *Traditional Cookery of the Cape Malay*. Cape Town: A. A. Balkema, 1954 (reprinted in 1978), pp. 13–33.

Hamilton, Cherie Y. *Cuisines of Portuguese Encounters: Recipes from Portugal, Madeira/Azores, Guinea-Bissau, Cape Verde, São Tomé and Príncipe, Angola, Mozambique, Goa, Brazil, Malacca, East Timor, and Macao*. New York: Hippocrene Books, 2001.

Houston, Lynn. "Serpent's Teeth in the Kitchen of Meanings: A Theory of South African Culinary Historiography." *Safundi, The Journal of South African and American Comparative Studies* issue 2, no. 3 (July 2000). http://www.safundi.com/articles/houston.asp.

Leipoldt, C. Louis. *Leipoldt's Cape Cookery*. Cape Town: W. J. Flesch & Partners, 1976.

Ramiaramanana, Bakoly Domenichini. "Malagasy Cooking." In *The Anthropologists' Cookbook*, ed. Jessica Kuper. New York: Universe Books, 1977, pp. 111–15.

Shaxson, A., P. Dickson, and J. Walker. *The Malawi Cookbook*. Blantyre, Malawi: Dzuka Publishing Company, 1999.

Sitole, Dorah, and *True Love* Magazine. *Cooking from Cape to Cairo*. Capetown: Tafelberg Publishers, 1999.

Smit, Sannie, and Margaret Fulton. *The South African Encyclopedia of Food & Cookery*. Sydney: Octopus Books, 1983.

Snyman, Lannice. *Rainbow Cuisine*. Hout Bay, South Africa: S & S Publishers, 1998, reprinted 2000.

Viljoen, Annemarie T., and Gertruida J. Gericke. "Food Habits and Food Preferences of Black South African Men in the Army (1993–1994). *Journal of Family Ecology and Consumer Sciences* 29 (2001): 100–115.

Wannenburgh, Alf. *Forgotten Frontiersmen*. Lansdowne, CapeTown, South Africa: Howard Timmins, 1980.

West, Martin. *Abantu: An Introduction to the Black People of South Africa*. Cape Town: C. Struik Publishers, 1976.

EASTERN AFRICA

Food and Agriculture Organization of the United Nations (FAO). "Action Plan to End Hunger in the Horn of Africa Unveiled." http://www.fao.org/WAICENT/OIS/PRESS_NE/PRESSENG/2000/pren0060.htm.

———. "Strategy to end hunger in the Horn of Africa." http://www.fao.org/NEWS/2000/001004-e.htm.

Gardner, Ann. *Karibu: Welcome to the Cooking of Kenya*. Nairobi: Kenway Publications, 1993.

Gonahasa, Jolly. *Taste of Uganda: Recipes for Traditional Dishes*. Kampala, Uganda: Fountain Publisher, 2002.

Guggisberg, Rosanne and traditional sources (recipes) and Elaine Mwango, comp. *Cooking with an African Flavour*. Nairobi: Mount Kenya Sundries, 1993.

Hamdun, Said, and Noël King. *Ibn Battuta In Black Africa*. Princeton, N.J.: Markus Wiener Publishers, 1994.

Harragin, Simon. "Health and Healthcare Provision in North West Turkana, Kenya." Overseas Development Institute, Pastoral Development Network, paper 36c, July 1994. Available as PDF file from http://www.odi.org.uk/pdn/papers/index1.html.

International Medical Corps (IMC), ReliefWeb. "IMC Responds to East African Drought." January 2001. http://www.reliefweb.int/w/rwb.nsf/0/6127d3cba1768455852569d0006f4b41?OpenDocument.

Karp, Ivan, and Patricia Karp. "Social Aspects of Iteso Cookery." In *The Anthropologists' Cookbook*, ed. Jessica Kuper. New York: Universe Books, 1977, pp. 101–6.

Kenyatta, Jomo. *Facing Mount Kenya: The Traditional Life of the Gikuyu*. London: Heinemann, 1979 (originally published 1938 by Martin Secker and Warburg).

Kuto, Grace. *Harambee! African Family Circle Cookbook*. Wilsonville, Ore.: BookPartners, 1995.

Maundu, Patrick M., and Maryan Imbumi. "East Africa." In *Encyclopedia of Food and Culture*, ed. Solomon H. Katz and William Woys Weaver. New York: Charles Scribner's Sons, 2002.

Mesfin, Daniel J., ed. *Exotic Ethiopian Cooking: Society, Culture, Hospitality and Traditions*. Rev. extended ed. Falls Church, Va.: Ethiopian Cookbook Enterprises, 1993.

O'Connor, Anthony. "The Changing Geography of Eastern Africa." In *The Changing Geography of Africa and the Middle East*, ed. G. P. Chapman and K. M. Baker. London: Routledge, 1992, pp. 114–38.

Shack, William, and Dorothy Shack. "Cooking in the Garden of Ensete." In *The Anthropologists' Cookbook*, ed. Jessica Kuper. New York: Universe Books, 1977.

Sharman, Anne. "Food and Recipes in Padhola." In *The Anthropologists' Cookbook*, ed. Jessica Kuper. New York: Universe Books, 1977.

Warren, Olivia. *Taste of Eritrea: Recipes from One of East Africa's Most Interesting Little Countries*. New York: Hippocrene Books, 2000.

CENTRAL AFRICA

Atsimadja, Felicité Awassi. "The Changing Geography of Central Africa." In *The Changing Geography of Africa and the Middle East*, ed. G. P. Chapman and K. M. Baker. New York: Routledge, 1992, pp. 52–79.

Brain, Robert. "Cameroon Koki: A Bean Pudding from Bangwa." In *The Anthropologists' Cookbook*, ed. Jessica Kuper. New York: Universe Books, 1977.

Cusack, Igor. " 'Equatorial Guinea's National Cuisine is Simple and Tasty,'—Cuisine and the Making of National Culture." Unpublished manuscript.

———. "Pots, Pens and 'Eating out the Body': Cuisine and the Gendering of African Nations." *Nations and Nationalism* 9, no. 2 (2003): 277–96.

Dounias, Edmond. "Weevil Larvae (Cameroonian Case)." In *Riches of the Forest: For Health, Life, and Spirit in Africa*, by the Center for International Forestry Research (CIFOR), 2004, pp. 9–12.

Eggert, M.K.H. "Central Africa and the Archaeology of the Equatorial Rainforest: Reflections on Some Major Topics." In *The Archeology of Africa: Food, Metals, and Towns*, ed. Thurstan Shaw, Paul Sinclair, Bassey Andah, and Alex Okpoko. New York: Routledge, 1993, pp. 289–329.

Ekoué, Sophie. *Cuisine et Traditions: Recettes D'Afrique*. Paris: Cauris Editions, 2003.

Feldman-Savelsberg, Pamela. *Plundered Kitchens, Empty Wombs: Threatened Reproduction and Identity in the Cameroon Grassfields*. Ann Arbor: University of Michigan Press, 1999.

Fernandes, Caloca. *Viagem Gastronômica Atravôs do Brasil*. 6th edition. Trans. Doris Hefti. São Paulo: Editora Senac São Paulo: Editora Estúdio Sonia Robatto, 2004.

Freyer, Bryna M. Curator, Smithsonian Institution. Personal communication on Central African Woyo pot lids. July 2004.

Gibbons, Ed (Doug Himes). "Central Africa." In *Encyclopedia of Food and Culture*, ed. Solomon H. Katz and William Woys Weaver. New York: Charles Scribner's Sons, 2002, pp. 21–27.

Hewlett, Barry S. "Cultural Diversity Among African Pygmies." http://www.vancouver.wsu.edu/fac/Hewlett/cultdiv.html.

Hladik, C. M., S. Bahuchet, and I. de Garine, eds. *Food and Nutrition in the African Rain Forest*. Paris: Unesco/MAB, 1990.

Jelliffe, D. B. "Parallel Food Classifications in Developing and Industrialized Countries." *American Journal of Nutrition* 20 no. 3 (March 1967).

Kingue, Angèle M. Associate Professor of French, Bucknell University. Personal communication on Cameroon. 30 June 2004.

Mukaruziga, Judith. Personal communication on Rwanda. 2004.

Rowlands, Michael. "The Consumption of an African Modernity." In *African Material Culture*, ed. M. J. Arnoldi, C. M. Geary, and K. L. Hardin. Bloomington: Indiana University Press, 1996, pp. 188–213.

Sarno, Louis. *Song from the Forest*. Boston, Mass.: Houghton Mifflin Company, 1993.

Steinberg, Jennifer Holland. Geographica: "Big Frog-Really Big," *National Geographic* 203 no. 6 (June 2003).

Index

About the Author

FRAN OSSEO-ASARE is an expert on food in West Africa, the founder and editor of betumi.com, a Web site on sub-Saharan food, and the author of a African cookbook for childern.